W9-BUQ-358

THE PRICE OF ADMISSION

THE PRICE OF

ADMISSION

How America's Ruling Class Buys
Its Way into Elite Colleges—and
Who Gets Left Outside the Gates

DANIEL GOLDEN

CROWN PUBLISHERS

NEW YORK

Copyright © 2006 by Daniel Golden

All rights reserved.
Published in the United States by Crown Publishers,
an imprint of the Crown Publishing Group,
a division of Random House, Inc., New York.
www.crownpublishing.com

Crown is a trademark and the Crown colophon is a
registered trademark of Random House, Inc.

Library of Congress Cataloging-in-Publication Data
Golden, Daniel, 1957–
The price of admission : how America's ruling class
buys its way into elite colleges—and who gets left
outside the gates / Daniel Golden.—1st ed.
p. cm.
Includes bibliographical references and index.
1. Universities and colleges—United States—Admission.
2. Education, Higher—United States—Costs.
3. College choice—United States.   I. Title.
LB2351.2.G65   2006
378.1'610973—dc22   2006012059

ISBN-10: 1-4000-9796-7
ISBN-13: 978-1-4000-9796-8

Printed in the United States of America

DESIGN BY BARBARA STURMAN

10 9 8 7 6 5 4 3 2 1

First Edition

For my family

CONTENTS

A Note on Academic Records

Since college admissions offices pay considerable attention to applicants' SAT scores, this book does too. The purpose of revealing students' test scores (as well as high school grades and class ranks) is not to embarrass individuals who fall below the norm of the colleges they attend but to document the extent of admissions preferences for alumni children and other favored groups.

SAT scores in this book are based on the old SAT, which awarded 200–800 points on math and verbal scales for a maximum 1600 score. The current SAT also includes a writing test, worth 200–800 points, for a top score of 2400. Whenever possible, SAT scores used in this book were confirmed by documents or sources besides the students themselves. The book takes no position in the long-running controversy over whether SAT scores are a useful way to evaluate college applicants and predict future achievement.

Private high schools, which many of the college applicants described in this book attended, do not formally rank students. However, many prep schools induct students with the best grade point averages—usually the top 20 percent—into an organization called the Cum Laude Society, which is roughly comparable to the National Honor Society. Hence, this book frequently uses Cum Laude status as a mark of whether college applicants ranked in the top fifth of their prep school class.

THE PRICE OF

ADMISSION

Introduction

THE TENNESSEE WALTZ

The United States would never develop an aristocracy, Alexis de Tocqueville declared in his classic 1835 study, *Democracy in America*. The fledgling democracy, he wrote, lacked primogeniture—the European custom of parents leaving all their wealth to their firstborn son. Without that practice, family fortunes in America would be divided among multiple descendants and gradually dwindle to nothing.

But the great French historian underestimated the ingenuity of America's upper classes, which have all too often enhanced their wealth—and power—across generations. Elite families, it turned out, didn't need primogeniture. They developed an indirect method of preserving their status: college admissions.

Despite the popular notion that top colleges foster the American dream of upward mobility and equal opportunity, the truth is quite different. While only a handful of low-income students penetrate the campus gates, admissions policies channel the children of the privileged into premier colleges, paving their way into leadership positions in business and government.

Even without primogeniture, the firstborn sons of Senate majority leader Bill Frist and former vice president Al Gore could count on a valuable inheritance: easy entry to America's foremost universities. Although their fathers are political foes, William Harrison Frist Jr. and Albert Gore III have a great deal in common. Both bear the full names of their famous fathers along with the pressure of public expectations and media scrutiny. Both have Tennessee roots but attended expensive Washington private high schools that cater to children of power. Both are stocky and played the same position—center—on their prep school football teams.

Both were middling students who preferred partying to homework and the company of jocks to scholars. Their academic records—and, in the teenage Albert Gore III's case, brushes with authority—would ordinarily have destined them for second-tier colleges. Yet both were admitted ahead of thousands of stellar candidates to their first and only choices, two of the nation's best and most selective universities, Frist to Princeton and Gore to Harvard, where their fathers had gone before them.

The two Tennesseeans waltzed into the Ivy League less on their own merit than on the basis of their paternal pedigrees. Princeton accepted Harrison Frist not because it believed in his intellectual potential but because his family had lavished tens of millions of dollars on a new student center, and his father was both a national figure and a former trustee of the university. In fact, Princeton's admissions staff gave Harrison the lowest ranking on its scale for evaluating applicants' academic credentials. Albert Gore III applied to Harvard in the fall of 2000; America's most prestigious university wouldn't pass up the son of an alumnus and former member of its board of overseers who stood several hundred disputed Florida votes away from being president of the United States.

Once enrolled in these premier universities, the two youths hardly distinguished themselves. Harrison may be best known at Princeton for joining a rowdy, hard-drinking social club, and both were arrested on substance abuse charges. If they appeared not to value an elite college education, it may be because they didn't earn their admission; it was delivered to them as a birthright.

Said Brandon Parry, a high school and college classmate of Frist's: "I don't think anyone ever doubted Harrison would get into Princeton."

———

THE IVY LEAGUES' embrace of the sons of Bill Frist and Al Gore underscores a reality elite universities pretend doesn't exist—that money and connections are increasingly tainting college admissions, undermining both its credibility and value to American democracy.

In a 1997 article, "The Pitfalls of a Pure Meritocracy," a Harvard senior admissions officer named David Evans portrayed the admissions process as such universities want it to be seen—wise graybeards assembling a talented freshman class of all viewpoints and backgrounds. "Subjective evaluations" giving "some bearing" to applicants' "personal qualities," he argued, are far superior to a "strictly merit-based system." To explain why these universities often pass over top candidates—high school valedictorians, students with perfect SAT scores, and the like—for seemingly lesser applicants, Evans compared a college to a symphony orchestra. Just as an orchestra cannot be composed solely of violinists, he argued, so a college should be a "symbiotic whole" where "the poet converses with the scientist and the conservative philosopher debates topics . . . with the liberal activist."

This appealing vision permeates the public perception of admissions and almost all of the dozens of books and thousands of newspaper and magazine articles written about the process. It provides a convenient excuse for arbitrary decisions: asked why it rejected a student, a college can say that he or she looked wonderful on paper but didn't fit into the mix. The image of a fair but fickle process also pumps up the applicant pool: every year, hoping against hope that they might be the right match, hundreds of thousands of high school seniors with impeccable academic records seek admission to ultraexclusive colleges that take fewer than one in five candidates, while their parents spend millions of dollars they can ill afford for tutors, test-prep classes, extracurricular activities, or fancy private schools to help beat the odds.

But this version of college admissions is fundamentally deceptive, as the orchestra analogy unwittingly reveals. To assemble its diverse array of musicians, an orchestra typically picks the best players on each instrument through blind auditions, eliminating any hint of favoritism. Imagine if the New York Philharmonic adopted the same selection criteria as Harvard, Yale, or Stanford. It would turn down a top violinist with a sublime sound in favor of a second-rate one with a screeching bow because his father had played in the orchestra himself, had endowed a rehearsal space (or was expected to do so once his son was chosen), was a famous screen actor, or controlled federal appropriations for the arts.

Like Harrison Frist and Albert Gore III, thousands of wealthy, well-connected applicants slide into elite colleges each year with little regard to merit or diversity. They benefit instead from what I call the preferences of privilege. Although how-to-get-into-college books, college-night recruiters, and college administrators ignore or downplay their importance, the preferences of privilege aren't just pivotal in close calls. They routinely allow an academically weak applicant to leap over a strong one and can represent an admissions boost equivalent to hundreds of SAT points at Ivy League schools and other elite colleges. The children of wealth and influence occupy so many slots that the admissions odds against middle-class and working-class students with outstanding records are even longer than the colleges acknowledge.

The preferences of privilege are nonpartisan: they benefit the wealthy and powerful across the political and cultural spectrum, Democrats and Republicans, supporters and opponents of affirmative action, left-wing Hollywood movie stars and right-wing tycoons, old-money dynasties and nouveau riche. They ensure each fresh generation of upper-class families—regardless of intelligence or academic qualifications—access to the premier colleges whose alumni hold disproportionate sway on Wall Street and in Fortune 500 companies, the media, Congress, and the judiciary. Once in college, moreover, these wealthy students are often tapped to join socially exclusive groups—eating clubs, fraternities, secret societies—where they hobnob with influential alumni and prospective employers. Recent members of Princeton's rarefied Ivy eating club, for instance, have included the niece of President Bush; the daughter of John Edwards, the 2004 Democratic vice presidential candidate; and the son of Senator Jay Rockefeller.

This book reveals the double standard that favors rich and well-connected students applying to the one hundred or so colleges and universities, mostly private institutions, that admit fewer than half their applicants and serve as the gateway to affluence and influence in America. These students fly first-class on the college admissions journey, enjoying direct access to admissions deans who accept them outright or sneak them in through side entrances such as deferred admissions, transfers from other colleges, and "special" status. They're forgiven transgressions that would doom other candidates, from missed application deadlines to drunken driving.

Top colleges and universities like to boast that they are "need-blind"— that is, they offer enough financial aid so that the students they admit can afford to attend. But they are not wealth-blind. They take a disproportionate number of students from prep schools, and have been known—as Duke University did under its late president Terry Sanford—to instruct recruiters specifically to pursue rich students. Motivated in the short term by the allure of gifts, colleges also fear that enrolling too many low-income students would create a poorer alumni base—and therefore reduce contributions—down the road.

Even as admission has become increasingly competitive in recent years, premier universities still extend special preference to alumni children. Children whose parents have given big money in the past or are likely to pony up upon admission are ushered to the head of the line. At nearly all top universities, the fund-raising office furnishes admissions with a list of these "development cases," who are often accepted even if they rank near the bottom of their high school classes or have SAT scores 300–400 points below some rejected applicants. University presidents generally have a right-hand man, from Joel Fleishman at Duke to the late David Zucconi at Brown, whose role, whatever his title, is to gratify key donors and alumni, including facilitating the admission of their children.

Colleges also fawn on the offspring of famous people who can raise a school's visibility, from Hollywood superagent Michael Ovitz to author David Halberstam and former *New York Times* publisher Arthur Ochs Sulzberger. They conciliate key faculty members with free tuition and an admissions break for their children. And while it's widely believed that the admissions preference for recruited athletes favors minority and low-income students, it actually tilts toward the white and wealthy. Offsetting minority participation in basketball, football, and track, prestigious colleges give an admissions edge to athletes in sports played mainly by upper-income whites; for instance, crew, squash, horseback riding, skiing, sailing, fencing, golf, and even—at Cornell University and the University of Virginia—polo. By spurring colleges to field women's teams in these sports, Title IX, the federal gender-equity law, has widened socioeconomic inequity and spurred an admissions and scholarship bonanza for rich women.

Put together, these preferences of privilege amount to nothing less than affirmative action for rich white people. As such, they should be part of any debate about affirmative action for racial minorities.

Like most Americans, I have mixed feelings about racial preferences; it is easier to justify lowering standards for an impoverished minority student from a single-parent home and inner-city high school than for an upper-middle-class minority applicant from a premier prep school, or for the student who is considered Hispanic only because he happened to be born while his father, perhaps a banker or diplomat, was posted to Latin America. But whether one is for or against affirmative action, it is important to frame that issue in context. Even as conservative critics paint affirmative action for college-bound minorities as giving African Americans, Hispanics, and Native Americans an unfair advantage over more capable white candidates, the truth is the reverse.

The number of whites enjoying preference far outweighs the number of minorities aided by affirmative action. At least one-third of the students at elite universities, and at least half at liberal arts colleges, are flagged for preferential treatment in the admissions process. While minorities make up 10 to 15 percent of a typical student body, affluent whites dominate other preferred groups: recruited athletes (10 to 25 percent of students); alumni children, also known as legacies (10 to 25 percent); development cases (2 to 5 percent); children of celebrities and politicians (1 to 2 percent); and children of faculty members (1 to 3 percent). Some applicants benefit from multiple preferences, that is, a legacy may also be an athlete.

These estimates might be conservative. Robert Birgeneau, chancellor of the University of California at Berkeley, told me that he once calculated the proportion of admissions spaces open to "regular students" at one Ivy League university, which he declined to name. His startling conclusion: students without any nonacademic preference are vying for only 40 percent of the slots. Birgeneau added that Ivy League schools typically understate the number of students whose alumni ties facilitated their admissions. For instance, most Ivies don't count grandchildren as legacies, even though alumni often give the most money—and thus wield the greatest sway over admissions—after becoming grandparents.

College administrators often defend the preferences of privilege by contending that the beneficiaries are "qualified" or "can do the work." But in college admissions–speak, those descriptions only mean that a student is likely to graduate. The vast majority of applicants to top colleges fit (or exceed) those descriptions, but only a small proportion are admitted. Since more than 90 percent of students at elite universities graduate, being "qualified" means meeting minimum standards—a far cry from being the best candidate for the slot.

Pressed further, these administrators say they need the preferences of privilege to keep up with their peers—to build laboratories and concert halls, fund faculty salaries and scholarships. If a college doesn't want to alienate well-heeled alumni and other parents whom it counts on as donors, the argument goes, it must admit their children as students, even if that means lowering standards. But there are many reasons to give to colleges, and whether and how much philanthropy would dwindle without an admissions quid pro quo is debatable. One of the country's best private universities, the California Institute of Technology, raises plenty of money without compromising admissions.

ALBERT GORE JR., Harvard '69, was a member of his alma mater's board of overseers from 1987 until he became Bill Clinton's understudy in 1993. The board's official responsibility is to maintain academic standards, but members and ex-members enjoy a side benefit that undercuts that goal: the admissions office relaxes standards as needed for their children.

From 1991 to 2001, all four of Gore's children enrolled at Harvard, defying the one-in-ten odds against admission. Asked about this success, a former Harvard official told me that the Gore children "floated up" for attention from the board of overseers. "Al's in the category of active alum," the official said. "He wasn't really ever in the position to give Harvard much political help, except along with other senators if there was a bill supporting basic scientific research. But he contributed fairly substantially in terms of volunteer interest. He was an overseer and he was a very strong adviser to the environmental program." A Gore spokesman declined comment.

Vice President Gore's three daughters were excellent students whose Harvard acceptances raised few eyebrows. Their younger brother, who had recovered from a near-fatal car accident as a six-year-old, was a different story. His parents sent him to St. Albans, a preparatory school located on the grounds of the National Cathedral and patronized by blue-blood families like the Guggenheims and Rockefellers. St. Albans aims to instill both learning and manners—its lower-school headmaster used to greet students at the door every morning and critique their handshakes with comments such as "Make it a little firmer"—and doesn't condone misbehavior. In 1996, it suspended eighth-grader Albert Gore III for smoking marijuana in a pastoral retreat called the Bishop's Garden during a school dance. Perturbed at the school's handling of the matter, the Gores transferred Albert to Sidwell Friends, a Quaker school and Chelsea Clinton's alma mater. In the summer before his senior year there, he was cited for driving nearly 100 miles per hour in a 55-mph zone.

Like St. Albans and most other prep schools, Sidwell Friends does not formally rank students. Classmates and others familiar with Albert describe him as intelligent but not studious. "Sidwell is a very competitive place," a classmate told me. "I wouldn't say he was one of the academic all-stars. He was obviously very bright, but it wasn't necessarily something people would have thought off the top of their head that he would go to Harvard. There were a few kids that really stood out, and he wasn't in that shining top ten."

Another Sidwell classmate said, "Al is a bright, bright person. In terms of work, some other students were putting out more work. A student may not have the best test scores or grades, but people talk about potential. I would hope that's what Harvard would see in a student like Al."

Unlike his sisters, who were all accepted to Princeton too, Albert did not seek admission there. He applied to Harvard in the fall of 2000, when his father was the Democratic candidate for president. Harvard officials may have sought assurances that he had outgrown his rule breaking. If so, that hope was misplaced.

After enrolling at Harvard in 2001, he was ticketed in September 2002 near a military base for driving under the influence. Charged with marijuana possession in 2003, he settled that case by agreeing to substance abuse counseling. Aside from playing junior varsity football as a freshman, he kept a low profile on campus; when he graduated from Harvard in 2005, his name wasn't even listed in the commencement program.

ELITE UNIVERSITIES "are skimming along in the upper atmosphere," former Yale president Benno Schmidt told me recently. "They don't even know what's down below. Some in the elite universities want to help, and a few actually roll up their sleeves and try. But most have no idea how total is the disconnect between a place like Yale and the one-third or more of the high schools in the U.S. that serve mostly poor kids."

This disconnect underscores an inconvenient truth about U.S. higher education's oft-proclaimed goal of diversity. Of all the sorts of diversity that elite colleges profess to seek, socioeconomic diversity counts the least. To build a freshman class that is balanced in other respects, colleges routinely sacrifice the interests of low-income families. They achieve the gender diversity required by Title IX largely by recruiting affluent female athletes, racial diversity by admitting middle-class blacks and Hispanics, and international diversity by pursuing jet-setters from Europe and the Middle East.

Opportunity is scarcer today for children of poverty than in living memory, and our higher education system is partly responsible. Even with recent tuition hikes, public institutions from state universities to community colleges still expand career opportunities for working-class students.

But private universities are another story. Although they are tax-exempt, nonprofit institutions subsidized by our tax dollars and receive billions of dollars in government funding and research grants, they are shirking their mission to unearth and nurture diamonds in the rough. Instead, they help to enshrine an American aristocracy. Income and wage gaps between the top and bottom strata have widened in the past quarter century; social mobility, once a defining American characteristic, is becoming as rare as the street corner phone booth. The country is largely ruled by what I call the "legacy establishment": President George W. Bush, the last two Democratic candidates for president, Senate majority leader Bill Frist, and four of the nine Supreme Court justices are either alumni children themselves or have legacy offspring, or both. Although polls show that most Americans oppose admissions breaks for alumni children, this establishment has repelled every populist challenge to the preferences that sustain it.

"A growing body of evidence suggests that the meritocratic ideal is in trouble in America," *The Economist* reported in a special issue in January 2005. "Income inequality is growing to levels not seen since the Gilded Age, around the 1880s. But social mobility is not increasing at anything like the same pace. . . . The United States risks calcifying into a European-style class-based society. . . . Everywhere you look in modern America—in the Hollywood Hills or the canyons of Wall Street, in the Nashville recording studios or the clapboard houses of Cambridge, Massachusetts—you see elites mastering the art of perpetuating themselves. America is increasingly looking like imperial Britain, with dynastic ties proliferating, social circles interlocking, mechanisms of social exclusion strengthening and a gap widening between the people who make the decisions and shape the culture and the vast majority of ordinary working stiffs."

Not all of this inequality, of course, can be laid at the door of higher education. The rich enjoy many advantages in American society. They lead longer and healthier lives, enjoy more travel and cultural vistas than less prosperous families, and attend the best elementary and secondary schools. But such advantages provide all the more reason not to make exceptions for underqualified students from rich families.

The fact is that the preferences of privilege enable wealthy candidates to nose out deserving working-class and middle-class students at elite colleges. The result is gross inequity: depending on the study, only 3 to 11 percent of students at America's most selective colleges come from families in the lowest income quartile. Asian American students, many of them immigrants and the first in their families to go to college, are disproportionately affected—rebuffed by what appears to be an informal quota system.

The casualties aren't just individual students but America itself. To stifle talent and exalt mediocrity is to weaken the country's economic competitiveness and political leadership. Voters unhappy with their choices for president in 2004 could blame Yale University. Both President George W. Bush and Massachusetts senator John Kerry were Yale legacies from well-off families. Both were mediocre students. Both belonged to Yale's secret Skull and Bones society, forging contacts that helped them in later life. And both continued family tradition by sending a daughter to Yale. Who's to bet that Vanessa Kerry and Barbara Pierce Bush, or Harrison Frist and Albert Gore III, won't face off on an election ballot some years hence?

RED-HAIRED, affable Harrison Frist attended St. Albans, where his father is on the governing board. St. Albans does not rank students but—unlike Sidwell Friends—maintains a chapter of the Cum Laude Society. According to a St. Albans spokesman, Harrison was not inducted into Cum Laude, signifying that he did not rank in the top fifth of his class. The Frist family declined comment.

"I've always felt a lot of jealousy and anger," said a St. Albans classmate who fell short of the Ivy League. "A lot of my classmates were getting into Harvard and Yale not because they had a 4.0 GPA or nailed the SAT but because their father had a connection with the dean of admission and had a famous last name. Harrison is a very nice guy, but he wasn't top 20 percent. He wasn't an intellectual. He was more of a jock type, a partyer on the weekends."

A high class rank is normally a prerequisite for Ivy League admission; more than 90 percent of freshmen at Princeton, for example, are in the top tenth of their high school classes. Indeed, when Harrison Frist applied to

Princeton under its early decision program in the fall of 2001, admissions officers were taken aback: his grades and test scores fell far below university standards. On Princeton's 1 (best) to 5 (worst) academic scale for applicants, he was rated a 5. On its parallel nonacademic scale, he was a 3 or 4, signifying extracurricular leadership in his school but not talent of a state or national scope.

Such applicants are almost always given a cursory look and rejected. Not Bill Frist's son. The senator, soon to be Republican leader, was already a Princeton alumnus, ex-trustee, and past recipient of a university award for championing science funding. Moreover, the senator's family—his father founded Hospital Corp. of America, the nation's largest owner of for-profit hospitals—had committed $25 million in 1997 to renovate a former physics building into the Frist Campus Center. Senator Frist, who opposes affirmative action for minorities in college admissions, apparently did not object to preferential treatment for his eldest son. No wonder that newly appointed Princeton president Shirley Tilghman advised her admissions staff that Harrison's acceptance was a high priority.

Four other St. Albans seniors had sought early admission to Princeton, all with stronger records than Harrison. Perhaps worried that rejecting any of the quartet would prompt outcries of Frist favoritism, Princeton accepted them all. This cover-up strategy—admitting a subpar candidate for institutional reasons and then defusing potential criticism from parents, teachers, or guidance counselors by taking every other higher-ranking applicant from the same school—is well known in admissions circles and even has its own euphemism: considering "context." More St. Albans graduates entered Princeton in 2002 than in the prior or subsequent years— and, since college admissions is a zero-sum game, fewer from other schools. One insider called it the "Frist effect."

Sherrie McKenna, director of college counseling at St. Albans from 2000 to 2005, said she was "as surprised as anyone" that Princeton took all five applicants but doubted that Harrison "carried" the others in with him. "I looked at that list and said, 'How are they going to turn down any of these boys?' Two were very top students. Two were very good students and recruited athletes. Harrison was a legacy."

Princeton was Jamie Lee's first choice too. He lived by the slogan "Go big or go home." To him it meant, as he wrote in his college application essay, "taking the biggest challenges, the biggest risks, not mindlessly or without calculation, but with confidence and with no other reward needed but success."

Not just Jamie's essay but his choices of where to send it exemplified this spirit. Disdaining his high school counselor's advice to include a safety school, he applied only to Princeton and six more of the country's most selective universities: Harvard, Yale, Stanford, Columbia, Dartmouth, and Massachusetts Institute of Technology.

He had reason to be cocky. Tall and dark-haired, with an English accent, a dry wit, and an air of regal reserve, Jamie was a superb student. Born in Hong Kong to an English father and Chinese mother, he grew up in London, where teachers marveled at his ability and his IQ was measured at 162, widely considered genius level. When his family emigrated to Greenwich, Connecticut, in 2003, he quickly established himself as a top student at Greenwich High, a premier public school. On his first tries, without a test-prep course, he scored the maximum on the PSAT, the SAT, and two of his three SAT II subject tests; on the third SAT II, writing, he missed by only 20 points, scoring 780 out of 800.

Nor was he merely a standardized-test machine; his problem solving displayed impressive originality. In 2005, Jamie won the Greenwich High award given to the senior who "demonstrates creative ability and inventiveness in math, who may take the unusual approach to a problem and come up with an unexpected answer." His creativity also emerged in music (the high school string ensemble performed his composition "Three Dances," with Jamie on cello) and mechanical design (he built an ingenious wooden cabinet with doors that automatically opened and closed a mobile rack for storing compact discs).

"He likes to be oppositional and play the devil's advocate," said his junior-year Latin teacher, Camille Fusco. "He's very independent in his thinking. On an essay question, he'd deliberately take the point of view I didn't want to hear. But he got away with it because he can take any view brilliantly."

He relished intellectual challenges. Before his multiple-choice final exam in advanced placement chemistry, the teacher offered an A-plus for the semester to anyone in the class who answered all sixty questions wrong—arguably as difficult as getting them all right, because it was impossible to know which choices were incorrect without knowing which were correct. The teacher made the same offer to his class every year, but no student had ever taken the risk and won. Jamie already had an A average in the class and would have aced the final the conventional way but couldn't resist a dare. Unfortunately, he carelessly answered one question right: his 1-out-of-60 final score lowered his semester mark to an A-minus.

Nor did he get away with going big in college admissions. Coming from England, where universities such as Oxford and Cambridge no longer ask applicants whether their parents were alumni, Jamie failed to weigh the preferences of privilege. Unlike many classmates in the affluent suburb, he was not a legacy, recruited athlete, or development case. The Lees are comfortably off—Jamie's father is a consultant to money managers—but couldn't afford a major gift; they rent half of a duplex on the less ritzy side of town. In admissions parlance, Jamie was "unhooked." And as Daniel Saracino, assistant provost for admissions at the University of Notre Dame, recently told me, so many spaces at elite universities are reserved for well-connected students that "the poor schmuck who has to get in on his own has to walk on water."

Through his mother, Jamie also belonged to a demographic group that colleges hold to a higher standard than any other: Asian Americans. Average SAT scores for Asian Americans admitted to the Ivy League are substantially above those for any other group, including whites; frustrated Asian applicants refer to any score below the maximum as an "Asian fail." Jamie's strengths in math and music played into an ethnic stereotype. In the age of diversity, colleges turn away Asian American whizzes in calculus and music for fear of overloading their "symbiotic whole" with too many students of the same race and interests. "I understood there'd be a bit of discrimination against Asians," Jamie told me.

Whatever the reason, none of the seven elite universities accepted Jamie, stunning his teachers, friends, and family. "I was really shocked he didn't get in anywhere," Fusco said. "I thought of him as a Harvard person." His English literature teacher, Brigid Barry, said she was also "very, very surprised. There's no doubt he's an outstanding student." She added that in eight years of teaching advanced placement English, she had seen the Ivy League schools admit many weaker candidates.

I became aware of Jamie's predicament on May 22, 2005, when I received an email from his father, Tim Lee, with the subject line "Exceptionally Gifted High School Student Rejected by Every College." It outlined his academic accomplishments and grim admissions news. Jamie had applied in the fall of 2004 to Princeton under an early decision program. Princeton, which had admitted Harrison Frist early, deferred Jamie until spring and then rejected him. Harvard, Stanford, and MIT rebuffed him too. Columbia and Dartmouth placed him on their waiting lists. But Columbia didn't pluck him from its list, and Dartmouth, which offered spots on its waiting list to 1,200 candidates, warned that it planned to admit very few of them.

Jamie's father and guidance counselor called the colleges, but their explanations were unsatisfying. According to Tim Lee, Marlyn McGrath Lewis, Harvard's director of admissions, told him that Jamie was an excellent student but that a number of better musicians had applied. When I asked her later whether Harvard judged Jamie by a higher standard because he was half Asian, she declined comment on his case but said Harvard had "long recruited Asian Americans." MIT, where the Lees had believed Jamie was a shoo-in, told the counselor that he hadn't displayed enough leadership. Jamie felt this was an unfair knock because he had entered Greenwich High as a junior, rather than spending four years there, and had to catch up in academic subjects such as American history.

Jamie planned to take a year off from school and devote it to writing and music composition. Instead, he finally fulfilled his Ivy League dreams, but only after using a hook of his own—the press. Just as college admissions offices are wary of offending donors and alumni, they also fear criticism by the media, particularly national outlets such as *The Wall Street Journal,* where I had written a series of articles on college admissions. With the Lees' permission, I contacted universities to which Jamie had applied, asking why they had overlooked such an exceptional candidate and raising the issue of anti-Asian discrimination. Six days after I emailed Dartmouth's admissions dean, Karl Furstenberg, he wrote Jamie, offering him one of a "very small number" of remaining places—twenty-two, according to a subsequent newspaper report—in the class of 2009. Jamie's good fortune, of course, is anomalous. Thousands of other brilliant students across America are spurned by elite colleges every year because they are unhooked.

HARRISON FRIST avoided the limelight at Princeton—even when student Democrats conducted a "Frist Filibuster" in the spring of 2005 to protest his father's plan to cut off debate on judicial nominations. Still, as Bill Frist's son, he was expected to join an exclusive "bicker" club, where he could hobnob with alumni, prospective employers, and the Princeton social elite. Any of the five invitation-only eating clubs along Prospect Avenue in Princeton would have beckoned to him, eager for the Frist cachet. He could have chosen his father's southern-genteel Cottage Club, or aristocratic Ivy, which welcomed three of his St. Albans classmates, including Brandon Parry.

Brandon told me that Ivy members have a direct pipeline to high-paying jobs at financial giants such as investment banking firm Goldman Sachs and management consultant McKinsey & Company. In February 2005, Brandon attended a Goldman Sachs recruiting event for internship applicants, which featured eight Princeton alumni working as Goldman analysts. Seven of the eight, Brandon said, had belonged to Ivy. "I thought, 'This is like an Ivy reunion,'" he said. "It's bizarre."

But instead of Ivy or Cottage, Harrison opted for the Animal House of Princeton clubs: Tiger Inn. Housed in a Tudor-style mansion, complete with stained-glass windows, elaborate fireplaces, and pool and poker tables, Tiger Inn is known for putting candidates through humiliating hazing rituals and for its wild parties; morning-after passersby often see an empty beer keg or two left in its front bushes. It was the last Princeton eating club to admit women, going coeducational in 1991 only after the U.S. Supreme Court refused to hear its appeal. Its website describes it as "a place to relax, talk with friends, study, play cards, shoot billiards, and notoriously (perhaps most importantly) enjoy beverages with fellow members."

"It's one of the more laid-back clubs," Timothy Prugar, then a Princeton junior and Tiger Inn president, told me on a radiant May afternoon in 2005, gesturing toward members sunning themselves on the lawn. "We have kids with 4.0s. We have kids who have to pick it up a little." He said that Tiger's reputation for hazing is a "relic of the past"; now the bicker, or application, process consists of "games to put people at ease so you can know them really well." Harrison Frist, he added, "is a humble kid. Just because people come from privilege doesn't mean they're privileged. Privilege is a state of mind."

So is inebriation. Classmate Brandon Parry told me that Harrison belonged not only to Tiger Inn but also to a fraternity known for "fairly aggressive" drinking. "My feeling is, it's college," Brandon said. "If you're not going to do it now, when are you?"

In May 2004, police stopped Harrison, then a sophomore, on Prospect Avenue near Tiger Inn at 1:35 a.m. After failing balance and blood alcohol tests, he pleaded guilty to drunken driving and related charges. He was fined, and his driver's license was suspended for seven months.

WITH OTHER Pulitzer Prize winners, Lee Bollinger stuck to the script. On the afternoon of May 24, 2004, in Low Library's majestic rotunda, the president of Columbia University called them to the podium, read their citations, shook their hands, and forked over their certificates and $10,000 checks, without editorializing.

Then it was my turn. President Bollinger read a citation that praised my articles for documenting the admissions edge given to children of alumni and donors. As I returned to my seat among my family and *Wall Street Journal* colleagues, he ad-libbed, "Never happens."

The quip evoked nervous tittering from the media poohbahs in the audience, some of whom likely hoped to wangle Ivy League slots for their own children. But I wasn't sure he was joking; I'd heard the same denial uttered with a straight face by too many other college administrators. I had learned that, in an age and society with few secrets, one of the last taboos among America's aristocracy is talking—or writing—about pulling strings in college admissions. Even at a reception before the Pulitzer ceremony, a fellow guest scolded me for criticizing this influence peddling: after what I had written, she wanted to know, how did I expect my then eleven-year-old son to get into a top university?

Growing up, I believed that America—and college admissions—were a meritocracy. My parents, both immigrants, exemplified upward mobility through education; they rose by their wits to earn doctorates and become tenured professors at the University of Massachusetts. Graduating from a public high school, I applied to two universities, Harvard and Cornell, and was admitted to both. (My older sister, a far better student than me, was already enrolled at Harvard, but that may not have helped my cause, because Harvard says it doesn't give preference to siblings.)

Back then, unhooked students had a better shot at the Ivy League. In 1974, when I enrolled, Harvard had 11,166 applicants for 1,600 seats in the freshman class. By 2005, the number of applicants more than doubled to 22,797—for about the same number of seats. Since Harvard and other elite universities with ballooning numbers of applications still make room for preferred groups, everybody else's chances have shrunk dramatically. An applicant with my credentials (1410 SAT score, top-10 class rank, one advanced placement course) wouldn't even be in the running at Harvard today unless he were a legacy, a development case, a recruited athlete, a faculty child, or a minority.

I didn't realize how much things had changed until, as an education reporter for *The Wall Street Journal*, I started looking into college admissions preferences in December 2002, after my boss warned me that I was missing "the biggest education story in twenty-five years." He was referring to the U.S. Supreme Court's agreeing to consider two lawsuits challenging affirmative action at the University of Michigan. As I scrambled to find a fresh perspective, he glumly pointed out, "Every angle's been covered."

But I soon unearthed a nugget. One of the rejected white students challenging race preferences at the university, Patrick Hamacher, had received an admissions edge himself because his mother was a Michigan alumna. His lawsuit rested on the notion that his rejection was unjust because Michigan accepted minorities with worse records than his. By the same reasoning, it would have been equally unfair to admit Hamacher and turn down applicants with better credentials who weren't legacies.

After my article on legacies was published, I learned about the preference for children of prospective donors. Duke University, I discovered, accepted at least one hundred nonalumni children each year due to family wealth or connections. As my research on admissions gathered steam, disillusioned college admissions staff and high school counselors pointed me to instances where money trumped merit. To my surprise, children of alumni and donors often talked openly to me about their experiences; they themselves wondered why they had been accepted, or felt guilty about displacing a less affluent friend or classmate with a superior academic record who had been rejected.

Ultimately, I wrote four front-page stories about the preferences of privilege. My series unleashed a torrent of reader emails, both pro and con, and follow-up coverage in the *New York Times,* the *Washington Post,* and other media. When a deeply divided Supreme Court upheld affirmative action in June 2003, Justice Clarence Thomas suggested in his dissent that national publicity about legacy preference may have tipped the decision. A few months later, Senator Edward M. Kennedy, himself a legacy, proposed that the federal government monitor preference for alumni children.

While administrators at several renowned universities stopped returning my phone calls, the strongest backlash came from Stanford University and the Groton School in Groton, Massachusetts. The elite university and prep school had one prominent trustee in common: Texas oil magnate Robert Bass, who had given $25 million to Stanford in 1991. I revealed—in an article examining how the preferences of privilege affected the college admissions outcomes of Groton's class of 1998—that Bass's daughter Margaret was the only one of nine Groton applicants admitted to Stanford that year, despite grades and test scores well below those of seven rejected classmates. A Korean American classmate, Henry Park, had scored 340 points higher than Margaret on the SAT, yet Stanford had spurned him.

Even before that article was published, lawyers for Groton began peppering the *Journal* with complaints that my efforts to contact the Basses—I had endeavored to get their side of the story—were invading the family's privacy. Then Stanford's vice president of public affairs, Gordon Earle, wrote to the Pulitzer Prize board as it was considering finalists, denouncing my work as "deliberately misleading and below an acceptable professional standard." Earle based his assault largely on a claim that I had taken a quotation from Stanford's then-dean of undergraduate admission, Robin Mamlet, out of context. When I had asked Mamlet if Stanford gave preference to donors' children, she had replied, "While I will certainly factor in a history of very significant giving to Stanford, it is essential to note that we have rejected many applicants whose parents are extremely wealthy, even applicants who are among the university's most generous donors."

Since elite universities have long denied favoring the rich—"Never happens"—my editors and I did not consider it "essential to note" that Stanford, which accepts only 13 percent of its applicants, had rebuffed many children of wealth. As space for the article was tight, I quoted only Mamlet's startling concession: "I will certainly factor in a history of very significant giving to Stanford."

After I embarked on this book, Groton denied me permission to use its library, and headmaster Richard Commons wrote two letters to Groton alumni, urging them not to respond if I contacted them. His efforts to stifle the flow of information backfired; following each letter, several alumni approached me to offer help.

Some of the *Journal*'s wealthier subscribers regarded my series not as investigative journalism but as a how-to guide. After its publication, I was contacted by a high-tech tycoon and his wife, whose daughter was applying to colleges. Given her so-so academic record, her prep school guidance counselor had recommended a second-tier university. But the parents had set their hearts on the Ivy League. How much money would they have to give, they asked, to make their dream come true?

I declined to name a figure and instead tried to discourage them from buying their daughter's admission into a top-tier university. All I could think about was the brilliant candidate—the Jamie Lee—who would be rejected to make room for her.

1

HOW THE "Z-LIST" MAKES THE A-LIST

Harvard's Payback
for Big Donors

On a mild evening in early spring, corporate executives, lawyers, oil barons, money managers, high-priced consultants, and heirs to Brahmin fortunes strolled unrecognized across Harvard Yard from their suites at the Charles Hotel or Harvard Inn. Hardly a black or Hispanic face could be seen as the gray-suited, gray-haired businessmen—some leaning on walkers, others spry and ruddy-faced, with athletic builds honed on Harvard crew or tennis teams—and women in silk scarves and slimming black pants made their way through an unmarked door into Annenberg Hall. There was no campus announcement of the gathering, and no press coverage allowed.

Bouquets of forsythia and tulips decked out the usually spartan fresh-man dining hall. The visitors enjoyed cocktails, wine, and appetizers—beef tenderloin, crab cakes, asparagus spears—as well as the attentions of Lawrence Summers, then Harvard's president. Several guests chatted about the latest show by the Hasty Pudding Club, the student theatrical society that puts on a musical burlesque every spring featuring Harvard men in drag.

Then a student band, perched in a balcony overhead, struck up "Ten Thousand Men of Harvard," and the group sat down to a candlelit din-ner. Wine refills put the crowd in an expansive mood, and they frequently interrupted Summers's after-dinner speech with applause. The sole exception was when he outlined his initiative to boost enrollment of students from families earning less than $40,000 a year by making their Harvard educations free. He appeared to wait for an ovation that never came. I interpreted the awkward silence to convey a message, perhaps even a threat: *If you make room for more low-income students by rejecting our children, we'll stop giving our millions.*

The April 8 dinner kicked off the 2005 annual meeting of what is likely the wealthiest advisory group in higher education: Harvard's Committee on University Resources. Little known and rarely mentioned in the media, COUR is not actually a committee in the usual sense—it doesn't formally make or advise on university policy—but Summers or any other Harvard president needs its support. It consists of Harvard's biggest donors, who form the financial backbone of an endowment that totaled $25.5 billion as of fiscal 2005, making it the nation's largest, more than $10 billion ahead of second-place Yale's.

Committee membership has tripled in the past fifteen years, propelled by the university's record-setting $2.6 billion fund-raising campaign, which lasted from 1994 to 1999 and relied heavily on multimillion-dollar gifts. "As a member of COUR, you will be asked to play a leading role in the proposed campaign," committee chairman Robert G. Stone Jr. told members in 1991 in the first issue of its newsletter. By 2004, COUR's 424 members, handpicked by university fund-raisers, included ten of *Forbes* magazine's four hundred richest Americans, led by Microsoft chief executive Steven Ballmer (2005 net worth: $14 billion), oil tycoon Robert Bass ($3 billion), and banker David Rockefeller ($2.5 billion). Most are alumni of Harvard's undergraduate college or its graduate programs, but not all; Bass, for instance, went to archrival Yale, followed by business school at Stanford.

To qualify for membership, donors must generally have given at least $1 million to Harvard—or be expected to do so—although a few smaller donors were picked for their prowess in raising large sums from wealthy classmates and business associates on Harvard's behalf. The seventy-three members of the group's inner circle, the executive committee, have typically given or raised at least $5 million, and sometimes much more.

A free dinner and a newsletter aren't the only signs of Harvard's gratitude to COUR members. The school summons top faculty to the committee's annual meeting to expound on such topics as nanotechnology and the science of aging. It names athletic facilities, research centers, faculty chairs, fellowships, and scholarships after donors.

And, in the most valuable reward of all, Harvard gives a massive admissions edge to their children, who flourish in a selection process that lacks conflict-of-interest rules and systematically favors the wealthy and well-connected. Although Harvard bridles at any suggestion that its slots are for sale, I found numerous instances in which a child's acceptance closely preceded or followed a major gift from the parents, giving at least the appearance of a quid pro quo. Most notably, a politically connected New Jersey real estate mogul with no Harvard ties pledged $2.5 million to the university only months before his elder son—a student below Harvard's usual standards—was admitted.

Harvard admits fewer than one in ten undergraduate applicants, turning down more than half of candidates with perfect SAT scores. Nine-tenths of its freshman ranked in the top 10 percent of their high school classes. Its graduate and professional schools boast similarly high standards: Harvard law school, for instance, accepts only 11 percent of applicants.

Children of major donors enjoy far better odds. By examining *Who's Who* entries, alumni records, and other sources, I found that 218 of 424 COUR members, or more than half, have had at least one child at Harvard. Many donors send more than one child to Harvard, bringing the total number of COUR members' offspring who have enrolled there over the years to at least 336. Nearly three hundred of these children attended Harvard as undergraduates, with most of the rest attending the law and business schools, which provide an entrée into the corridors of American power.

Since, by my count, at least eighty COUR members either do not have children or their children have not reached college age, the number of COUR offspring who have gone to Harvard works out to 336 children of about 340 eligible members—an astonishing enrollment rate of one child per major donor. Given that the typical married couple in the United States has one or two children, that wealthy women tend to have fewer children than the average, and that many children of COUR members never apply to Harvard at all, a conservative conclusion would be that the university welcomes well over half of applicants from the families of its biggest donors.

Through their easy access to Harvard, the children of COUR members don't just gain intellectual polish. They also acquire a prestigious career credential and high-powered friends and spouses, consolidating their families' place in the American aristocracy. "Last year we completed a double 'hat trick' when my youngest daughter, Morgan, married Harvard classmate John Stafford," investment banker Ralph Hellmold, a member of the Committee on University Resources, boasted to his Harvard classmates on their fortieth reunion in 2002. "Thus, each of my three daughters has not only graduated from the college, but married her own Harvard man."

Executive committee member James O. Welch Jr., former vice chairman of RJR Nabisco Inc. and a Harvard alumnus who endowed a professorship in computer science, leads the way in the admissions sweepstakes, with six sons who graduated from Harvard. Welch declined comment. Similarly, Finn M. W. Caspersen's generosity has not gone unrewarded in admissions to Harvard Law, a school whose preference for children of well-heeled alumni was satirized in *Legally Blonde*. The heroine of the hit 2001 comedy, played by Reese Witherspoon, learns from a classmate that her dim-witted ex-boyfriend, Warner Huntington III, "got wait-listed when he applied. His father had to make a call."

Caspersen, a Harvard Law alumnus who also sits on the COUR executive committee, formerly headed consumer lending giant Beneficial Corp., which specializes in making high-interest loans to consumers with poor credit. He and his wife have endowed several faculty chairs at the law school and donated to its library, where the rare-book room is named after them. Caspersen, who now runs a private investment firm, chairs a

$400 million fund-raising campaign that the law school launched in 2003. Four Caspersen children—Finn junior (who also has a Harvard bachelor's degree), Erik, Samuel, and Andrew—have enrolled at Harvard Law. The Caspersens declined comment.

Professor David R. Herwitz, who served for years on the law school's admissions committee, told me that Caspersen's sons were fine students and "totally admissible." He added, "Any school, particularly one with a long tradition, becomes something of a family. What kind of a crazy world would it be if people who had gone to the school and made contributions would be told: your kid is very close, but not close enough?"

UNDOUBTEDLY SOME children of COUR members were superb candidates whom Harvard might have admitted even if they were unhooked. For others, the preferences of privilege outweighed test scores or grades below Harvard norms. These fortunate candidates with marginal credentials—like many minorities aided by affirmative action—are often saddled with self-doubt, wondering if they deserved their Harvard admission.

Most COUR children at Harvard have been legacies—a group to which Harvard acknowledges giving at least a small admissions boost. Harvard accepts one third of alumni children, nearly four times its overall admission rate. Legacies constitute 13 percent of the student body. William Fitzsimmons, dean of admissions and financial aid at Harvard, who has been a guest speaker at COUR meetings, told me that he personally reads all applications from alumni children. He said the average SAT score of legacies admitted to Harvard falls just a couple of points below the school's overall average, and that he uses legacy status as a tie-breaker between comparable candidates. Asked how he defends a policy so little rooted in merit, Fitzsimmons, a 1967 Harvard graduate, said the school's alumni "volunteer an immense amount of their free time in recruiting students, raising money for their financial aid, taking part in Harvard Club activities at the local level, and in general promoting the college." He added, "They often bring a special kind of loyalty and enthusiasm for life at the college that makes a real difference in the college climate . . . and makes Harvard a happier place." Therefore, he said, "when their sons and daughters apply, we review their applications with great care and will give a 'tip' in the admissions process to them."

Loyalty and volunteerism aside, the biggest reason for Harvard's legacy preference is money. Alumni donations drive Harvard's endowment, and the ability and willingness of graduates to donate to the university influence the size of the preference given to their progeny. The better than one-in-two admission rate for COUR members' children in my survey indicates that children of big alumni donors enjoy more than the tie-breaker edge Fitzsimmons describes. This finding corroborates a 1991 study by David Karen, now a professor at Bryn Mawr College, which concluded that alumni children at Harvard lose most of their admissions advantage if they apply for financial aid. In other words, if alumni want their children to have an admissions edge at Harvard, they should become bankers, lawyers, or dentists—not social workers, teachers, or ministers. "My interpretation was that if you couldn't parlay a Harvard degree into an income sufficient to pay for your kid's education, Harvard was less likely to make the same mistake twice," Professor Karen told me.

The boost for children of alumni on the University Resources committee can amount to far more than a couple of SAT points. Harvard alumnus and Boston venture capitalist Craig L. Burr, a member of the Committee on University Resources, gave his alma mater at least $1 million in the mid 1990s; his son, Matthew, applied in 1998. Matthew Burr ranked fourth in his class at the Groton School but had an SAT score of 1240. Three-fourths of Harvard students have SAT scores of 1380 or higher, and the average freshman score is about 1470. Matthew applied to one other college, Williams, which rejected him.

"I just don't test well," Matthew told me. He wrote an application essay about a family safari to Kenya—a likely tip-off, if one were needed, of the Burrs' wealth to admissions readers. His Groton counselor, he said, made it clear to him that his family connection would "help out" with Harvard admissions.

Craig Burr told me his donation to Harvard had "absolutely nothing to do" with his son's acceptance. "Matthew did not need any help because he had phenomenal grades," he said.

"I was qualified in getting in to Harvard," Matthew said. "At the same time, I do think legacy helped me. I don't think legacy is a fair criterion for people to get into college. But for me, that was the way it was."

Like Matthew Burr, Jessica Zofnass had excellent grades in prep school but an SAT score (1410) below the Harvard average. Jessica, who enrolled in 2004 (followed by her sister Rebecca in 2005), is the daughter and granddaughter of Harvard alumni; her father, COUR member Paul Zofnass, endowed a scholarship in environmental studies. "I don't think I got into Harvard for my SAT scores," Jessica told me. "Hopefully it wasn't just legacy. More of what I did at Choate [Wallingford, Connecticut, prep school Choate Rosemary Hall] was being well rounded, captain of a lot of sports teams, president of the French Club.

"It's really exciting for me to be here. But it's a very unjust society if the people who already have the benefits and the advantages and already have a wonderful life get an additional leg up. I'm very torn. If I were born into a family that was less advantaged, I would feel very bitter about the legacy status."

Paul Zofnass, a financial consultant to environmental firms, donated between $250,000 and $500,000 to Harvard in 2003–4, when Jessica was a senior at Choate, and says he is also "very committed" to raising donations from his Harvard classmates. Zofnass told me Jessica "clearly had the credentials for someone to get into Harvard. I've also known plenty of kids who were every bit as good as her and they didn't get in. Why? My involvement helped a little bit. Had I had nothing to do with Harvard, she probably would have gotten in, but I'm not sure."

Another COUR member's son, a Harvard undergraduate, told me that he graduated in the middle of his prep school class with an SAT score in the 1300s—"not too good by Harvard standards," he acknowledged. His father, an alumnus, donated more than $1 million to the 1990s campaign, plus half a million in his son's freshman year. Still, the student said he felt no qualms over his admission.

"Definitely legacy was a factor, but I don't feel like someone else should be here instead of me," he said. "I don't feel guilty. A lot of people I know at Harvard are very, very, very, very intelligent, but they just sit on their asses. With my work ethic and potential, test scores that may be a little less than some others shouldn't get in the way of possibilities for me and my life." He said his father donated to Harvard out of love for the institution, not to sway admissions.

Most of these upper-class legacies went to prep schools, where they participated in aristocratic pastimes such as squash, crew, and sailing. Largely played by affluent whites, these sports offer a college admissions entrée unavailable to most public school and inner-city students. Some of the COUR children were skilled enough—and had the right pedigree—to impress Harvard coaches who submit lists of potential recruits to the admissions office.

Frances Cashin followed her father, COUR executive committee member Richard M. Cashin Jr., not only into Harvard but also onto its crew team. Once a standout rower for Harvard and the U.S. Olympic team, Cashin is managing partner of the investment firm One Equity Partners. He and his wife, Elizabeth, also a Harvard graduate and University Resources committee member, have given generously to Harvard, including at least $1 million during the 1990s campaign and a $5 million pledge in 2004. Frances, a fifth-generation Harvard legacy, scored 1440 on her SATs, slightly below Harvard's average, and ranked in the second quartile of her class at Deerfield Academy, a western Massachusetts private school. She rowed on the Deerfield girls' crew team but was not heavily sought after by college coaches. She said other Ivies did not pursue her because they expected her to go to Harvard.

Shortly after her junior year at Deerfield, Frances told me, her father arranged for her to meet Fitzsimmons, the Harvard admissions dean. The dean does not officially interview applicants but chats informally with at least one hundred a year—many of them, like Frances, children of key alumni. She and the dean talked for half an hour during her lunch break from a summer rowing camp on the Charles River. Frances told me that

Harvard men's crew coach Harry Parker, her father's former mentor, and women's coach Liz O'Leary, a former Olympic teammate of Cashin's, recommended her as a recruit for the crew team. She enrolled at Harvard in 2003 and rowed on the women's second varsity boat in 2004–5.

Frances told me that legacy preference is a "valid thing for a college to do. Any college has to be careful about the students it lets in from a social perspective. If you let in too many of any one group, it can affect social cohesiveness. At one time, Harvard had too many Asian American students." As described in Chapter 7, Harvard admissions has long slighted Asian Americans, holding them to a higher test-score standard than whites. Frances did not explain how Asian American students, who for years have made up between 15 and 20 percent of the Harvard student body, hurt the university's cohesion. Instead, she continued, "It's important to Harvard to have people who know what it means to work hard, make good friends, and go out at night. A lot more alumni children are well-rounded kids, probably because they come from more stable families." Frances's first cousin, Elizabeth Demers, enrolled at Harvard in 2005 from Phillips Academy Andover and also joined the crew team.

The combination of a well-connected family and an upper-crust sport ushered in Elizabeth Berylson, granddaughter of former Harvard governing board member Richard A. Smith, a movie theater and department store magnate who reaped $648 million from the sale of Neiman Marcus in 2005. Elizabeth did not rank in the top 20 percent of her class at Milton Academy but showed enough talent on the squash court to be recruited by Harvard coaches. Her mother, Harvard alumna and COUR member Amy Smith Berylson, endowed a professorship in engineering during Elizabeth's freshman year, 2004–5. Elizabeth, whose older brother also went to Harvard, declined comment, saying she was "running out the door to play squash."

Not all of the COUR members' children who enrolled at Harvard were legacies. Some were development cases—children of wealthy non-alumni whom Harvard viewed as potential donors. While Harvard has never officially confirmed that it gives preference to such applicants, insiders say that, as at most universities, these candidates are included on a list of priority applicants that the development office sends to admissions.

Although her father, oil magnate Robert Bass, is a Yale graduate and her mother went to Smith College, Anne Chandler Bass (known as Chandler) entered Harvard in 1996 from the Groton School. Harvard administrators say Chandler, who was also accepted at Stanford, has a vivacious personality and athletic skill; as a freshman, she played field hockey for Harvard. Still, a former official told me, Harvard admitted her "in the hope of favors yet to come."

Those favors did arrive. After his daughter enrolled, Robert Bass became cochairman of Harvard's parent fund-raising committee, and he and his wife, Anne T. Bass, later joined the Committee on University Resources. Following their daughter's graduation in 2000, the Basses gave $7 million to endow two professorships. Government Professor Michael Sandel, who had been one of Chandler's teachers, was named Harvard's first Bass professor in 2002. Chandler herself received a Harvard fund-raising award that year.

Legacy preference at Harvard is supposed to be limited to a graduate's children. Yet the impact of major donors—alumni or not—on Harvard admissions extends far beyond the 336 students from their immediate families. They lobby, often successfully, for children of relatives, friends, neighbors, and clients. William Fitzsimmons, who himself served a stint in Harvard fund-raising as executive director of the Harvard College Fund from 1984 to 1986, immediately before becoming admissions dean, is receptive to such donor overtures. The late COUR chairman Robert Stone— a shipping executive who served on Harvard's governing board from 1975 to 2002 and chaired the search committee that picked Summers as president—told me in 2005, a year before his death, that he sometimes recommended candidates to Fitzsimmons.

"I never write a letter for a kid unless he comes around to talk to me," said Stone, two of whose children went to Harvard. After interviewing these candidates in his New York office, Stone told me, "I give my impressions to the admissions office. Is he hungry? Will he contribute to the class? Will he come to Harvard?" Asked about his batting average in gaining admission for applicants he recommended, Stone said modestly, "Pretty good."

COUR member Thomas Payette, a Boston architect, acted as an intermediary for a Japanese client who owned a construction company and wanted his son to attend the Harvard Graduate School of Design. According to Payette, a design school graduate who sent two of his own children there, the Japanese builder donated $1.25 million apiece to Harvard and Massachusetts Institute of Technology around 1990 to induce them to admit his son, a less than stellar applicant. Payette did not recall whether the gift swayed MIT, but said the youth was accepted to Harvard's landscape architecture program, which had more openings than other design school divisions.

I asked Payette whether COUR members pony up to Harvard to boost their children's chances for admission. "I imagine there's a little of that," he said. "We don't talk about it much. Right now most of us are at an age—it's our grandchildren we worry about."

THE ACCESS enjoyed by COUR members points up a fundamental problem with Harvard admissions. Other selection systems in our society have built-in protections against conflicts of interest. Doctors conducting clinical trials of promising drugs don't know which patients are given the new medications and which are taking a placebo. Cities hire police officers and firefighters based on civil service exams. Judges disqualify themselves from cases if they have personal or business relationships with lawyers or litigants, while the voir dire process ferrets out biased jurors. But Harvard— tied with Princeton for first place in *U.S. News & World Report's* 2006 ranking of America's best universities—relies on the discretion of its admissions staff to ensure that each applicant gets a fair hearing. With few safeguards against a rigged system or even natural human biases, it's hardly surprising that well-connected candidates edge out unhooked applicants.

Every year, Michael Holland runs the Boston Marathon with his close friend admissions dean William Fitzsimmons. "We have a long time to talk about everything," said Holland, a money manager and member of the Committee on University Resources. He and Fitzsimmons, he added, "go all the way back to college." Holland graduated from Harvard in 1966, a year before Fitzsimmons.

Neither Holland nor Fitzsimmons has ever regarded their friendship as a reason for the dean to remove himself from considering the applications of Holland's children. On the contrary, Holland said, Fitzsimmons personally interviewed one or two of his sons. Three of Holland's six sons enrolled at Harvard.

Fitzsimmons "doesn't recuse himself," said Holland, who endowed a scholarship fund at Harvard; he and his wife donated between $500,000 and $1 million to the Harvard campaign in the 1990s and between $250,000 and $500,000 in 2000–1. "Just the opposite. They look for any input from people. If you have a nephew or a niece applying, and you have a piece of information, they want to know it."

Fitzsimmons told me he knows so many Harvard alumni that it would be impractical for him to withdraw from considering their children's applications. "We say to anybody, whether it's a Harvard person or not, if they feel they can add something to a student's application, send it in," he said. "We're in the information business. If you have someone who knows Harvard well and knows the student well, they can add something useful in terms of a match between the two."

Like the dean, a significant portion of Harvard's undergraduate admissions staff consists of alumni who often know a legacy applicant's parents or siblings. Those familiar with admissions deliberations say it's quite common to hear such comments about a candidate as "He may not look great on paper, but his father was a late bloomer too."

Fitzsimmons dismissed such comments as irrelevant: "You don't admit or not admit somebody because their older brother was a terrific person." However, Lloyd Peterson, a former Yale admissions officer who now counsels applicants as vice president for education at College Coach Inc., said elite universities should be concerned about conflicts of interest. "It's difficult to sit in a room with a bunch of admissions officers at a place like Yale or Harvard and have 15,000 kids come across your desk and you not know any of them," he said. "There's a level of clubbiness that goes on behind closed doors."

Unlike Harvard's undergraduate admissions, its law school does have a conflict-of-interest policy. According to Professor Elizabeth Warren, who chairs the school's five-member admissions committee, members who know a student or a student's family cannot vote on that candidate. Such recusals take place "a handful of times" each year, she said.

"The purpose is to avoid being an insider's club," Warren said, while acknowledging the tension between that goal and the school's policy of giving preference to alumni children. "Lawyers may be more sensitive to conflict questions than most disciplines. We worry a lot about unarticulated and unintentional biases built into a system."

Harvard undergraduate admissions could reduce favoritism by eliminating weak applicants at an early stage of the process. Instead, anyone weeded out by a first cut can be resurrected later. "Everybody in the world is still in play until the last committee meeting at the end of March, when the letters go out," Fitzsimmons said. Since outstanding applicants would survive the winnowing anyway, this fluidity elevates connections over merit. "Who do you think is being brought back?" Peterson asked. "It's not a kid named Gonzalez from [California's Central Valley]. The kid's going to be named Rockefeller or Vanderbilt." He estimated that if the first cut were final, the number of children of COUR members admitted would drop in half.

Instead, hooked applicants get the nod at the last minute from the admissions committee—which at Harvard, as at most elite universities, is largely composed of admissions officials and faculty. As one former Harvard official described these deliberations, "It comes down to the last day and you have twenty tickets still to give. You're tipping people in and out. It's not over till it's over. You're weighing the black kid from Harlem or the Appalachian kid against the alumni son."

Such last-minute horse trading has a long history at Harvard. Half a century ago, Albert F. Gordon came out a winner. The son of Albert H. Gordon, a Wall Street financier and Harvard graduate who was already on

his way to becoming one of the university's biggest donors, the younger
Al applied in 1955 despite breaking the honor code at St. Paul's School in
Concord, New Hampshire, where he had been caught cheating on a chemistry final exam. It didn't help that he failed geometry as well. "I was a lousy
student," Gordon confided over breakfast in November 2004 at an inn just
outside Harvard Yard. "There's no one who ever had as much tutoring as I
did through all my school years."

Nevertheless, Gordon said, his father's influence prevailed. Wilbur
Bender, then dean of admissions, had made up his mind to reject the
younger Gordon until, on the last day of deliberations that year, Delmar
Leighton, then Harvard dean of students, made a rare appearance before
the admissions committee. "I only have to tell you one thing," Leighton
said to the committee. "Albert Gordon has to be on the list."

Gordon scraped through Harvard—"I had to sweat every exam," he
said—and had a successful career as an investment banker at Kidder,
Peabody & Co., the firm his father had rescued from collapse during the
Great Depression. Albert H. Gordon, who turned 104 in 2005 but remains
active, has given $30 million to Harvard. The younger Al has chipped in
with another $5.3 million to the university, where his daughter, three sib-
lings, and four nephews and nieces also enrolled. Al used to belong to the
Committee on University Resources; three family members remain on the
committee, including his father and a sister on the executive committee.
"The committee is nothing more than a meat market," Al said. "They parade you around, and if you don't give enough, your kid won't get in."

Al said the admissions wheeling and dealing hasn't changed much
since he applied to Harvard: relatives and friends whom he or his father
recommends often find their way into the student body. While acknowledging that this kowtowing to donors is unfair to outsiders who aren't part
of the club, he said it's vital to sustaining fund-raising and alumni loyalty.

"This is why I do what I do for Harvard," he said. "They were damned
decent to me. So they get rewarded, big-time. This is why Harvard is loved
by so many people. Guys that do very well, that get through Harvard very
easily, they could care less."

ANNIE GRAYSON was not inducted into the Cum Laude Society at Hotchkiss, a Lakeville, Connecticut, boarding school. Although Hotchkiss does not officially rank students, a person familiar with her record told me that Annie's grades placed her slightly below the middle of her class. Her SAT score was in the 1200s, at least 200 points under the Harvard average.

Harvard would give short shrift to an unhooked applicant with those credentials. But Annie was the daughter of Boston-area venture capitalist Bruns H. Grayson Jr., a Harvard alumnus and member of the Committee on University Resources. Her mother, Perrin, also graduated from Harvard. In 2003–4, Annie's senior year at Hotchkiss, her parents gave Harvard at least $1 million. In his thirtieth-anniversary report to his classmates that year, Grayson, quoting the poet Robert Browning, noted that he has "plenty of money, money enough and to spare."

When Annie applied, Harvard placed her on its waiting list. Then, shortly after her Hotchkiss graduation, Harvard notified her that she had been admitted—but with a twist. She could not enroll with her fellow high school graduates at Harvard that September; instead, she had to wait a year, until fall 2005, before entering as a freshman. The Grayson family declined comment for this book.

If wealthy or well-connected applicants aren't admitted to Harvard in the standard fashion, they need not despair. Like Annie Grayson, they may be placed on the "Z-list"—a Harvard admissions office term for a little-known policy that compromises standards in the interests of alumni and donors, enabling their children to enter America's most famous university by a side door. The Z-list consists of twenty-five to fifty well-connected but often academically borderline applicants accepted on condition they defer enrollment until the following fall—when they occupy slots that could otherwise be given to outstanding but unhooked applicants.

Harvard also wait-listed Annie Grayson's Hotchkiss classmate Katherine Campo but didn't offer her deferred admission. Katherine, who enrolled at Brown instead, was a top student at Hotchkiss and a member of the Cum Laude Society and had a higher SAT score than Annie. "Annie was a great kid, really enthusiastic, outgoing," Katherine told me. "She deserves to go anywhere. But in terms of actual numbers, there are a ton of people who should have gotten in over her. She wasn't at the top.

"Personally, I don't like" preferences for children of alumni and donors, Katherine added. "It should all be based on merit. If I didn't know Annie, I would be angry and bitter. The frustrating thing is knowing there are really smart kids who don't have the opportunity."

The *Harvard Crimson* reported in 2002 that 72 percent of students on the "Z-list" are alumni children. My research showed that quite a few children of COUR members deferred admission for a year, sometimes more than one child in the same family. Annie Grayson's sister, Lucy, who graduated from St. Paul's School in New Hampshire in 2001, delayed a year before entering Harvard.

Ashley Hobbs—daughter of COUR executive committee member Franklin W. Hobbs IV—took a year off after graduating from Hotchkiss, where she didn't rank in the top 20 percent. Her father, an investment banker, was elected to Harvard's board of overseers in 2000; among other donations, he gave Harvard between $250,000 and $500,000 in 2003–4, when Ashley was a sophomore.

"In my experience, students on the Z-list were connected kids, sometimes but not always academically weaker," Susan Case, former college counselor at Milton Academy, told me. "I could usually predict who might end up with that option by seeing the family's history."

Harvard says that the Z-list isn't meant specifically for children of alumni and donors, but for all students whom it would like to take off the waiting list but can't find beds for. "The idea is that when we finally run out of spaces every year, we'll offer twenty, thirty, forty people the chance to come a year from now," admissions dean William Fitzsimmons told me. If there is a preponderance of alumni children, he said, it's because they're more dedicated to Harvard and more familiar with the deferral option than other applicants; they'll hang on longer, hoping to make the Z-list, rather than enrolling at another university.

Fitzsimmons said that the Z-list originated in the late 1970s as part of an effort by Harvard to encourage students to take a year off before college. According to admissions insiders, the list gradually evolved into a legacy program. For Harvard, deferral was a no-lose proposition: either it would discourage underqualified legacies from enrolling without actually rejecting them, thus preserving both academic quality and donor goodwill, or the students would mature in their year off, readying them for Harvard. It turned out that most Z-listers were willing to wait for a Harvard education. Twenty-four out of thirty-four students on the list in 2003, and forty out of forty-eight in 2004, accepted the deferred admission, according to Fitzsimmons.

Harvard touts deferral in an essay, "Time Out or Burn Out for the Next Generation," which it sends to Z-listed students and features on its admissions website. Written by Fitzsimmons and two other Harvard officials, the article contends that a year off helps students relax and mature. "Perhaps the best way of all to get the full benefit of a 'time off' is to postpone entrance to college for a year," they write. "After all the places in the current class are filled, a small number of outstanding applicants have been offered the opportunity to come to Harvard for the subsequent academic year. . . . The results have been uniformly positive."

Harvard does not tell students how to spend the interim year. Wealthy legacies often sign up for expensive backpacking expeditions or sailing trips. Michael Meighan, director of programs for Sea-mester, a Sarasota, Florida, outfit that charges students $14,500 to sail for eighty days in the Caribbean on a traditionally rigged schooner and learn leadership and team-building skills, told me that at least three students deferred by Harvard had spent part of their year off in its programs. One was Ashley Hobbs, who participated in "Club Snork n' Fun" during her Caribbean voyage. "After her sailing days here, she will travel to Italy for the spring and then begin school at Harvard in the fall," the organization's newsletter reported.

For well-connected students, the Z-list isn't the only roundabout route to a Harvard degree. Instead of deferring for a year, they can enroll somewhere else and then transfer in. In general, students at other colleges who seek to transfer to Harvard face even more daunting odds than freshman applicants; Harvard typically admits only 5 percent of its one thousand transfer candidates a year. But, as in freshman admissions, children of alumni and donors enjoy a marked preference in the transfer process.

Richard L. Menschel, a Harvard Business School graduate and a senior director at Goldman Sachs, cochaired Harvard's $2.6 billion campaign in the 1990s and sits on the COUR executive committee. His wife, Ronay Menschel, also a COUR member, is a former deputy mayor of New York City. They have given generously to Harvard's business school, school of public health, and art museums. The Menschels' two older daughters, Charis and Sabina, both went to Harvard. The third, Celene, was not in the top 10 percent of her class at her fashionable New York City prep school, Nightingale-Bamford.

She matriculated in 2000 at Connecticut College in New London, Connecticut, where she flourished academically and on the women's cross-country team. After two years, she was admitted to Harvard as a transfer—an unusual leap from a respectable liberal arts college to America's premier university. According to Connecticut College, only one student in its five prior classes had transferred to Harvard.

Ned Bishop, track coach at Connecticut College, told me that Celene was reluctant to leave. While she starred on his team, he said, she wasn't a standout at Harvard, which competes in a tougher division. "I got some impression, in terms of running, she wished she had still been part of our team," he said. "My sense of her transferring was just the family connection to Harvard. She felt a little bit of family obligation to go to Harvard if she could."

THE ACADEMIC and status differences between children of COUR members and unhooked students persist even after the chosen few enroll at Harvard. They share one campus but move in separate worlds. The donors' children lag behind scholastically and forge ahead socially. Coming from the same fashionable prep schools or neighborhoods, playing the same upper-class sports, they often end up living together, eating together, and hanging out together in Harvard's exclusive "finals clubs."

Long dominated by prep school graduates and athletes, Harvard's semisecret finals clubs, like the eating clubs at Princeton, offer a party scene and behind-the-scenes job network for the affluent. COUR executive committee member Ernest Monrad, a Boston money manager who has endowed two Harvard chairs, recalled that he got his start after law school at a Boston firm because he and the senior partner both belonged to the Fox club. "It got me the interview," Monrad said. Two of his sons and a grandson have followed him to Harvard, and all three joined finals clubs: AD, Fox, and Fly. "I've got two grandchildren up for admission" to Harvard now, he told me. "I'm just going to stay away. They know my name, I think."

University Resources committee members Richard Cashin Jr. and Jonathan Kemper, a Kansas City banker, graduated from Harvard in the same year, 1975. Cashin was in the Owl Club, Kemper in the Phoenix. Nearly thirty years later, their daughters, Frances Cashin and Charlotte Kemper, were Harvard roommates. "Last year, I was at a dinner table, and we were all legacies there except one girl," Charlotte told me. "She said, 'Maybe I should leave.'" Although Charlotte can't belong to her father's club, which remains all-male, she said she occasionally goes to parties there.

At universities with significant dropout rates, just graduating is a mark of academic achievement. But it's much tougher to get into Harvard than to graduate from it; 97 percent of entering freshmen emerge with a degree. Thus, the honors—or lack thereof—awarded students upon graduation offer a better yardstick for measuring scholastic prowess. By examining honors data on 192 COUR members' children who graduated from Harvard since 1980, I found that they were more likely to graduate without honors and less likely to attain the top two categories of distinction (magna and summa cum laude, aka high and highest honors) than the Harvard average. Typically, the number of Harvard students who receive high or highest honors exceeds those graduating without honors. In my sample, the reverse was true. About one-fifth, or thirty-nine children of donors, earned summa or magna degrees, while more than one-fourth, or fifty, graduated without honors, including three of James Welch's six sons. (The balance, 103, graduated with honors—cum laude.) Overall, only one-tenth of Harvard graduates were not given honors in 2004, down from 22 percent in 1990.

The lackluster performance of the donors' children may reflect their lesser high school credentials. Alternatively, they may be less motivated to excel in the classroom than other students because their financial security is ensured.

There are, of course, conspicuous exceptions to this pattern. Elizabeth, Fernanda, and Charlotte Winthrop come from the twelfth generation of their family at Harvard, where a dormitory is named Winthrop House. Both of their parents are Harvard graduates; their father, investment adviser Grant Winthrop, is on the Committee on University Resources. But the sisters haven't coasted on their blue-blooded pedigrees. All three were top students at Nightingale-Bamford before entering Harvard. Elizabeth graduated summa cum laude in 2001, winning a fiction prize for writing the best short story by an undergraduate. Fernanda graduated magna cum laude in 2004, the same year that Charlotte enrolled.

In high school, Charlotte told me, she was valedictorian and senior class president and edited the literary magazine. Her SAT score was 1480—about Harvard's average. After her junior year at Nightingale, at her father's instigation, she met with Fitzsimmons. "We mainly talked about travel," she said. "I have a big interest in Southeast Asia. I'd like to think I would have gotten in had I not been a legacy. But there are so many qualified people who apply that I'm sure it helps."

Another Harvard legacy from Nightingale-Bamford, Elizabeth Niemiec, became disillusioned with the snobbish club scene of the campus jet set. Her father, investment banker David Niemiec, and her mother, Melanie Niemiec, are both Harvard graduates and COUR members. A top Nightingale student with a 1520 SAT score, Elizabeth was also admitted to Pomona and Williams colleges and Wesleyan University. Although she preferred Pomona, her parents persuaded her to go to Harvard. While she was applying there, a staff member in the development office who had been a classmate of her father's showed her around campus and introduced her to the head of Harvard's environmental science and public policy department, her field of interest. During her freshman year, 2000–1, her parents gave Harvard between $250,000 and $500,000.

As a freshman, Elizabeth recalled, she "just wound up spending time with other girls who had gone to the small private schools in New York. It was easier. We had something in common. And all the guys I knew freshman year were people I might have met at my prom and their friends, people they met at their finals clubs."

Elizabeth chose to live in a group or "block" with five other legacies, all but one from New York. In their sophomore year, all six joined the Bee, a finals club for women. Clubs such as Bee sprang up because the traditional finals clubs remain all-male; they severed ties with Harvard rather than admit women. The Bee's president, Molly Krause, was the older sister of one of Elizabeth's blockmates, and made sure they were all invited—or "punched," in club jargon. Molly's father, Peter Krause, managing director of the Greenhill investment banking firm, is on the University Resources committee; he and his wife, Alice, both nonalumni, co-chaired Harvard's parent fund-raising program.

As a junior, Elizabeth roomed with Fernanda Winthrop and Molly's younger sister, Christina Krause—a trio of daughters of COUR members. Fernanda and Christina were the Bee's "punch masters," deciding who would be invited to join the club. "It drove me crazy," Elizabeth said. "When I was on the other side of it, and all the members were talking about the reasons not to let so-and-so in, or to let so-and-so in, it was horrible. I was hiding in my room. I totally removed myself from the Bee and my block and branched out more." She moved in with a working-class student from Michigan before heading to Mexico for a semester of field work.

Elizabeth graduated in 2004 and became a researcher in the white-collar-crime division of the Manhattan district attorney's office. She plans to go to medical school. Admissions preference for children of alumni and donors, she believes, "isn't fair at all. They push people out of the pool perhaps before they should, and keep others in the pool that maybe shouldn't be.

"I didn't really run into many geniuses" at Harvard, she continued. "There are a lot of people who are legacies I know that are really smart and did really well at Harvard. The people who have the most social conscience and are interested in discussing ethics are generally not the legacies. I was in a peer-counseling group for rape and sexual assault victims—we answered phones, took drop-ins from students having emotional issues. The group of women that I met there were fascinating and great. They were also less likely to be legacies than the people I ran into in other circles."

CHARLES KUSHNER had big ambitions—for his business and his children. The New Jersey real estate developer once proclaimed that he wanted to be "one of the largest owners in the country." He also yearned to send his two sons to the country's most famous university.

Kushner applied the same strategy to fulfilling both of these goals: buying access. His success—and subsequent downfall—suggests that elite universities are just as susceptible as politicians to the lure of big money. They also demonstrate that Harvard, despite its nod to alumni loyalty and tradition, will bend admissions standards as far for the child of a wealthy nonalumnus with no prior affiliation to the university as for any legacy—provided that the parent ponies up a suitable donation.

Kushner's real estate empire, worth more than $1 billion, grew from a construction business started by his father, a Holocaust survivor, to encompass 25,000 apartments, 5 million square feet of industrial, office, and retail space, and thousands of acres of undeveloped land in the mid-Atlantic region. He protected his expanding domain by becoming one of the country's biggest political contributors. From 1997 to 2002, according to the *Bergen Record,* Kushner, his family, and his business associates directed at least $3.1 million to political committees and politicians, including more than $1.5 million to James McGreevey, who was elected governor of New Jersey in 2001. The Kushner circle's largesse to Democrats rivaled the lavish giving by Enron Corp. to George W. Bush and other Republicans before the Texas energy trading giant self-destructed in 2001. Starting before they had even reached voting age, Kushner's two sons and two daughters contributed nearly $300,000, the *Record* reported.

Kushner's home and headquarters became a compulsory stop for prominent Democrats visiting New Jersey, including President Clinton and Vice President Al Gore. Governor McGreevey stocked his administration with Kushner cronies and nominated the real estate baron to chair the Port Authority of New York and New Jersey, which controls lucrative development contracts in the New York area. Kushner was never confirmed; he stepped down in the face of legislators' demands to question him about potential conflicts of interest.

Kushner's philanthropy wasn't limited to politicians. He also gave prodigiously to various charities, including Harvard. In 1998, according to two sources familiar with the gift, the New York University alumnus pledged $2.5 million to Harvard, to be paid in annual installments of $250,000. Harvard then named Kushner and his wife, Seryl Stadtmauer Kushner, to the Committee on University Resources.

At the time of the pledge, Kushner's older son, Jared, was starting the college admissions process at the Frisch School, a Jewish high school in Paramus, New Jersey. A senior in 1998–99, Jared was not in the school's highest academic track in all courses, and his test scores were below Ivy League standards. Frisch officials were surprised when he applied to Harvard—and dismayed when he was admitted.

"There was no way anybody in the administrative office of the school thought he would on the merits get into Harvard," a former school official told me. "His GPA did not warrant it, his SAT scores did not warrant it. We thought for sure, there was no way this was going to happen. Then, lo and behold, Jared was accepted. It was a little bit disappointing because there were at the time other kids we thought should really get in on the merits, and they did not. I believe that Jared, for the longest time, didn't want to talk about any of this, because he felt a little bit upset or guilty that he may have taken somebody else's place. One of the things the Ivies ask is, 'Was this student in the most challenging courses offered in the school?' We could not answer that question yes."

Margo Krebs, who was director of Frisch's college preparatory program at the time, said, "Jared was certainly not anywhere near the top of his class. He had some very strong personal qualities. He's a very charming young man with a great deal of poise, the sort of kid you would look at him and say, 'This is a future politician.' It was an unusual choice for Harvard to make."

Kalman Stein, the current school principal, arrived at Frisch the year after Jared graduated. "I can tell you he was in good classes, took some advanced placement classes, had some decent grades," Stein told me. "Isn't that the norm: you give enough money to a college and you get your kid in?"

Along with his wealth, Kushner may also have used his political connections to sway Harvard. A source close to the family told me that New Jersey senator Frank Lautenberg, to whom Kushner and his family gave nearly $100,000 from 1992 to 2002, turned to Massachusetts senator Edward Kennedy to boost Jared's Harvard prospects. Senator Kennedy, a Harvard alumnus whose family has been associated with the university for three generations, is said to have contacted admissions dean William Fitzsimmons, who then spoke with Kushner. A spokeswoman for Senator Kennedy said the office has no record of any involvement with Kushner, and that the senator makes admissions calls only for family members.

However it was arranged, Kushner was granted an audience with Neil Rudenstine, then Harvard president. "He was very interested in trying to start a scholarship program for low-income and middle-income students," the former president told me. "He seemed quite committed and sincere about it." Rudenstine, who referred Kushner to the development office, said that "the issue of admissions never came up, nor was I aware of the fact that he had children."

Rudenstine wasn't the only Ivy League president whom Kushner cultivated. In addition to his seven-figure pledge to Harvard, the real estate tycoon donated smaller amounts to Cornell and Princeton. At his request,

Hunter Rawlings, president of Cornell from 1995 to 2003, toured Kushner Yeshiva High School in Livingston, New Jersey. The developer was on the school's board and had pledged $1 million to rename it after his parents.

"All I remember is that Charlie came to Cornell once for a visit," Rawlings told me. "He said he was very involved in a school in New Jersey. I made a trip there. Charlie just wanted me to see the school and meet some teachers." Kushner also told Rawlings, the ex-president recalled, that "he would love it if students from the school could be considered at Cornell."

The developer may have hoped that Cornell would favorably consider one Yeshiva High student in particular: his second son, Joshua. Like his brother, Joshua Kushner was not an academic standout. Rabbi Jeremy Luchins, chairman of the Kushner Yeshiva science department, said Joshua took a second-level science track rather than the grueling honors classes he teaches. The rabbi described Kushner's children as "hard workers. They may not be academic stars, but they do well in whatever track they're in, by dint of sweat." But if the developer viewed Cornell as Joshua's insurance against a Harvard rejection, he need not have worried: after graduating from Yeshiva High, Joshua enrolled at Harvard in 2004.

Kushner didn't neglect his alma mater either. His major gifts to New York University coincided with the matriculation of two of his children there. Kushner gave $3 million to endow an undergraduate deanship at NYU in July 2001; his daughter, Dara, enrolled that fall. In October 2002, Kushner was appointed to NYU's board of trustees. In June 2003, his real estate company leased three floors of the famous Puck Building in SoHo to NYU at below-market rates. That same month, Jared Kushner graduated from Harvard. He then entered NYU's law school, ranked one of the nation's top five law schools by *U.S. News & World Report*.

Kushner also discussed giving the Puck Building outright to NYU. The city valued the building, which is listed as a New York City landmark on the National Register of Historic Places, at $18.6 million in fiscal 2006 for property tax purposes; its actual value on the market would likely be much higher. The donation was never consummated, as the developer's profligate purchasing of political access came back to haunt him.

In June 2004, Kushner agreed to pay $508,900 to the Federal Election Commission as a civil penalty for making campaign contributions from business partnerships without obtaining the partners' agreement. Six weeks later, the governor whose political career Kushner had bankrolled resigned in a sex scandal. McGreevey revealed that he was gay after his former homeland security aide, Golan Cipel, threatened to sue him for sexual harassment. Kushner himself had employed Cipel at one time and sponsored the Israeli's U.S. work permit. On August 18, 2004, less than a week after the governor's resignation, Kushner pleaded guilty to federal charges of tax violations, illegal campaign contributions, and retaliating against a witness—his own sister, Esther Schulder, who was cooperating with federal investigators. The developer had paid a prostitute $10,000 to seduce his brother-in-law, William Schulder, and then sent his sister a tape taken by a hidden camera of the motel room encounter. As part of the tax probe, federal authorities subpoenaed records of Kushner's giving to Harvard.

Kushner stepped down from the presidency of his company and the NYU board. In March 2005, the real estate czar who had capitalized on his riches to dominate New Jersey business and politics, ingratiate himself with one president of the United States and two Ivy League presidents, and engineer his sons' admission to the nation's best-known university was sentenced to two years in federal prison.

2

RECRUITING

THE RICH

Development Admits
at Duke

Jean Scott switched from teaching history at Duke University to directing its undergraduate admissions office in 1980 with the dream of selecting the best possible freshman class.

Then she found out about the cardboard box.

Twice a year, after evaluating Duke's first and second round of applicants, Ms. Scott would lug a box—of the size that, in her prior job, she might have stacked with English-history texts for her bookshelves—a quarter mile down Chapel Drive from the admissions building to President Terry Sanford's spartan office on the second floor of the administration building. There, she would unpack its contents: applications of candidates whom she had intended to reject but who were on a list of students the president had sent her for special consideration. He had chosen them not because they showed academic promise he feared might otherwise go unnoticed but because they were the children of corporate titans expected, in the event of a favorable decision, to contribute to the university endowment. Duke, one of the South's best universities, aspired to national preeminence—and it needed money to get there.

Over lunch or coffee, the president and the admissions director hashed over the folders one by one. Scott would justify each rejection—one applicant was close, but she had denied two thousand just like him;

another was a real stretch; she doubted whether a third could do college work at all. Sanford, a former North Carolina governor, was too cagey a manager, and too courtly a southerner, to give orders, but she learned to read his signals, to distinguish between the instances when he was just going through the motions for a friend and when he wanted a student admitted no matter what the credentials. She won some battles, lost others, and occasionally compromised: an unimpressive but potentially lucrative applicant might be required to attend a summer transition program before freshman year, or enroll elsewhere for a year or two to demonstrate a capacity to pass college courses before being taken as a transfer.

"There was more of this input at Duke than at any other institution I ever worked for," said Scott, now president of Marietta College, a liberal arts college in Ohio. "There were certainly students who got in because they were a high priority" for fund-raising. "I would have been very pleased to have the best class as determined by the admissions office. But the world isn't like that. I got a little frustrated."

BY THE time Marianna "Maude" Bunn applied to Duke for the fall of 2001, Jean Scott had long since moved on, Terry Sanford had died (in 1998), and applicants were tracked by computer. But one thing hadn't changed: children of prospective donors still got a break.

Maude fell in love with Duke's Gothic-style campus on her first visit, during spring break as a high school junior. "It just felt right for me," she told me. Whether she was right for Duke was a tougher question. She lacked the outstanding academic record expected of an applicant to one of the nation's best and most selective universities. Duke accepts fewer than one-fourth of its applicants; 75 percent of its students score above 1320 on the SAT, and 88 percent are in the top tenth of their high school class.

Despite solid grades at her boarding school, the Lawrenceville School in Lawrenceville, New Jersey, Maude was not inducted into its chapter of the Cum Laude honor society, indicating that she did not rank in the top 20 percent of her class. As for her standardized tests, "when I first took the SATs, my scores were really, really low," she said. After studying with a tutor once a week over the summer, she "did a little better" but still below the Duke average. Her extracurriculars—school sports, dorm treasurer, working on the yearbook—were unexceptional; she joked with Protestant friends about starting a "WASP Club." She wrote her college application essay about *Afterlife*, an independent Japanese film that, she says, "affected me."

Maude also did not stand to gain from any of the standard admissions preferences. She was not a minority, a recruited athlete, or legacy; her father and several other relatives were Princeton graduates. But she did enjoy one attribute of potential appeal to Duke—family wealth. Although Maude grew up in the ritzy Chicago suburb of Lake Forest, Illinois, her ancestors hailed from the downstate city of Springfield. The family had dominated Springfield business since the time of Abraham Lincoln (said to be an early customer of a bank founded by the Bunns in the 1850s); the Bunn name is to Illinois's capital what du Pont is to Delaware. Besides banking, Bunn ventures in Springfield included a watch factory, an electric company, a grocery wholesaler, and, most notably, Bunn-O-Matic Corp., the coffeemaker company founded by Maude's great-uncle.

Moreover, the Bunns had the kind of philanthropic track record that warms the hearts of college fund-raisers. At Lawrenceville, alma mater of more than a dozen family members, Maude studied at the Bunn Library— opened in 1996 and fully equipped for the digital age—and her father, Willard "Googan" Bunn III, was a trustee.

Duke's development office flagged Maude's application, and she was accepted. Her parents promptly became cochairmen of a Duke fundraising effort aimed at other parents of the class of 2005. As of December 2004, her parents had donated at least $10,000 to Duke in two separate years.

Maude's mother was well aware from a briefing given to the parent fund-raising group by Duke admissions officials that her daughter's record did not meet the university's usual academic expectations of near-perfect SAT scores and a plethora of advanced placement courses. "That wasn't Maude," Jeanette "Cissy" Bunn told me in 2003. "Maude, she's bright, she has good grades, but she doesn't meet the superstar status. She has not written books, she has not performed with the city ballet. Those [super-stars] are the kids applying to all these schools, millions of them, gifted, wonderful kids. Most of us have normal kids. We're very grateful. I'm not cavalier, which is why I do the parents' thing.

"The only thing Maude wanted in life was to go to Duke. They were kind enough to take her. My child was given a gift, she got in, and now I'm giving back.

"Did my normal child take the place of somebody who could really make a difference in the world? Sure, yes. To an extent. But there are so many things you can lose sleep over. I'm happy for me and my child."

SINCE HIRING Terry Sanford as president in 1969 and getting serious about its national ambitions, Duke has enrolled thousands of privileged but underqualified applicants with no prior ties to the university, in the expectation of parental payback. This strategy has helped elevate Duke's endowment, undersized compared with those of rivals such as Harvard, Yale, and Stanford, from 25th in 1980 ($135 million) to 16th in 2005 ($3.8 billion), generating more funds for scholarships, buildings, and faculty. But these gains have come at a price—the integrity of Duke's admissions process.

Duke is not alone in making this trade-off. While legacy preference is primarily a fund-raising tool, universities justify it with rhetoric about preserving valuable traditions and rewarding loyal volunteers. There's no such justification for the students known as "development admits"—the children of wealthy nonalumni. They are the dirty little secret of college admissions. These students are often substantially underqualified and have no familial connection to the school. Their strongest advocates come from the development, or fund-raising, office, and their primary qualification is the money their parents are expected to give to the school upon acceptance.

Colleges, which understate the extent of legacy preference, often deny that they have development admits. Just as great newspapers guarantee the objectivity of their reports by separating selling of advertisements from the gathering of information, so great universities profess to safeguard the quality of their student bodies by constructing a firewall between fund-raising from admissions.

In reality, there is no such wall—not even a shallow trench. Almost every university takes development admits, and the practice is increasingly prevalent, fueled by larger economic forces. Reflecting the growing income gap in American society, the ranks of the *über*-rich are multiplying. The number of billionaires on the *Forbes* magazine list of the 400 richest Americans increased from 13 in 1982 to 374 in 2005. Like other nonprofits, colleges want a piece of that action—and the easiest way is to admit these moguls' children.

Until recently, relatively few colleges emphasized raising money from nonalumni parents. Their attitude has been that alumni give for a lifetime, while parents give only while their children are in college. Plus, parents already paid tuition. But with corporate and government money declining as a proportion of total higher education support since the mid-1980s, and with the number of people who could afford a major gift on top of tuition swelling, college development officers began looking beyond their traditional alumni constituency to nonalumni parents and other potential donors with whom they could claim a connection, however remote.

For appearances' sake, most colleges are careful to avoid making explicit deals or promises while the application is under review. But once the student is admitted they're quick to solicit contributions or invite parents to join a fund-raising group. Duke and other colleges deny selling slots—"There's no quid pro quo, no bargains have been struck," Duke's director of development communications, Peter Vaughn, told me—but there's a mutual understanding that one good turn deserves another.

When pressed to justify development admits, college administrators sometimes claim a social benefit to ensuring that children of the rich enjoy an elite education. These students will someday inherit considerable wealth, the argument goes, and a good education will incline them to use it or give it away more wisely. But this argument doesn't account for what economists would call the "opportunity cost," or forgone benefits, of this policy. To make room for the unexceptional rich, elite colleges turn away brighter, upwardly mobile applicants who may take advantage of their education to accumulate just as much wealth by starting a business or making a scientific advance that enhances the health and welfare of society. Like legacies, development admits are held to a lesser standard—not whether they are the best candidates in the pool but whether they can graduate—and take the place of more deserving students, including those from low- or middle-income backgrounds.

Top universities ranging from Stanford to Emory say they occasionally consider parental wealth in admissions decisions. "We do advise the admissions office about applications coming from the children or grandchildren of significant donors," Yale president Richard Levin told the university's alumni magazine in 2004. "Which doesn't mean that they are automatically admitted!" At New York University, the associate provost for admissions, the head of fund-raising, and the president's chief of staff meet every Monday to discuss a three-page list of about forty applicants whose parents are leaders in business, politics, media, and entertainment. "The list comes from different places," said Barbara Hall, associate provost for admissions. "A dean may put us on to somebody, the board of trustees, the president, the development office, whatever. If it's a close call, the decision will go in favor of the student."

Students who eschew a development edge may suffer for their scruples. In 1998, despite her mother's urging, Caroline Braga decided not to tell Brown University that one of her maternal ancestors, William F. Sayles, endowed Sayles Hall on campus in 1881. Despite a 1430 SAT score, she was rejected and went instead to Georgetown, which accepts a higher proportion of applicants than Brown. "I was a little bit naive," she said. "In an ideal world, I wouldn't include preferences. In the real world, you use whatever tools you have to get where you want to go." Michael Goldberger, Brown director of admission from 1995 to 2005, acknowledged that "having a building named after your family on our campus would be a plus factor."

The length of a college's development list depends on the school's financial well-being and alumni resources. Traditional elite schools, such as Harvard or Yale, reap so much money from alumni that they rarely bother to chase any but the richest nonalumni children. On the other hand, for young, aggressive universities without a long-nurtured and deep-pocketed alumni base, development admits offer a quick endowment fix, as well as an opportunity to jump-start a family pattern of giving.

Although it had earlier roots as a Methodist college, Duke was not established as a university until the 1920s. From 1994 to 2003, according to the Council for Aid to Education, Duke received only 20.5 percent of its nongovernmental revenue from alumni, far less than Princeton's 54.6 percent, Yale's 52.7 percent, and Harvard's 41.8 percent. Instead, Duke has cultivated wealthy nonalumni by giving breaks to their children who fall below its rigid admissions standards.

In the late 1990s, at the height of a fund-raising campaign and a soaring stock market, Duke relaxed its standards to admit more than one hundred applicants a year who would have been turned away without pressure from the development office. More than half of them enrolled, constituting an estimated 3 to 5 percent of Duke's student body of 6,200. Many of their grateful fathers and mothers joined Duke's parent fund-raising group, which year after year led all universities nationwide in unrestricted gifts to its annual fund from nonalumni parents.

"A Duke education is too valuable an asset to squander," former Duke president Keith Brodie told me. "University presidents are under greater pressure than ever to raise money. I suspect many of them have turned to admissions to help that process."

Duke's pandering to rich applicants may have fostered divisions within its student body and between the university and the surrounding community. According to annual student surveys conducted by *The Princeton Review*, members of different races and social classes interact less at Duke than at most other major universities. Such tensions flared painfully in spring 2006 when three members of Duke's virtually all-white men's lacrosse squad were indicted in connection with the alleged rape of a black single mother, a student at a predominantly black university nearby, who had been hired to dance at a team party. All three athletes came from affluent suburbs and attended exclusive private high schools.

Duke's thirst for development admits also left it vulnerable to a con artist. In the late 1980s, a continuing-education student calling himself Baron Maurice Jeffrey Locke de Rothschild cut quite a figure at Duke, driving expensive cars, buying champagne for frat parties, befriending top university administrators, and boasting about his famed European banking relatives. When the local banks called in his chits, the baron turned out to be Mauro Cortez Jr., a Mexican American of modest means from El Paso, whose assumed surname had been a shrewd ploy to vault him into an elite university. In 1991, the not-so-nobleman was sentenced to three years in prison for bank fraud.

BEFORE STUDENTS from affluent families can be admitted, they have to apply. That doesn't happen only by chance. Colleges shape the economic status of their applicant pool through recruiting. To attract rich candidates, they target promotional mailings to families in the wealthiest zip codes, or send admissions staff to stir up interest at elite private and suburban high schools.

Bates College, a liberal arts school in Maine that prided itself on its lack of snobbishness, discovered around 1980 that egalitarianism was getting expensive. Its loyal alumni couldn't afford major gifts, its students were financially needier than those of rivals such as Bowdoin and Middlebury, and the number of college-bound teenagers from its traditional base in rural and suburban New England public schools was declining. According to Susan Tree, director of admissions from 1979 to 1991, Bates reacted with a twofold strategy—recruiting more intensively at private schools while placating liberal faculty by also seeking minority and inner-city students.

"Bates wanted to admit children of people with a history of philanthropy, and it influenced where we chose to travel to recruit," Tree said. "Bates did not have as strong a history at the big independent schools where heavy hitters tend to send children. We began in the late 1970s being more intentional about developing our relationships with independent schools where there are lots more of these people." Tree herself began mining private schools in metropolitan New York, where Bates was little known. The tactic worked, she says; applications soared from 2,300 to 4,000 a year as Bates raised both its stature in the prep school world and its endowment. But it lost a certain modesty in the process, she says: "It's become much more elitist in its self-image."

Tree says Bates did lower academic standards for some wealthy prep school applicants, but she defends their admission. "I remember one wonderful Bates family which sent three children to the college, each of whom was out of the profile," she told me in an email. "We admitted them because of our relationship with their independent schools and faith that they would succeed at Bates and make some valuable contributions. The schools were ones we were hoping to do more business with and, while not proven scholars, it was clear that these kids were leaders and viewed very positively by the faculty and their peers. We were right and never regretted the decisions. The parents became avid supporters of the college. There was never any thought in the mind of the admission staff ahead of time that this family would do anything for the college—but they certainly did."

Prep schools—which admit their own legacies and development cases—understand only too well what recruiters are seeking. Eager to place as many graduates as possible at top institutions, prep school counselors help colleges identify development admits, often through an unobtrusive phrase or two in a letter of recommendation stating that the parents have been generous to the prep school and are likely to give to their child's college as well. The prep school's fund-raising office may call the college to reinforce the message.

In return, colleges often tip off prep schools in advance about which students they intend to take. Colleges also consult the school counselors about whether they can get away with accepting a low-performing student from a wealthy family while rejecting a standout of lesser means. Taking a development case "out of context," as this practice is euphemistically known, can hurt a college's reputation if it isn't handled deftly. Colleges sometimes accept a high-achieving applicant they don't really want, just so they can take an underqualified development case without causing too much consternation among classmates and parents. Or they tell the prep school that the development prospect must achieve a certain minimum SAT score to be admitted.

"If ten students apply from a school, you don't want to take numbers one, two, and eight," said Jean Scott, the former Duke admissions director. "Occasionally, we'd go back and take someone stronger who was on the bubble, for whom a rejection would be extraordinarily painful. You want to make the kid who worked hard and got a 95 average feel they were treated with something resembling justice."

A last-minute intervention by university fund-raisers can reverse a pending rejection. Susan Tree, who became director of college counseling at Westtown School in Pennsylvania after leaving Bates, recalled "one year when on a Monday in March, Wesleyan told me that a particular senior would not be admitted. Three days later the student told me joyfully that he received an admission letter. . . . I went to my office and called my liaison in admissions and said, 'Is this a mistake?' He (a rookie) said, 'Oh no,' they had received a call from the development office and the decision was changed."

How much does it cost to buy your child's way into college? Educational consultants say a five-figure donation—as low as $20,000—is enough to draw the attention of a liberal arts college with an endowment in the hundreds of millions. At an exclusive college, it can take at least $50,000 with some assurance that future donations will be even greater. At top-25 universities, a minimum of $100,000 is required; for the top 10, at least $250,000 and often seven figures.

It's considered crass for wealthy parents to approach college officials directly with a financial proposal while their child is applying. "Everyone in my position was offered bribes," said Mary Anne Schwalbe, former associate dean for admissions at Harvard. Parents would come in for their child's interview, she said, and then ask to speak to her privately. "They would say, 'Not only will I give Harvard $1 million, but I'll give you and your husband a house or a cruise,'" Mrs. Schwalbe recalled, laughing. "I'd come home and Douglas [her husband] would say, 'Do it!'"

Parents have better luck negotiating through intermediaries—the prep school's development head, a friend on the university board of trustees, or an independent college counselor. Steven Roy Goodman, an independent counselor who advises students on college admissions, said that as long as his clients are "in striking distance" academically, his job is to facilitate their admission to the college of their choice by any legitimate means—including playing the development card. His method, he said, is to find the college's "weak link"—what it needs most that the parents can provide. "I try to see if there are any resources the parent has that could be helpful: cash, internships, a foundation or job-related things," he said. Once he's analyzed how the parents can be useful, he calls a contact at the college to say he's advising a potential development case and says, "Here are the credentials. The parents could be involved in this sector or that sector." His follow-up depends on the response he gets. In one case, he said, a client wanted to go to a well-regarded liberal arts college but was "barely in striking range." The student applied early and was deferred to the regular pool, whereupon his father, a lawyer, offered to give in the range of $75,000–100,000 to the college and have his firm sponsor internships for students and host forums on campus. The applicant was admitted.

Goodman likened such pledges to colleges to a political action committee's contributions to political candidates. In each case, there is rarely an explicit deal: the candidate does not promise to enact the giver's agenda, any more than the college agrees to admit the student. But in both situations, the donor buys access and a sympathetic hearing—and a skeptic might wonder if there is any real difference between this understanding and a formal quid pro quo. For applicants and parents who want to believe in the incorruptibility of college admissions, it's hardly a reassuring analogy.

THE FAMILY of oil tycoon Robert Bass illustrates the power of fundraising priorities in admissions to elite colleges. Billionaires' children are like top quarterbacks: they go anywhere they want, displacing students with more potential but smaller bankrolls. They don't need 4.0 GPAs or longstanding legacy ties to get into the selective university of their choice. Once enrolled, they enjoy a range of coveted extracurricular perks—from memberships in clubs and fraternities to a seat on the bench of a premier varsity team—and gain the credentials and inside contacts to extend their family's wealth into the next generation.

In the late 1930s, Robert Bass's great-uncle, Sid Richardson, discovered the Keystone oil field in West Texas. It became the wellspring of a family fortune that soon caught the Ivy League's attention. Sid's nephew and business partner, Perry Richardson Bass, and Perry's four sons—Sid, Edward, Robert, and Lee—all graduated from Yale. All five made *Forbes* magazine's 2005 list of the 400 richest Americans; Robert ranked 73rd in the United States and first among Basses with $3 billion. His children didn't follow Robert to New Haven, or their mother, Anne, to Smith College. They opted for three other top 10 universities—Harvard, Stanford, and Duke. At each of those institutions, their parents have become among the biggest donors.

The Bass children became accustomed to development preference at an early age; all four attended elite prep schools where their father and/or mother have been donors and trustees. In 1993, Duke admitted the eldest Bass child, Christopher, from Middlesex School in Concord, Massachusetts. Three years later, while Christopher was still an undergraduate, the Basses pledged $10 million to the university.

In a subsequent article lauding the fund-raising prowess of Duke's then-president, Nannerl O. Keohane, the *Raleigh News & Observer* linked Christopher's admission to the donation: "In the case of this year's Bass family gift, Keohane's courtship began when the school recruited the son three years ago. The parents were invited to join the board of visitors for Trinity College, sort of a mini-board of trustees whose job it is to support the school that enrolls about 80 percent of undergraduates. Duke then showered the family with little amenities such as tickets to basketball games." In 2001, the Basses gave another $10 million, and two years later Anne Bass became a Duke trustee.

As noted in a previous chapter, Harvard snared another sibling—Chandler Bass, who enrolled in 1996 from the Groton School in Groton,

Massachusetts. Her father then became cochairman of Harvard's parent fund-raising committee and later endowed two professorships there.

Robert Bass has been even more generous to Stanford. After joining its board of trustees in 1989, he and his wife donated $25 million in 1991 and have made other substantial gifts in subsequent years. Two of their children, Timothy and Margaret, enrolled there. Because their father holds a degree from Stanford's Graduate School of Business, Timothy and Margaret did enjoy legacy preference under university rules. But that connection was hardly sufficient to explain the size of Margaret's admissions break.

Of nine applicants to Stanford from the Groton School in 1998, Margaret Bass was the only one accepted. Yet, according to a document from Groton's college counseling office, most of the rejected Groton applicants had superior academic records to hers. Her grades placed her in the middle of her Groton class, and she had an SAT score of 1220, lower than seven of the other eight applicants to Stanford. Three-fourths of Stanford freshmen have scores of 1360 or better.

Robert Bass and his daughter referred me to a family lawyer, Martin London, who said Margaret's record on the Groton document was inaccurate, but declined to be specific. (Twenty other Groton graduates said the document accurately listed their academic records, and another person familiar with Margaret's record at Groton said her data were correct.) Her roommate at Groton, Claire Abernathy, said Margaret is a "great writer," and "I'm sure her admissions essay was fantastic."

Margaret Bass graduated from Stanford in 2002. The next year, I asked Robin Mamlet, then Stanford admissions dean, about Margaret's admission to the university. Mamlet acknowledged that the university's development office supplied her with names of applicants whose parents had been major donors. She said a history of family giving is factored into an admissions decision but that Stanford has often rejected children of donors.

Tim Bass was three years ahead of Margaret at Groton, where his grades were slightly weaker than hers, according to people familiar with his record. Tim did distinguish himself on the gridiron, where he started for

Groton for three years and earned all-league honors. But it's a huge leap from starring in a prep school league to playing in the Pacific-10 conference, a proving ground for future pros. Tim Bass wasn't fast enough to play for Stanford—and his coaches and teammates knew it. But they also knew who his father was, which might have helped him make the team.

As a Stanford applicant, Timothy sent information about his high school football record and game video to football coaches, and asked to join its team. His request was handled "at the highest levels of the athletic department and the development office," according to a person familiar with the matter. Timothy made the squad as one of a handful of "walk-ons"—players without athletic scholarships. For three college football seasons, from 1995 to 1997, Timothy Bass wore uniform number 25 for Stanford University. But he rarely played. When the five-foot-eleven, 186-pound strong safety made his only career tackle, players and coaches on the Stanford sidelines cheered.

London, the family lawyer, said that Stanford recruited Tim Bass to play football. "Tim was recruited by Stanford and several other schools solely and exclusively because of his football skills," according to London.

However, Tyrone Willingham, then Stanford coach, said he did not recruit Tim Bass. Willingham described Tim as a "modest athlete" who requested an opportunity to walk on.

William Harris, then Stanford's defensive coordinator, said Tim lacked the speed to cover opposing receivers. "If you're trying to beat USC, you've got to have some talented people," he said. Harris, now a high school coach, said he was unaware of why Tim made the team, but said college administrators often plead with football coaches to take children of prominent families: " 'We've got Ted Kennedy's nephew here or whoever. He plays football. He'd like to try to walk on.' If you've got some spots, which normally you do, if you've got extra uniforms, it's not a problem."

Tony Vella, a teammate of Tim Bass at Stanford, said, "You could tell, once you got on the field, he might not have been a Division I football talent." Vella added that he and his teammates "found it a crack-up" when they graduated from Stanford that Robert Bass, as board chairman from 1996 to 2000, signed their diplomas. Tim, who graduated in 1999, was "ribbed a little bit, nothing too drastic," Vella said. "He's actually a very humble kid."

THE PHOTOGRAPH on the cover of the *New York Times Magazine* on Sunday, November 18, 1984, represented a personal triumph for Terry Sanford, then nearing the end of his fifteen-year stint as Duke president. Under the headline "Hot Colleges and How They Get That Way," the photo portrayed students in Duke sweatshirts walking across the campus quadrangle. The accompanying story actually gave more space to other colleges in vogue, from Brown University to the United States Military Academy at West Point. But it began by featuring a prep school senior who wanted to go to Vanderbilt University and lamented that "everybody's really pushing . . . Duke." Farther down, the article noted that Duke was "one of the hottest colleges" for students in Greenwich, Connecticut, an upscale New York suburb, but was largely overlooked by seniors at Boston Latin School, a "high-powered school populated primarily by poor and minority students."

Sanford had been hired to transform Duke into a national institution, and the *Times* coverage seemed to be powerful evidence that he had delivered on that commitment. Interviewed by the newspaper, Sanford offered a banal explanation for Duke's popularity: its emphasis on liberal arts. But he knew better. Duke's chic image in prep schools and wealthy suburbs, its anonymity among poor and minority students, and the newspaper's decision to feature Duke on the cover could be linked to his policy of recruiting and admitting offspring of rich or powerful families—including the daughter of the newspaper's publisher and the son of the editor in chief of the *Times* magazine.

This strategy came naturally to Sanford. As a moderate Democrat who stood for civil rights and racial integration and sought to bring the South into the American mainstream, he had many influential friends and admirers in politics, business, and the media. He was even considered for the presidency of that ultimate establishment body, the Ford Foundation.

When Sanford assumed Duke's presidency in 1970, he later said, he thought he "could elevate Duke to national and international status." But he lacked resources. The school was facing a budget deficit, its endowment was inadequate, and its alumni were too young to leave money to Duke. "Terry said, 'What we need is some first-class funerals,'" said his biographer, Howard Covington.

To increase donations, Sanford turned to admissions—and to someone who understood the prep school world: Croom Beatty, a teacher and fund-raiser at a boys' boarding school in Asheville, North Carolina, whose own children attended elite northern private schools. They had been friends ever since Sanford's governorship, when his son, Terry Sanford Jr., was a pupil in Beatty's history class. Now retired in Asheville, Beatty recalled in a telephone interview that Duke's student body in the early 1970s was heavily composed of middle-class public school students from the northern and mid-Atlantic states. Turned down by Harvard or Yale, they applied to Duke because it kept its tuition relatively low, and were admitted largely on the basis of high SAT scores. "They would come down, they would study, and go back," Beatty said. After graduating, they "didn't connect with Duke," and their giving was insufficient.

Sanford wanted more public school students from North Carolina and more private school students from other states. At his urging, Beatty scoured the nation's prep schools for applicants whose families could fill Duke's coffers. Although his title was associate director for admissions, Beatty combined admissions and fund-raising in a way that reduced the supposed barrier between the two functions to rubble. "I handled the private schools," he said. "I would go and visit and come back. I basically kept a list of people whom it would be in Duke's best interest to have them come. It wasn't that large, maybe about twenty-five names." When the families visited campus, Beatty and his wife entertained them at their home, and if the applicants were particularly important, he would tell Sanford, who would review the files. For these students, Beatty said, a subpar SAT score was not necessarily a barrier to admission if they showed leadership qualities.

Beatty's names weren't the only well-heeled candidates requiring delicate handling by admissions. The development office supplied its own list, and Sanford passed along names accumulated from his contacts. Joel Fleishman, a Duke public policy professor, vice chancellor, and longtime Sanford confidant, also identified prospects. All told, former admissions director Jean Scott estimated, "a couple of hundred" applicants a year were given special attention as children of prospective donors.

Beatty initiated Duke's parent fund-raising committee, institutionalizing the implicit understanding that parents would reward the university for admitting their children. "Parents have more interest at that given time than anyone," Beatty said. "They care. Their child is being educated, they're more attuned. I find alums only get very excited at twenty-five-year or fifty-year intervals."

Word soon spread in private school circles that Duke was hunting for development admits and wasn't too concerned about their credentials. "There was definitely a sense that people who had money and had been in contact with somebody at Duke were siphoned into the process," said Mary Anne Schwalbe, college counselor at the Dalton School in Manhattan from 1979 to 1985. "They received a preference even if they didn't have a strong record. I would say to the parents, 'Duke is a long shot. I would recommend a less competitive school in the South.' The parents would say, 'I've been in touch with somebody there, and it's looking good.'"

Beatty said his recruiting made major inroads for Duke—particularly at what he called "socioeconomically high-end" schools in the Dallas area. The "Duke Dallas" campaign, in which Beatty brought top university administrators to woo students and parents, quadrupled applications from those schools. "We really worked Dallas," he said. Such courtship was effective; along with Yale, Duke has the lowest proportion of students on financial aid (40 percent) among the nation's top 10 universities.

Beatty's excursions paid particular dividends among families that had traditionally attended Yale. In the mid-1960s, Yale briefly experimented with reducing legacy preference before yielding to an alumni backlash. Perhaps worried that their alma mater would turn down their children, some alumni were exploring other options. Duke raided Yale families such as the Mars candy bar clan, the Kohlers (Wisconsin makers of plumbing fixtures), and the Wrigleys of chewing gum fame. William F.

Wrigley Jr., son of a Yale alumnus, graduated from Duke in 1985 and now sits on the board of visitors for the university's Nicholas School of the Environment. He's also chief executive of the family company and in 2005 was the 65th richest American, with a net worth of $3.4 billion, according to *Forbes* magazine.

Beatty recalled another applicant whose family connections made her stand out: Cynthia Fox Sulzberger, daughter of Arthur Ochs Sulzberger, then publisher of the *New York Times* and now chairman emeritus. She enrolled at Duke in 1982 from the Dalton School, where she wasn't a top student. Her admission "worked out magically," Beatty said, alluding to the magazine cover story, published while Cynthia was a Duke undergraduate. "Certainly she was on a development list. We were trying to do things in public policy, and the Sulzbergers were important people."

I found no evidence that Sulzberger intervened in any way in the magazine article. However, an editor close to the article had his own stake in Duke's goodwill. The son of Edward Klein, editor in chief of the magazine from 1977 to 1988, was applying to Duke at the time of publication. Alec Klein, a strong student at one of New York City's best public high schools, was admitted but enrolled at Brown instead; a former colleague of mine in *The Wall Street Journal*'s Boston bureau, he is now a distinguished reporter for the *Washington Post*. Neither the Sulzberger nor Klein relationship was disclosed in the article.

Michael Winerip, the author of the article, told me that editors wanted a reference to Duke moved up to the opening section, making it more plausible to feature Duke in the cover photo. "I do believe, in retrospect, they were trying to position Duke near the top of the piece to get that cover on it," Winerip said. "I don't think it had anything to do with the Sulzbergers. In my twenty years at the *Times,* I've never seen any instance of the family using the paper that way. My suspicion is that Klein ordered up Duke."

Edward Klein now writes a weekly column for *Parade* magazine. He is the author of two books about the late Jacqueline Kennedy Onassis and of a 2005 biography of Hillary Clinton, *The Truth About Hillary.* He acknowledged he chose the cover photo (in consultation with the executive editor at the time, Abe Rosenthal) but said that his son's application to Duke had no impact on the cover or article, and that Yale was his son's first choice.

"If I were trying to help my son, if I was willing to be unethical enough to use the magazine to do so, the story I should have done was a story about Yale," Klein said. Several of his friends, including *New York* magazine founder Clay Felker, had gone to Duke, and "it was just on my radar screen that Duke was coming up strongly."

Klein told me he "may have been aware" Cynthia Sulzberger was going to Duke, but said that knowledge also did not influence his handling of the article. "That would have had no bearing. Punch [Arthur Ochs Sulzberger] never, ever picked up the phone and called me on any story. He never asked any favors."

Catherine J. Mathis, spokeswoman for the *New York Times,* told me, "These events took place in 1984, and there's a danger of fallacy in applying 2004 standards retroactively. We are much more sensitive nowadays to the ethical desirability of disclosing connections, even if they have not influenced the journalism. Mr. Sulzberger was not aware that the magazine was going to run the story and was not thanked by Mr. Sanford or Duke officials after it appeared."

In any event, Duke's admission of Cynthia Sulzberger—and other relatives in the ensuing years—paid off in a more traditional way. In 1998, Sulzberger and family members pledged $700,000 to Duke's Center for Child and Family Policy. And the basement of a building on Duke's east campus houses the Cynthia Sulzberger Interactive Learning Lab.

TEXAS ENTREPRENEUR Milledge "Mitch" Hart III, cofounder of Electronic Data Systems Corp., didn't know anyone at Duke in 1981. But that changed quickly after his daughter told him it was one of her top two choices. He called a former Duke dean, Robert Krueger, who had run unsuccessfully—with Hart's strong backing—for the U.S. Senate from Texas in 1978. Krueger assured his supporter that he would introduce him to the right person at Duke: vice chancellor Joel Fleishman.

Fleishman met Hart and his wife and daughter at the airport and escorted them to the president's house, where the family stayed for three nights. Hart described it as an exhilarating visit in which he, Sanford, and Fleishman talked politics until 3 a.m.

Hart's daughter enrolled at Duke—followed by three more of his children, as well as many other students he's recommended. Hart said all of them were competitive academically. In 1986, after Hart pledged $1 million to a fund-raising campaign led by Fleishman, Duke established the Hart Leadership Program, which educates students about leadership skills. He also served a term on Duke's board of trustees.

"Joel is one of my four or five closest friends in the world." Hart said. No matter where Hart happens to be on his birthday, he added, Fleishman calls him every year to sing "Happy Birthday" to him.

Fleishman has held numerous titles at Duke—from senior vice president to founding director of the Institute of Policy Sciences and Public Affairs to professor of law. Fleishman was Duke's fifth-highest-paid employee in 2005, earning $532,684 in salary, benefits, and deferred compensation. His impressive curriculum vitae also touts a wide variety of outside affiliations with nonprofit foundations and boards, as well as lucrative directorships on boards of companies whose chief executives are Duke donors and parents. But his fifteen-page resume has one important gap: it says not a word about Duke undergraduate admissions. Yet in his heyday under Sanford, and to some extent under ensuing administrations, Fleishman played a key role at the vortex of development and admissions. Like Croom Beatty, he breached the supposed wall between the two functions and helped funnel children of wealth into Duke's student body, preempting slots that might otherwise have given a leg up to outstanding students from less cushy backgrounds.

Fleishman's and Beatty's roles were complementary. Both enjoyed friendships with Sanford dating back to his governorship—Fleishman had been his legal assistant—and carried out his bidding as president, usually outside bureaucratic channels. Although Fleishman never worked in the development office, he chaired Duke's 1983–92 fund-raising campaign, which raised $221 million. While Beatty recruited wealthy students in the hope that their parents would give, Fleishman tirelessly courted potential donors—and, if necessary, pushed to admit their children.

Jean Scott, the former admissions director, recalled conversations with Fleishman about candidates. "I'm sure he had input into the president's list or the development list or both," she told me. Harold Wingood, a former senior associate director of admissions from 1986 to 1992, said Fleishman would add names to the development office list: "If necessary, Joel would call either me or the president's office."

Fleishman "was so useful to the place because he knew everybody," recalled a former administrator in Duke's fund-raising office. "He knew the Clintons. He gave an awful lot of TLC to the fat cats. When really wealthy guys' kids were coming to be shepherded through the application process," he would take care of it.

Fleishman declined an interview for this book, but he is said by his wide circle of friends to have a brilliant mind, unusual charm, and varied interests. Lean, balding, and athletic-looking, he was once offered the presidency of Brandeis University. He sends holiday cards featuring his own translations of the Psalms. He's also an oenophile who wrote a monthly wine column for eight years for *Vanity Fair*—and who courted Duke donors with vintage selections. While chairing the capital campaign in 1992, for instance, Fleishman conducted a wine tasting at the fortieth wedding anniversary of investment banker and Princeton alumnus James Gorter and his wife, Audrey, parents of two Duke graduates. The Gorters later endowed a professorship at Duke with a gift of more than $1 million.

"Joel used to give very expensive bottles of wine and put them on his university expense account, which was rather generous," recalled former president Keith Brodie, who succeeded Sanford. "There was this flow and nurturing of these donors with these bottles of wine. Because they were millionaires, you had to buy an expensive bottle."

There is no indication that Fleishman traded admissions support for corporate directorships. However, his friendships with Duke givers provided a valuable entrée into businesses far afield from the academic milieu. Take, for example, the story of two of fashion designer Ralph Lauren's children, David and Dylan, who graduated from the Dalton School in Manhattan in 1989 and 1992, respectively, and enrolled at Duke while Fleishman ran the fund-raising campaign. A person familiar with their records described David as a "B-plus" student with SAT scores in the 1100s, who likely needed a development boost for Duke admission. Dylan was stronger academically, with better grades and SATs in the 1200s. Both were active in student government, sports, and other extracurricular activities.

Sondra Feig, then Dalton's college counselor, said the Laurens had "learned an important lesson" when Brown University turned down their older son, Andrew, in 1986–87. (Andrew, who had a B average in high school and a lower SAT score than his siblings, enrolled at Skidmore College and later transferred to Brown.) For David and Dylan, Feig said, the Laurens hired an independent college counselor and contacted Duke officials. "They learned who to go to and how to do it. That's what did it for Duke."

Phyllis Steinbrecher, the Laurens' independent counselor, said she knew Fleishman and had dealt with him on development cases. "Duke was looking for wealthy kids," she recalled. She said she frequently approaches colleges on behalf of clients who want to donate. "The code words you use are, 'This is a development family.' Of course there's influence. Everybody knows what they're buying. I'm sure almost every school has a connection between their admissions office and their development office."

Ralph Lauren himself attended City College of New York, long a gateway to the middle class for striving immigrants and working-class students. He was a regular guest at dinners Fleishman hosted on Duke's Parents' Weekend for parents of students he had "shepherded through," Brodie told me. "The Laurens would come frequently when they were in town. There was a closeness there."

Lauren eventually pledged a six-figure gift to Duke. In 1999, Fleishman became a director of Polo Ralph Lauren Inc. As of June 2005, he was earning $35,000 a year as a director, plus $7,500 as chairman of its compensation committee and $2,000 per meeting. He also owned or held options to buy 34,500 shares of Ralph Lauren stock, worth at least half a million dollars, public filings show.

Also during the fund-raising campaign, three children of Peter Nicholas, cofounder and chairman of Boston Scientific Corp., enrolled at Duke. Nicholas and his wife, both Duke graduates, have since become among its biggest donors—almost $130 million in total—and Nicholas served as chairman of the Duke board from 2003 to 2005.

In October 1992, Fleishman joined the Boston Scientific board, for which he's paid $50,000 a year, plus $10,000 to chair the audit committee. As of January 2006, he owned or had options to buy more than 140,000 shares of Boston Scientific stock, worth more than $2 million.

J. David Ross, a former vice president for advancement at Duke and now a fund-raising consultant, said Fleishman was a close friend of the Nicholas family: "I used to go to parties at the Nicholases' and Joel was always there." Ross told me Fleishman sits on more corporate boards "than a lot of people, especially for nonpresidents," but added that the directorships weren't a payback for facilitating admissions of executive offspring. "He brought enough prestige and savvy" to the companies, Ross said. Boston Scientific declined comment.

Fleishman is also on the board of a North Carolina insurance holding company, James River Group, and as of August 2005 held 23,347 shares of the firm, worth at least $600,000. Fleishman knew its cofounder and chief executive, J. Adam Abram, through Brandeis, where Adam Abram's late father, Morris, had been president. Fleishman was a Brandeis trustee in the 1990s. J. Adam Abram, a Harvard graduate, has donated six figures to Duke and in 2000 joined the board of visitors of Duke's public policy institute, which Fleishman founded. Fleishman remains a faculty member and director of a center for ethics at what is now called the Terry Sanford Institute. In 2003, Abram's son, Benjamin, enrolled at Duke.

Benjamin Abram said in a 2004 telephone interview that he had strong credentials, including a 1400 SAT score, a class rank in the top 10 percent at East Chapel Hill High School in North Carolina, and outside activities ranging from student body president to member of a comedy improvisation troupe. Plus, he said, he is a legacy because his mother has a Duke doctorate. Among other schools he considered, he was placed on the waiting list by Harvard and Washington University in St. Louis and accepted by University of Chicago and Johns Hopkins University.

Benjamin's family hired an independent counselor to guide him through college admissions, Steven Roy Goodman. Goodman declined comment on Benjamin's case but said he has sometimes contacted Fleishman on behalf of wealthy applicants seeking a development edge at Duke.

Benjamin acknowledged it was likely that Fleishman had pushed for him: "I guess Dad talked to Joel, and Joel put his own bidding in." He added that Fleishman had offered to be his faculty adviser if Benjamin came to Duke and majored in public policy, as Benjamin wound up doing. He said he was about to begin his studies with Fleishman.

"The admissions process has a lot of different, not entirely merit-based considerations," Benjamin told me in our first conversation. "For me, what's important to my sanity is how much I make a name for myself here; how much I do to improve Duke as an institution." Later, Benjamin called back and said he had taken time during an exam break to jot down his reflections in his journal about his admission to Duke: "What it comes down to, ultimately, is that there are many, many qualified applicants for only so many spots. Did my application get special attention? Sure. But I am still a qualified, competent student and I am holding my own in vigorous classes at Duke. Everyone's applications have something that sparkles to them, and part of that for mine may have happened to be my name." His father declined comment.

As of March 2006, Benjamin was still holding his own academically at Duke with a 3.165 average, just above a B. The junior was active in campus politics as copresident of Duke Democrats, and he had been elected senior class president. He was also doing his part to improve relations between Duke and the urban neighborhoods around it by working with a homeless Durham fourth-grader.

Another Duke donor admired Fleishman's taste in fine wines. New York financier Marshall Cogan, an early Wall Street associate of Citigroup chief executive Sandy Weill, was a friend and political supporter of Terry

Sanford. Although Cogan was a Harvard man, his mother attended Duke, as did his daughter Stephanie. Cogan and his wife served on the Duke parents committee from 1985 to 1989, and later gave a professorship to Duke in his mother's name.

In 1986, the same year his daughter graduated summa cum laude from Duke, Cogan took control of New York's famed 21 Club. Also that year, Fleishman became the club's "wine consultant," a title he held until 1989, according to his curriculum vitae. Ken Aretsky, who managed the restaurant from 1986 to 1995, told me he never knew about Fleishman's employment, and that it must have been a private arrangement between the connoisseur and Cogan.

"I don't remember Joel being on the payroll at all," Aretsky said. The club had its own sommelier. "We didn't need Joel." Cogan, who stayed close to Fleishman and attended a party honoring the former 21 Club consultant on his seventieth birthday, declined comment.

TERRY SANFORD'S handpicked successor was nothing like him. While Sanford enjoyed hobnobbing with the rich and famous, Keith Brodie, who took over in 1985, was a psychiatrist who preferred improving Duke's faculty to sweet-talking donors. Appalled by Sanford's interference in what he thought should be a professional and merit-based process, Brodie distanced himself from admissions and the Sanford loyalists who had wielded it as a fund-raising tool. "He looked askance at my work. He wanted admissions to be totally separate from development," recalled Croom Beatty, who soon left Duke. Although Fleishman continued fund-raising, Brodie rebuffed his desire to be named university chancellor. And Mitch Hart left the board of trustees after a dispute with Brodie over how much influence the donor would wield over the leadership program.

"It was the sense of Dr. Brodie that the old system was rife with abuses," Harold Wingood, senior associate director of admissions from 1986 to 1992, told me. "Undue consideration was given to children of donors."

Richard Steele, whom Brodie brought in to replace Jean Scott as admissions director, said he never carried a box of development case folders to the president's office. "That changed from day one," Steele told me. "Dr. Brodie stepped aside from admissions decisions. He was scrupulously consistent about that." Steele also prohibited development officers from lobbying his staff on behalf of wealthy applicants, requiring that all names be directed to him.

Steele said that his first two years on the job were "kind of rugged" because of a rash of complaints from trustees and donors about their diminished influence over admissions. "They weren't used to this system," he said. "I did a lot of phone work trying to warn them. Some were very angry. It was quite a change in expectations for them."

Under Brodie, Wingood said, the development office would push for about one hundred students at a mid-March meeting with admissions. The discussions were "rough rounds," said Wingood, now dean of admissions at Clark University in Worcester. "It could take a whole day to review one hundred kids. Sometimes there were raised voices. Sometimes there were tears." John Piva Jr., who headed development, was "aggressive," Wingood says. "He had his must-haves."

Wingood estimates that thirty to forty students would be upgraded from being rejected to the waiting list, or from the waiting list to being admitted. "We'd take students in some cases with SAT scores 100 points below the mean, or just outside the top 15 percent of their class," he said. "They weren't slugs, but they weren't strong enough to get in on their own." Steele put the number at fifteen to twenty students.

Christoph Guttentag, Duke admissions director from 1992 to 2005 and currently dean of admissions, contended Wingood and Steele underestimated the number of students admitted "because of the advocacy of the university's development office" in the Brodie era, and that it was actually about ninety a year.

Brodie's approach was academically sound but politically inexpedient. Criticized for a lack of fund-raising zeal, he was replaced in 1993 by Wellesley College president Nannerl O. Keohane, who had a proven knack for making the dough rise. Top development officials at Duke were "practically doing handstands" when she took over, one ex-administrator recalled. "She was known to be very good to fund-raising."

"Duke's under-capitalization relative to its peers and competitors was very much on our mind," John Chandler, leader of the presidential search committee, later told Duke's alumni magazine. "It was music to our ears to hear Nan say, 'I enjoy raising money,' and her record at Wellesley in raising money was a very considerable factor in our turning to her as our first choice."

President Keohane did not disappoint. One of her first moves was to expand the development office's cramped headquarters on Campus Drive. She spearheaded a campaign that officially began in 1998 with a goal of $1.5 billion—and raised nearly $2.4 billion by the end of 2003. As the campaign heated up, so did development pressure on admissions. Duke admitted about 125 nonalumni children in 1998, and again in 1999, who had been tentatively rejected or wait-listed before family connections were taken into account. By 2000, when Duke accepted ninety-nine such students, the flood of development admits was causing alarm on campus, with some faculty and administrators worrying that it was diluting the student body's intellectual vitality. In November 2000, a report to trustees by a university committee on admissions called for a one-third reduction in such admissions. Duke did not provide data on development admits for 2001 or 2002. By 2003, as the fund-raising campaign wrapped up, the number dropped to fifty-eight.

"The number had slowly been climbing," committee member Phillip Jones, associate professor of mechanical engineering, told me. "That's just not something that we wanted to continue doing. It restricts your ability to admit maybe the kid that's going to become the next Picasso."

Keohane told me in an email that she didn't intentionally increase the number of wealthy applicants given an admissions edge. She said, "It is possible that the numbers drifted upward during the campaign" because "more people in development expressed interest in candidates. But this was certainly not a policy directive or even a conscious choice." Keohane, who stepped down from Duke's presidency in 2004 and joined Harvard's governing board the next year, also acknowledged that the preference for children of prospective donors is "disproportionately favorable to white students."

At its peak under Keohane, the Duke system worked this way: through its own network and names supplied by trustees, alumni, donors, and others, the development office identified five hundred or so likely applicants with rich and powerful parents who were not alumni. It cultivated them with campus tours and basic admissions advice, and relayed the names to the admission office, which returned word if any of the students forgot to apply so that the development office could remind them to do so.

The development office then winnowed the initial group to at least 160 high-priority applicants. Although these names were flagged in the admissions office computer, admissions readers evaluated them on merit, without regard to family means. About thirty to forty were accepted, the others tentatively rejected or wait-listed. During an all-day meeting in March, admissions director Guttentag and Piva, senior vice president for development, debated these remaining cases. Just as Sanford and Scott had done long before, Guttentag and Piva weighed the students' academic shortcomings against their families' likely giving. The outcome was the same as it had always been; most of the 120 were admitted. If the two were at loggerheads over a particular applicant, Duke's provost acted as referee.

Guttentag told me that students admitted for development reasons graduate at a higher rate than the overall student body, although their grades are slightly lower. Nevertheless, Rachel Toor, a Duke admissions officer from 1997 to 2000, recalled in her 2001 book, *Admissions Confidential*, that Guttentag "never wanted to admit these kids and had to fight to be able to keep them out. He usually lost." Students recommended by development were, she wrote, "the weakest portion of our applicant pool . . . The director had to reserve a number of places in the class for these kids, places that could easily have been filled by regular kids."

Once these children of privilege enrolled, so did their parents—in Duke's parent fund-raising committee. Committee members usually give at least $1,000 to Duke, and the national chairman and eight cochairmen (two for each of the four classes at Duke) donate more, including at least two seven-figure gifts endowing faculty chairs.

The daughter of an investment banker, Caroline Diemar scored 1190 on the SATs, more than 200 points below the Duke average, despite having a private tutor. Caroline, who attended a private school in New Jersey, applied early to Duke for the fall of 1999 and was deferred to the spring. She then buttressed her application with recommendations from two family friends—one a member of the parents committee, another a major Duke donor—and was accepted. In the summer before her freshman year, Duke enlisted her parents as members of the parent fund-raising committee for her class; they later became cochairmen. Her father, Robert Diemar, declined to say how much he has given to Duke. "We support all of our five children's schools," said Diemar, a Princeton alumnus, adding that Duke accepted his daughter on merit.

At Duke, Caroline joined a sorority and took up rowing, and was on the women's crew team for three years. A sociology major with a 3.2 grade point average, below the 3.4 average of her senior class, she was looking for a job in advertising or marketing when I chatted with her early in 2003.

"I was networking anybody I met that had a connection with Duke," Caroline told me about her college admission process. "Everybody has a thing to make them stand out. I didn't have athletics, I didn't have race, I wasn't the artistic person, I didn't play an instrument, I wasn't in student government. I knew I could do it. I just needed something that could make me stand out." The lesson she learned: "Networking is how you go about everything."

FOR CAROLINE DIEMAR, using connections to get into Duke was a personal initiative. For Maude Bunn, it was a hometown tradition.

The Bunns are part of a close-knit group of families in affluent Lake Forest, Illinois, that has dominated the higher echelons of Duke's parent fund-raising committee. The suburban network illustrates how the wealthy, by operating in tandem, exert influence over the college admissions process as if choosing members for an exclusive country club—inevitably muscling out working-class applicants and other outsiders.

In addition to Maude's father, Lake Forest luminaries on the committee have included department-store heir Marshall Field V, who has given six figures to Duke; Paul Clark, chief executive of Icos Corp., a biotech firm; and Robert DePree, chairman of cornmeal maker House-Autry Mills Inc. Bunn, Clark, and DePree and their spouses were all committee cochairs for their children's classes. (Billionaire William Wrigley Jr., a Duke alumnus and donor, also lives in Lake Forest.)

Asked why he is on the committee, one Lake Forest father said, "It's important to give one's time and resources to help worthy nonprofit institutions. At Duke, the endowment is smaller than its peer institutions, yet the school's performance consistently ranks in the top 10. They're doing a great job with the dollars they have.

"Plus, they've delivered for my daughter."

The Lake Forest couples are social friends, serve on many of the same Chicago-area boards, and typically send their children to the same private elementary school, Lake Forest Country Day. They write recommendations to Duke for each other's children. Once a child from this network is admitted to Duke, his or her parents typically join the parents committee, donate to the university, and vouch for the children of friends and neighbors when they apply. In Lake Forest, not fulfilling these obligations would be considered as rude as forgetting to RSVP to a wedding. At Duke, their children maintain the ties; the daughters of Field, Clark, and DePree, for instance, all joined the same sorority.

"It perpetuates itself," Ashley Clark told me. "It was nice knowing older girls in my sorority."

Susan DePree, Robert's wife, told me that the Lake Forest parents have assumed key responsibilities on the Duke committee because they are accustomed to and expert at organizing and raising money for civic causes. The committee, she said, is a "pretty intimate group" but not "clubby." It has unusual access to Duke administrators, including briefings from Christoph Guttentag.

"We're just passing along this job," Mrs. Bunn said. "Those of us in

Lake Forest were all on a lot of the same boards in Chicago. There's some perception that we can get the job done. We have gotten the job done pretty well."

Lake Forest wasn't always a Duke stronghold. James Gorter, retired chair of investment management firm Baker Fentress—the same man for whom Joel Fleishman conducted an anniversary wine tasting—remembered that "there were very few people from Lake Forest going to Duke" when his daughter, Mary, enrolled there in 1977 (followed by his late son Kevin, a 1987 graduate). Gorter, who said Duke wasn't aware of his business stature when Mary applied, did his part to enlarge the Lake Forest pipeline, joining the parent committee, endowing a professorship, and recommending children of his friends.

"We got to know a lot of the people there not only in the admissions department but also in the fund-raising groups," said Gorter. "They're very caring, which I don't think is true in all educational institutions. I really believe there is a much greater caring for and responsiveness at Duke if you recommend somebody. Even if they don't take them, they tell you why. They go out of their way to make sure they tell you exactly what's going on. Parents are very important to Duke. It's a very family-oriented place."

Gorter said his batting average on recommendations was "pretty good." Among those he backed was Abigail Field, Marshall Field's daughter. Field, in his turn, recommended Maude Bunn, as did the Clarks.

"We have a lot of family friends who have kids above me at Duke," Maude explained when I interviewed her in 2003, during her sophomore year. "They wanted to help me out and write letters and stuff. After I got in, my parents were asked to do fund-raising for Duke and they were saying, 'Yeah, we owe it to all these people.' "

Maude, who was studying art history and anticipating a career in fashion, told me she initially felt "very, very awkward" at Duke because her admission "wasn't necessarily on my own merits." But she soon adjusted. "The more time I've spent here, I feel more and more confident—they didn't have to take me if they didn't think I was equal to all the other students they are admitting. I'm doing just as well as everybody I know if not better." She graduated from Duke in 2005 with a bachelor of arts degree.

In 2004, yet another child from the same Lake Forest circle entered Duke: Josephine Terlato, from a prominent wine distributing and producing family. Her grandfather, Anthony Terlato, chairman of Terlato Wine Group, was an early importer of pinot grigio to the United States. Her father, William, a graduate of Loyola University in Chicago, is president of Terlato Wine Group and Paterno Wines International, which markets one out of every ten bottles of wine over $14 sold in America, according to its website. Like the Clarks and other Duke parents, the Terlatos have been active on behalf of Lake Forest Country Day.

At Lake Forest High, a premier public school, Josephine Terlato was in the top 15 to 20 percent of her class, qualifying for the National Honor Society but not the Cum Laude Society, which is limited to the top 9 to 12 percent there. Her SAT and ACT scores, she said, were "right in the norm for Duke." She applied early, was deferred to the regular pool, and then admitted. She was also accepted at Georgetown and the University of Michigan but was turned down by Columbia University and Boston College.

She wrote her essay about the family business—perhaps alerting admissions readers to her affluent upbringing. "I started getting involved a few years ago by going to wineries we own in Napa Valley and France and working there," she said. "I talked about how I've grown up in that type of culture."

Josephine said she knows the Fields, Bunns, and other Duke families but didn't solicit their recommendations. "My recommendations were all from teachers and people I had worked with in community service," she said. "I thought that if I were going to get in, I would want to be assured I could handle the workload and what was expected of me as a student." A few months after she was admitted, her parents joined Duke's fund-raising committee—at the invitation, Josephine said, of the Bunns.

3

THE **FAME**

FACTOR

Celebrity Children
at Brown

The show business headliners of yesteryear rarely made a fuss about their children's schooling. They gave them tap shoes and singing lessons and put them on the stage or screen as soon as they were old enough to remember their parts. By contrast, today's pop culture icons, from Kevin Costner to Bette Midler, send their young to exclusive prep schools and premier colleges, most of which make academic allowances for celebrity children. Thus the glitterati parlay transient name recognition—the fifteen minutes of fame promised by Andy Warhol—into a secure position in America's aristocracy. For Hollywood celebrities, "It's not that their son or daughter is getting a great education," says James Rogers, former director of admission at Brown. "It's how much they can puff their chests at a Beverly Hills cocktail party."

Depicted in a February 1998 article in *Vanity Fair* as the "School for Glamour," Brown University is the elite college best known for pursuing scions of the famous. And rarely has Brown sacrificed academic standards for Hollywood luster more blatantly than it did in courting power broker Michael Ovitz.

In October 2004, Michael Ovitz was getting skewered nationwide. His former employer, Walt Disney Co., was on trial, sued by shareholders who were furious that it had paid him $140 million in severance for a fourteen-month stint as president. His former Disney boss and close friend, Michael Eisner, had described him in one memo that surfaced in the case as a "psychopath" who "cannot tell the truth."

But on Brown's hillside campus in Providence, Rhode Island, Ovitz's cinematic clout insulated him from criticism. If the former talent agent who cofounded Creative Artists Agency no longer reigned in Hollywood, he could still dazzle Rhode Island with his Rolodex—and burnish his crumbling reputation with an Ivy League luster. On the evening of Saturday, October 23, nearly three thousand students and parents overflowed Brown's basketball gym, filling the grandstands and folding chairs set up on the floor, to hear Ovitz banter with longtime friend and client Dustin Hoffman. Ovitz had invited the movie star, whom he addressed as "Dusty," to Brown. The event—billed as "A Conversation with Dustin Hoffman, Moderated by Michael Ovitz"—was the culminating attraction of Parents' Weekend. It offered an intimate glimpse of celebrity likely to leave parents grateful and inclined to donate.

Three giant screens behind the speakers magnified their contrasting images. Ovitz looked scholarly in a conservative suit, while Hoffman wore corduroys and an open-necked shirt, with his glasses slipping down to the end of his nose. As master of ceremonies, Ovitz bowed to Brown ("Every single time I'm on this campus, I'm invigorated by the creativity and individuality") and described the importance of risk taking to the creative process ("There is no success without multiple failure"). He also led applause for Dusty's film clips, off-color stories, reminiscences about schooling ("Nobody flunks acting, it's like gym"), and advice for President Bush ("Go to the shrink!"). In return, Hoffman alluded to the shareholder lawsuit only to praise his "friend for twenty-five years": "Whatever his controversies have been . . . he protected the artist."

Brown president Ruth Simmons also saluted the mogul-turned-moderator. She described Ovitz as the "exemplar of a Brown parent who, without being asked, comes forward to help."

In reality, the renowned deal maker didn't have to be asked to bring Hoffman, because Ovitz owed Brown a favor. Like Disney, the Ivy League university paid dearly for Ovitz—not in cash, but in college admissions.

Ovitz might never have become, in President Simmons's words, "a true friend to Brown" if the university had not made an admissions exception for the eldest of his three children.

In promoting the event on its website, Brown described Ovitz as "P'05"—in other words, parent of Brown senior Kimberly Ovitz, who sat in the front row. President Simmons herself singled out Kimberly for praise, crediting her with suggesting Hoffman's appearance. But Kimberly was not the first Ovitz child to attend Brown; her brother Christopher held that distinction. Despite a mediocre academic record and a middle-school suspension for swinging a baseball bat at a female classmate, Christopher Ovitz applied to Brown from a Santa Monica, California, prep school in 1999. His candidacy prompted intense debate within the university's administration over how far it should bend standards even for the son of the man often called the most powerful in Hollywood. With Brown ever eager to boost its endowment, then as now the Ivy League's lowest, then-president E. Gordon Gee and his development staff pushed for Christopher. In the end, Christopher was admitted as a "special student," a rarely used designation that required him to pass some classes before the university committed to enrolling him as a full undergraduate.

Chris lasted less than a year at Brown, but the university soon reaped the benefits of his admission. In January 2003, Michael Ovitz emceed his first campus conversation with an A-list celebrity, director Martin Scorsese. Ovitz hailed his longtime client as "a man who never compromised" and "the greatest filmmaker we have today." Nine hundred students packed the auditorium and four hundred more were turned away. The following winter, Ovitz hosted a reception for Simmons at his Brentwood mansion, adorned with his superb collection of modern art. Among the guests were Brown parents Hoffman and Danny DeVito.

Brown administrators hoped that the standing ovation for Hoffman and Ovitz at Parents' Weekend would ultimately yield a more tangible asset. As President Simmons reminded the crowd, Brown parents "are among the most generous in the country." Hoffman's parting remark to the audience appeared to reflect an awareness that Brown's flexible admissions standards had made the evening possible. Hoffman told the student body, "Some of you worked harder than others to get here. Some of you, not unlike myself in high school, didn't work that hard."

CELEBRITY CHILDREN, such as Christopher Ovitz and his Hollywood peers, don't have to work that hard to be admitted to most elite universities. Just as they command the best table at a restaurant or front-row seats at a premier sports event, so they expect—and receive—special attention from starstruck colleges. So too with well-known teenage actors and models. Child actors whose cuteness had faded used to scrounge for parts in TV commercials and B movies; now, like *Wonder Years* star Fred Savage and his brother Ben of *Boy Meets World,* they go to Stanford.

And their good fortune has consequences. The vast majority of precocious stars and celebrity offspring are well-off whites, tipping the socioeconomic scale at top-tier colleges further toward the privileged. Every academically weak child of a sitcom stalwart or TV newscaster admitted takes the place of a brighter student from a more anonymous background.

Universities don't have a separate preference category for teen celebrities, who constitute a small number of applicants in any given year. Instead, they're treated as a subset of development admits. Whether famous in their own right or their parents', they're lumped in with children of business tycoons or corporate directors on the list that the fund-raising office provides to admissions.

For instance, New York University's development list includes applicants it calls "notables," mostly from the spheres of entertainment and politics. "You look at the application and Daddy is a leading playwright or a Hollywood producer," said Barbara Hall, associate provost for enrollment management. "You pick up on those. If it's a close call, the decision will go in favor of the student." Among recent notables at NYU: omnipresent twin actresses Mary-Kate and Ashley Olsen. "Politically, it's the astute thing to do," Hall added. "You don't want the president to go to a meeting in Washington and find out he's denied the child of the Speaker of the House and he didn't know it."

While universities pursue other development cases with a view to a parental donation, that's not the primary reason why they lower standards for celebrity children. Most celebrities are not major donors to higher education and have often frustrated colleges that hope otherwise. With a few exceptions—such as Bill Cosby, who with his wife, Camille, gave $20 million to Spelman College in 1989—they're used to lending their names rather than wallets to social causes. They also tend to maintain expensive lifestyles and are solicited by so many organizations that they don't build close relationships with any of them. "The glitterati of that sort are more than happy to appear at your dinner and be honored at a major event, but they are not terribly generous as a group," said Terry Holcombe, former vice president for development and alumni affairs at Yale. "They have a million excuses."

For colleges, celebrity is a coin of the realm, convertible into prestige and publicity. Premier universities look to these children to generate attention—the favorable buzz that can boost applications, draw coverage in *People* magazine and other media, thrill alumni, and turn a place such as Brown into a "hot" school despite a lagging endowment and blue-collar surroundings. Children of the famous carry with them the aura of their parents, of course, but they do more than that: they bring their parents in tow. In the incessant academic competition for newsworthy speakers at commencement exercises and other ceremonies, colleges often grab the limelight and one-up their rivals by enlisting celebrity parents, who interrupt their busy schedules and waive their usually hefty fees in gratitude to the institutions that admitted their children.

"There are a lot of really rich people. It's not the richness schools are looking for, necessarily, it's the cachet," said Seppy Basili, vice president of learning and assessment at Kaplan Inc., the test-prep company. The speaker at Basili's own graduation from Kenyon College in 1982 was actor Alan Alda, whose daughter also graduated that year.

College counselors say that celebrity status is worth at least 100 SAT points at Brown and other selective colleges. Vincent Garcia, counselor at Campbell Hall School in North Hollywood, a popular prep school for movie industry families, said college admissions representatives who visit Campbell Hall to speak to prospective applicants and their families are sometimes "unnerved" and "overwhelmed" by the presence of celebrity parents whom they've idolized. If a university has a strong filmmaking or television program, he said, parents who are directors or screenwriters often enhance their son or daughter's chances by offering to share their expertise if their child is admitted.

"It's usually communicated by the parent to the college development office or even to the film department," Garcia told me. "The parent would meet with the director of a particular department and say, 'I'd really love to play an active role in helping you with the students who have questions, or come on campus and talk about my experience transitioning from acting to directing.'"

Foremost among Campbell Hall celebrities were Mary-Kate and Ashley Olsen. Neither was inducted into the school's Cum Laude Society, signifying they did not rank in the top 15 to 20 percent of their class at Campbell Hall. Yet both enrolled at New York University, where 63 percent of freshmen are in the top tenth of their high school classes. When they were choosing a college, "I got more attention from admissions directors than I ever had before," Garcia says.

Michael Pagnotta, a publicist for the Olsen twins, said they did "quite well" academically in prep school, but declined to be more specific. "When colleges examined their achievements not just as actresses but as businesspeople and fashion designers, the admissions people felt it would be terrific to have them," he said. In October 2005, Mary-Kate took a leave of absence from NYU, which Pagnotta said was unrelated to academics.

Colleges accommodate celebrity children every step of the way. They're treated like guests at a four-star hotel with university officials acting as concierge. Rather than being interviewed by an underling, these students may meet with the university president or admissions dean. When Steven Spielberg's stepdaughter, Jessica Capshaw, sought an interview with Duke University, she didn't even have to leave her home. Duke admissions director Christoph Guttentag, explaining that he happened to be in California anyway, made a beeline for the Spielberg residence and interviewed her there. Despite this house call, Jessica—described by people familiar with her record as "reasonably well qualified" and "perfectly solid" but not an academic standout—enrolled at Brown in 1994.

Even if celebrity applicants don't want red-carpet treatment, they have little choice. Julia Halberstam's heart was set on attending Brown, but she pleaded in her 1998 application essay to be judged on her own merits and not as the daughter of David Halberstam, Pulitzer Prize–winning writer of *The Best and the Brightest* and the baseball book *Summer of '49*.

"I am really just someone who did not want to get in for the wrong reasons," Julia told me. She ranked in the middle of her prep school class and had a 1340 SAT score, about 50 points below Brown's average. She said she "really excelled" in English and history in high school but had Cs in subjects such as math and science that didn't interest her. "I put in as much effort as I could to separate myself, to not be my last name."

Ordinarily, Brown does not interview applicants on campus; they meet with alumni representatives across the country. But when Julia and her father visited Providence, Brown admissions director Michael Goldberger met with them personally—and spent most of the time talking baseball with the writer. His daughter was so infuriated that, at her insistence, she had a second interview with another Brown official. "It was just me and him and we talked and it was great," she said.

When I ran her story past Goldberger in 2003, he told me that he met with one hundred applicants and their parents a year, strictly as a courtesy. He said ten to fifteen of them were celebrities, donors, or alumni. No records were kept of the conversations, he said, and they had no effect on the admissions decision. Goldberger resigned as admissions director in 2005 to become Brown's athletic director.

Julia Halberstam was admitted to Brown, graduated in 2002, and through the Teach for America program taught kindergarten at a school in Greenville, Mississippi. She remained troubled by the thought that she got in because of her father. "I don't know if I got into Brown because of my father's celebrity—I'll never know," she told me in 2003. "I was very aware of it and uncomfortable with it." She believes colleges should consider an applicant's race and social class—not celebrity status. "Not everyone has the same childhood that I did," she said. "There's a difference between not knowing and not being able to learn."

Despite Julia's misgivings about benefiting from influence, she did use one family connection in the hope of boosting her Brown chances. At her request, former Brown president Vartan Gregorian recommended her. Although Gregorian had recently left as president, he retained some clout with Brown admissions.

"I have known Julia since she was a child," Gregorian told me. "She would come on her father's shoulders to my Christmas parties. I always said to her, 'When the time comes, if you need a recommendation . . .' " He added that he had recommended to Brown the granddaughter of another well-known writer, E. L. Doctorow.

It's hardly surprising that some celebrities think getting into an elite college is as easy as crashing the line at a chic nightclub. In the 1980s, Tatum O'Neal, the youngest Oscar winner in history, visited the Brown admissions office and expressed interest in enrolling—even though she had scant formal education before dropping out of a Beverly Hills school. Asked how she expected to be academically competitive, she answered, referring to fellow child star Brooke Shields, "I just decided, 'Princeton had Brookie, so Brown needed me.' " In the end, she decided not to apply.

For celebrity applicants such as fashion model Lauren Bush, niece of President George W. Bush, there's no such thing as a deadline. In February 2002, a month after Princeton's application deadline had passed, Lauren contacted the university through her personal college adviser and asked permission to apply. The adviser explained that Lauren had changed her mind about her college plans after falling in love with Princeton on a recent visit. Sure enough, Princeton granted her special dispensation to apply. Despite SAT scores considerably below the typical Princeton student and a B average at the Kinkaid School in Houston, she was admitted. A person familiar with Lauren Bush's application to Princeton acknowledged that "her credentials were a cut below," but says Fred Hargadon, then dean of admission, was a political conservative "looking to inject personalities not from the liberal elite." Lauren—who also submitted to colleges a poetry collection entitled *Me*—was accepted by a second Ivy League university as well: Yale, the president's alma mater. (Her father, Neil Bush, graduated from Tulane University.) Once at Princeton, Lauren became a member of its most exclusive eating club, Ivy, joining Catharine Edwards, daughter of Senator John Edwards, the 2004 Democratic candidate for vice president.

Eyebrows were also raised when Lauren's younger brother, Pierce George Mallon Bush, enrolled in fall 2004 at Georgetown, considered one of the nation's top 25 universities. Pierce's academic struggles had been publicized by his own father, Neil Bush. Because his son had been misdiagnosed with attention deficit disorder, Neil Bush told interviewers, Neil had cofounded an education software company offering a computer curriculum for Pierce and other "hunter-warrior types" who don't enjoy reading.

"I did pretty good in elementary school," Pierce, appearing with his father, said on Fox News's *Hannity and Colmes* show in September 2002. "And I got up to the middle school level, and I started running into some trouble just because I wasn't quite that interested in what was being thrown across the table, if you know what I'm saying. . . . Once you pick stuff that you're interested in, and that's like the thing, my grades have improved a lot."

That same month, on CNN's *Connie Chung Tonight*, Chung asked Neil Bush: "Now, your son is a straight-A student, isn't he?" Bush replied, "Well, he's not a straight A. I think he's doing very well this year, though."

The president's brother declined to be interviewed for this book but said in a voice-mail message, "Despite the burden of these two children being offspring of Neil Bush, they've managed because of their merit to get into two fantastic universities. Both are doing very well at their respective universities and both are very happy. Frankly, it's my contention that the universities are lucky to have them as students."

No university in the country has practiced celebrity admissions more assiduously or successfully than Brown. Over the past twenty-five years, it has attracted, among others, children of Democratic Party poohbahs, including two presidents (John Kennedy and Jimmy Carter; Bill Clinton's daughter, Chelsea, visited Brown but opted for Stanford), three presidential candidates (Walter Mondale, Michael Dukakis, John Kerry), and a vice presidential candidate (Geraldine Ferraro). Among entertainment notables, it has drawn children or stepchildren of two Beatles (Ringo Starr, George Harrison), two Grammy Award winners (James Taylor, Carly Simon), an Emmy Award winner (Candice Bergen), and at least seven Academy Award winners (Marlon Brando, Steven Spielberg, Dustin Hoffman, Jane Fonda, Kevin Costner, Tim Robbins, and Susan Sarandon)—not to mention nominees Diana Ross, Richard Burton, David Mamet, Louis Malle, and Lee Strasberg. Fashion has been represented in the student body by children of designers Calvin Klein, Diane von Furstenberg, and Ralph Lauren. Allegra Beck, daughter of Donatella Versace and niece of the late Gianni Versace, enrolled at Brown in 2004. In addition, Brown has garnered its share of teen performers—such as actress Leelee Sobieski, who appeared in *Never Been Kissed* and *Eyes Wide Shut.*

Academically, Brown's celebrity students lag behind their more obscure classmates. The top 20 percent of Brown seniors graduate with high honors. Yet of thirty-three Brown graduates from famous families whom I checked, not a single one received such honors, according to university records. Four of the thirty-three, or 12 percent, graduated with honors in their majors: Vanessa Vadim (Jane Fonda's daughter), Alexandra Kerry (John Kerry), Cosima von Bulow (Claus von Bulow), and Rhonda Ross (Diana Ross). By contrast, nearly 30 percent of all Brown students achieve distinction in their majors.

But the success of celebrity children isn't only judged by grades or honors. Even though Brown has the Ivy League's lowest endowment ($1.8 billion in fiscal 2005), their visibility—and their parents'—has helped transform it from the "doormat of the Ivies," as it was sometimes labeled, to one of the nation's top destinations for bright students with a creative or artistic bent.

Ovitz and Hoffman, who weren't paid for their Brown appearance, are not the only prominent parents to headline events there. The late King Hussein of Jordan spoke at commencement when his son, Prince Faisal, graduated in 1985. Recent Parents' Weekend headliners at Brown included

MSNBC talk show host Chris Matthews (father of Michael Matthews '05), *Doonesbury* cartoonist Garry Trudeau (father of Ross Trudeau '06), and the late *Superman* actor Christopher Reeve (father of Matthew Reeve '02), while actor-director Tim Robbins (stepfather of Eva Amurri '07) spoke at an Ivy League film festival there.

ON PARENTS' Weekends, Brown students are accustomed to seeing actor/director Danny DeVito and his wife, Rhea Perlman (who played the barmaid Carla in the sitcom *Cheers*), at a coffeehouse or at student theater productions featuring their daughter Lucy, or Kevin Costner, in cowboy hat and boots, tailgating before a Brown football game. On one such occasion, the Oscar-winning director of *Dances with Wolves* vied with his daughter's classmates in Beirut—a drinking game in which cups of beer are arranged in a pyramid and the object is to throw Ping-Pong balls into them.

Brown has long contended that it has no calculated plan to appeal to celebrity children; they simply fall into the university's lap. "We did not go out in search of these kids," Robert Reichley, retired executive vice president for university relations, told me in his home on the edge of Brown's campus. "We did not cultivate them as you might a fine quarterback. They came in over the transom."

Whether by accident or design, Brown has positioned itself perfectly to attract students from famous families. Sometimes labeled the "alternative Ivy," it blends Ivy League prestige with relaxed curricular requirements. Some Brown faculty and administrators evince an unusual sympathy for celebrity children. Richard Fishman, a visual arts professor and director of the Creative Arts Council, which sponsored the Hoffman-Ovitz event, went so far as to call them an "oppressed minority."

Brown has other gateways for celebrity children besides freshman admissions and Chris Ovitz's "special student" status. Several children of prominent parents have transferred from other colleges to Brown, which is easier to get into as a transfer than as a high school senior. Brown accepts more than one-quarter of transfer applicants, compared with 17 percent of freshmen applicants. Because Brown does not offer financial aid to transfers, they tend to come from wealthy families, as do Andrew Lauren, son of Ralph Lauren; Kimberly Ovitz, who came from New York University; and Princess Theodora, daughter of the deposed King Constantine of Greece. The princess transferred from Northeastern University in Boston, an urban school that specializes in providing workplace experience for students and doesn't traditionally cater to royalty. According to a person familiar with her situation, Theodora (whose family lives in England) chose Northeastern because it has a strong alumni base and reputation in Greece, even though it offers only a modest program in theater, her area of interest. After her freshman year, she decided that she wanted more extensive coursework in the arts and humanities and applied for a transfer to Brown, which her older brother, Prince Nikolaos, had attended. Although few Northeastern students transfer to the Ivy League, a considerable step up in prestige, Brown admitted her.

Over the years, foreign royalty has been represented in the student body not only by Princess Theodora of Greece but also by the offspring of, among others, King Hussein of Jordan and the Aga Khan. Two children— Tatiana and Alexandre—of wrap dress inventor Diane von Furstenberg and Prince Egon von Furstenberg of Austria also attended Brown. The university's popularity among international students, not all of them royalty, is perhaps not surprising since Brown was one of the first Ivy League schools to pursue them. In 1978, former admissions director James Rogers recalled, he advised Howard Swearer, then Brown president, that the number of American high school graduates was expected to taper off as the baby boom generation reached adulthood. "I suggested that international students add a great deal to campus, and we should make a concerted effort to recruit them," Rogers recalled.

Swearer agreed, and a Brown admissions staffer began to visit private and international high schools in Europe and the Far East each year and send back names of potential applicants. Rogers would follow up with an annual trip to London, Paris, Athens, and Rome, holding a "Brown Night" in each city. "It started a lot of international buzz," Rogers said. "The more cosmopolitan group was our audience in the beginning. People who had heard of Brown would be those who had the means to send their children there. I'm sure it helped fund-raising."

Within five years, Rogers said, the proportion of international students in Brown's freshman class doubled from one in twenty to one in ten. Since leaving Brown, he has operated his own counseling service for international students—including, he said, "a number of Saudi royals."

UNTIL THE late 1960s, Brown wasn't on the international—or even national—map. "I played basketball, and we had two kids on our team from Atlanta," recalled *Providence Journal* columnist Bill Reynolds, a 1968 Brown graduate. "They were almost exotic. Everybody else was from New England, New York, or New Jersey. Then somebody made a very conscious marketing strategy to be favorable to children of celebrities."

Brown's evolution into a celebrity campus began in 1969, when it adopted a curriculum eliminating the distribution requirements that compelled students to take classes across the academic spectrum. To ensure a well-rounded education, most universities require students, whatever their major, to take at least one course in the humanities, social sciences, and sciences. Brown's "New Curriculum," which also reduced credits needed to graduate and let students take any course on a pass-fail basis rather than for a grade, enhanced its appeal to artistic students who hoped never to open another math or science text.

"To any person who is brought up in advantaged circumstances or had European schooling, American distribution requirements look awfully jejune," former Brown dean of admissions and financial aid Eric Widmer told me in his office at Deerfield Academy in Deerfield, Massachusetts, where he is the headmaster. "They want to take ownership of their education, and Brown allowed them to do that. So Brown was more appealing to celebrities than a university that spoon-fed them."

Julia Halberstam, for instance, recalled that "Brown was just the perfect fit for me, because of the curriculum. There are no requirements.

I never wanted to look at a number again." More recently, Tess Curtin Lynch, daughter of the actress and comedienne Jane Curtin (*Saturday Night Live, Third Rock from the Sun*), aspired to Brown as a refuge from math and science. As a student at the Harvard-Westlake School in Los Angeles, she acted in school plays and was published in the literary magazine. Her grades were solid but not outstanding: "Everything was brought down by math," she told me over the phone in 2004. Brown's lack of requirements, she said, was "a huge part of what made me want to go there."

The first time Tess took the math SATs, she scored 550 out of 800—well below Brown's standards. Her college counselor at Harvard-Westlake School told her she would need at least 600 to be competitive. Her family hired a tutor, who came to her house once a week and helped lift her score to 660 (along with a 700 verbal mark). "Probably a quarter of my classmates at Harvard-Westlake had the same sort of tutoring," Tess said. She applied early to Brown, was deferred to the regular pool, and then admitted.

Tess Lynch, who enrolled in 2001, acknowledged the dual advantage of her parentage: not only is her mother well known but her father, Patrick Lynch, is a Brown alumnus. "Probably that played a bigger part than my mom," she said. She also had a recommendation from Brown alumna Nancy Josephson, an influential Hollywood agent.

"I'm willing to admit I had the best possible set of circumstances," said Tess, who majored in English at Brown with a focus on creative writing. "I was very lucky. I don't know what my situation would have been without these steps up. I'm very, very pro-affirmative-action. I wouldn't want to go to school where all the people were just like me."

The "New Curriculum" caught a higher education wave, boosting Brown applications and allowing it to be more selective in admissions. Then, in 1979, Brown cemented its rising stature with a stunning coup: the enrollment of the late John F. Kennedy Jr.—son of the assassinated president and crown prince of a political dynasty. "John-John" was widely expected to follow his father, grandfather, and sister to Harvard. But Harvard was leery of his mixed academic record in private school (first at the Collegiate School in Manhattan and then at Phillips Academy in Andover), while John wanted to escape his family's long shadow—and math classes. His quantitative skills were shaky, and Brown's strong theater program appealed to him.

James Rogers, then Brown's admission director, recalled that John considered the state universities of Virginia and Vermont as well as Harvard and Brown. "I personally and other people in the office worked very hard with Andover in this case," said Rogers. "We talked a great deal about what would be in his best interest. Other colleges were involved in these discussions. We believed, and Harvard also said, going to Harvard would not be in his best interest simply because of all the ghosts. In the end, it came out that most everybody agreed that Brown would really be a very good place for him, which was then passed on to his mother [Jacqueline Kennedy Onassis]. She kind of bought it." Bruce Breimer, then and now director of college guidance at the Collegiate School, recalled that Onassis sought his advice about Brown, and he reassured her that it was the right match for her son. After graduating from Brown in 1983, John enrolled at New York University law school, and then exposed his scholastic deficiencies by failing the state bar exam twice.

In twenty years (1969–88) as Brown's admissions director, Rogers said, "the greatest advantage to Brown I was able to achieve was the admission and matriculation of John. People began to talk about Brown. If somebody who had as many admissions options as he had would choose Brown, there had to be some reason."

At Brown, female students and faculty swooned over the handsome Kennedy; one history professor walked from the front of her class to John's seat in the next-to-last row of the lecture hall to compliment him on his haircut, according to a former classmate. At the same time, the administration shielded him from the media. Robert Reichley, who headed university relations at the time, recalled that he refused to answer any questions about John—even such innocuous inquiries as what classes he was taking or what his major was. Every interview request was forwarded to John himself, who turned virtually all of them down. Media photo opportunities at his freshman registration and his graduation were restricted. By refusing to exploit John for publicity, Brown gained favor among other celebrities.

"All the celebrity kids here wanted to be invisible," said Reichley, who earned a mock "William Tecumseh Sherman prize" from the *New York Times* for repeatedly saying no to questions about John. "That's one reason many of them came to Brown. They said Brown protected them and didn't use them."

Even Reichley couldn't keep some celebrity students out of the public eye. Brown's next presidential offspring, Amy Carter, who enrolled in 1985, neglected her classes in favor of political protest. She was arrested during demonstrations against South Africa's apartheid regime and CIA recruitment. After being given grades of "incomplete" for failing to finish several courses, she left Brown during the 1987–88 academic year at the university's suggestion. "She spent a lot of time on issues that might better have been spent on academic life," Reichley said. Her Brown classmate Vanessa Vadim, daughter of Jane Fonda and director Roger Vadim, also made headlines for an arrest; she was accused of obstructing government administration, loitering, and disorderly conduct when her boyfriend was arrested on a drug charge. Vanessa, who was sentenced to do three days of community service, graduated in 1989.

A third celebrity in that entering class of 1985 stayed out of trouble herself—but owed her fame to her father's status as defendant in the most widely followed criminal case of the decade. Cosima von Bulow was the daughter of Claus von Bulow, a Danish-born aristocrat accused of attempting to murder his wife, Sunny—Cosima's mother—at the family's Newport, Rhode Island, mansion by injecting her with a dose of insulin that left her comatose. He was convicted in 1982, but the Rhode Island Supreme Court overturned the verdict and he was acquitted on retrial in June 1985.

While Sunny's two children by her first marriage believed Claus was guilty, Cosima supported her father. Fortuitously for her, so did Anne Brown, a von Bulow family friend and widow of John Nicholas Brown, whose family founded Brown University. Anne Brown surprised high society by appearing as a character witness for Claus in the 1982 trial, testifying, "Claus no more tried to murder Sunny than the man in the moon. He didn't marry her for her money. He married her for her beauty."

Most of Cosima's friends expected her to seek shelter from the scandal by going far away to college, but Brown University's New Curriculum appealed to her. "No one could understand why I wanted to go to school in Providence," Cosima told me by phone from her London home. "I liked the fact that I was going to be able to concentrate on subjects that were my strengths rather than waste time on core curriculum."

Cosima said she excelled academically at two prep schools; "I'd like to think I would have gotten into Brown anyway." To bolster her chances, she turned to Anne Brown for a recommendation. Brown's letter to the admissions office began, Cosima recalled, "Having turned down fourteen of my sixteen grandchildren, I think you now owe me a favor."

Anne Brown died in November 1985 at the age of seventy-nine. Cosima majored in comparative literature at Brown and graduated in 1989 with honors for her thesis on novelists Marcel Proust, Henry James, and Virginia Woolf. She moved to England after graduation, married Neapolitan nobleman Ricardo Pavoncelli, and has two children. She's been "a big supporter of Brown," she said. Cosima has kept Anne Brown's letter ever since in her father's house in Denmark.

IN 1989, the same year that Vanessa Vadim and Cosima von Bulow graduated, Brown installed a new president who was well equipped to attract more celebrity students. Vartan Gregorian, an Iranian-born immigrant of Armenian descent, was a media darling himself. After climbing through the academic ranks to become provost of the University of Pennsylvania, he had in 1981 assumed the presidency of the New York Public Library, where his ebullient personality transformed a stodgy institution into a chic place for charitable donations. Celebrity-conscious and chronically under-endowed, Brown coveted Gregorian's fund-raising prowess and his legions of high-profile friends and library donors—many of whom now looked to him to facilitate their children's admission to the Ivy League.

The new Brown president "came into New York City all the time and tapped every person who had made major donations to the public library," said Sondra Feig, former college counselor at the Dalton School in Manhattan. "Some of their kids were totally over their heads to go near Brown. They didn't want to go to Brown, but they were entertained in Providence. They left after a very short time."

In one instance, Feig said, Gregorian intervened in admissions on behalf of the daughter of a New York entrepreneur and library donor with Hollywood ties. The applicant, who was dyslexic, had mediocre grades at Dalton and left Brown without graduating.

The young woman told me that Gregorian was a close friend of her parents and that she had known him since she was seven years old. Soon after he became president of Brown, she said, he invited her to enroll. "I was thrilled with the opportunity Vartan was giving me," she said. "He took a great risk with me. My understanding was he was allowed two students a year he could have in. That was it. He could override anybody." Shortly after entering Brown, she said, she encountered an admissions official at an open house. "He told me, 'You're the student we didn't want,'" she said. "It was a very not fun experience."

Gregorian acknowledged facilitating her admission but said such intercessions on his part were rare. "I tried as much as possible to keep out of the admissions process," Gregorian, now president of the Carnegie Corporation of New York, told me during a lengthy conversation in Carnegie's Madison Avenue offices. "If as president I wanted someone admitted, I could have phoned and said, 'Admit him.' I seldom if ever did that."

He said that the children of the famous flocked to Brown not because of an administration strategy to give them an admissions edge but because of their anonymity on campus, the flexible curriculum, and the "esprit de corps" of the student body. He added that as Brown reached a critical mass of contented celebrity parents, they sang its praises to other notables with teenage children. "Once you had a cadre of five or ten celebrities, they became recruiters for Brown," he said. In particular, he said, Anna Strasberg—widow of Brown acting teacher Lee Strasberg and mother of two Brown graduates—promoted the university to friends, including the late Marlon Brando, whose daughter Petra went to Brown.

Nonetheless, Gregorian was keenly aware that Brown's endowment was only one-tenth of Harvard's. Hoping to narrow that deficit, he corralled the son of one of America's wealthiest men, billionaire Gordon P. Getty. William Paul Getty—son of Gordon and grandson of oil magnate J. Paul Getty—graduated in 1989 from the Groton School, where he was considered an average student, and enrolled at Brown. At the time, Gregorian was a trustee of the J. Paul Getty Trust—he served on its board from 1988 to 2000—and a close friend of William's mother, Ann Getty. Ann had joined the board of the New York Public Library in 1985 and given the library $1 million in Gregorian's honor. Gregorian said the Gettys had asked him where to send their children for college, and he had recommended several universities, including Brown. "I wanted Gordon Getty's children to come to Brown," Gregorian said. "I told admissions, 'The Gettys' son is applying, and I know them very well.' " He said the Gettys made no financial commitment in return: "I have no quid pro quos."

His intervention failed to produce the desired results, either for Brown or for the family. William Paul Getty, nicknamed Billy, "dropped out in six months," Gregorian said, adding that he didn't know why. He wrote a recommendation for Billy, who was interested in transferring to the University of Southern California.

Billy's parents did not make a significant gift to Brown, even though Gregorian again courted his father, a composer of classical music, by using university money to establish a Gordon Getty fund for visiting composers. Asked whether the Gettys would have contributed if their son had graduated, Gregorian sighed and said, "Maybe." Reached at his California home, Billy Getty declined comment.

SOPHIA LOREN was looking for admissions help. Her son Edoardo Ponti, who had attended high school in Switzerland, was applying to Brown University, but the legendary Italian actress didn't know anyone there. Then a friend who ran a dance studio, and whose own children had gone to Brown, gave her a name: David Zucconi. Zucconi, a Brown administrator, squired Loren and her son around campus, introducing them to other Brown officials. Sure enough, Edoardo was accepted—but the future movie director chose the University of Southern California's film school instead.

Edoardo was one of the few who got away from Zucconi. Although he held various titles in the admissions, development, and alumni offices during forty-four years as a Brown employee, one of his jobs was always the same: behind-the-scenes liaison to the rich and famous whose children were seeking admission. Zucconi ran interference for the families, lobbied for the students with the admissions staff, and looked after their happiness once enrolled—all in the hope of attracting money and attention to his beloved Brown. His advocacy ushered in many a well-connected student with second-rate qualifications, likely depriving stronger but unhooked candidates of slots.

Just as most celebrities don't book their own airplane flights or tennis courts, they also don't generally negotiate their children's college admissions. But their own entourage often lacks expertise in this area. Thus they need a coach, an adviser, an inside guide—someone like Zucconi.

"He got some kids into Brown, pushing, one way or another, who should never have been there," recalled William Nicholson, a former Brown admissions officer. "Usually they were children of great wealth or alumni. I would try to accommodate him. Sometimes the kids whom he referred were godawful. I'd call him and say, 'Dave, you've got to do some screening.' "

"Alumni would pass his name along" to celebrities who "wanted to get their sons or daughters in," said his older brother, Mario Zucconi, who lives on Long Island. "He was out with Walter Matthau. He had drinks with Walter Cronkite. He was out to dinner with Jane Fonda." Through Dave's contacts with wealthy alumni and business executives as well as celebrities, Mario said, "you cannot believe the money that he solicited or Brown received. Half-a-million- and million-dollar gifts were commonplace."

One such gift came from Fonda. According to Nicholson, Zucconi helped guide her daughter, Vanessa Vadim, through the admissions process. Nicholson said Vanessa "did not need a lot of push" and would have been a strong candidate anyway. Zucconi became friendly with Fonda and took her to lunch at Brown's faculty club. A year later, she called him to say she was delighted with Vanessa's freshman experience and wanted to repay Brown. According to Nicholson, she gave $750,000 anonymously for minority scholarships. (In 1991, Fonda would gain another Brown connection by marrying broadcasting mogul Ted Turner. Expelled from Brown in 1960 for having a female student in his room, Turner received honorary degrees from the university in 1989 and 1993 and became a major donor and trustee.)

"I spoke to Zucconi several times about some of my development cases," said Bruce Breimer, director of college guidance at the Collegiate School. "He would interview the kids, write a report, pave the way, let the admissions office know the prominence of the family. The buzz was, he's the guy to go to."

Most universities have a "guy to go to," but Dave Zucconi showed unusual gusto in the role. A barrel-chested former football player with a bone-crushing handshake, a booming Bronx accent, and a facial resemblance to actor Jason Robards, the 1955 Brown graduate invariably dressed in a blazer and one of his collection of ties adorned with the university seal. According to the student newspaper, the *Brown Daily Herald,* he drove a large white Cadillac convertible that he often parked on campus in prohibited zones. Students knew him for the lobster dinners he threw for football players and other favorites, while alumni in the United States and abroad often heard him speak at Brown functions and sought his advice on their children's applications.

Zucconi was blessed with total recall for the names and faces of Brown alumni, particularly athletes. As master of ceremonies at Brown, he would delight these alumni by recalling their long-faded exploits on the basketball court or gridiron. "He made everybody feel important," said *Providence Journal* columnist Bill Reynolds. "People came back to campus after twenty years and didn't know anyone; he knew them."

Raised in a third-floor walk-up, the son of Italian immigrants, Zucconi did not come from wealth himself. But his lack of social polish, combined with his gregariousness and eagerness to please, endeared him to the late Beatle George Harrison and his wife, Olivia, who contacted him when their son, Dhani, applied to Brown. (In his application essay, Dhani described playing music onstage with his father and Eric Clapton—a reminder to Brown admissions officers, if one were needed, of his family's celebrity.) Later, Zucconi traveled to England with the Brown crew team, including Dhani, for the Henley regatta, and the Harrisons invited him to visit them.

Zucconi loved regaling his friends with the tale of that visit. When he and his wife arrived at the Harrisons' home, a man working in the garden ushered them in and Mrs. Harrison greeted them. As she began serving tea, the gardener, still in his work clothes, joined them. After much pleasant conversation, the Zucconis said good-bye. Leaving the house, a bewildered Zucconi asked his wife, "Where was George? Why was the gardener with us?"

"That was George," his wife said.

Chris Matthews turned to Zucconi when the *Hardball* host's older son, Michael, was applying to Brown. Michael was not ranked in the top 20 percent of his class at St. Albans School in Washington, D.C., according to the school. His father said that Michael had strong grades, test scores, and extracurricular activities, including starting a film club at St. Albans and working for an AIDS orphanage in Kenya.

Matthews said that Lisa Caputo—a 1986 Brown graduate, former press secretary to First Lady Hillary Clinton, and frequent *Hardball* guest—steered him to Zucconi. The two men talked periodically during the admissions process, but Matthews said he didn't know whether Zucconi played a role in Brown's acceptance of Michael, who enrolled in 2001. "It's all a mystery to me what happened behind those doors," Matthews said. "I was thrilled when he got in." Brown gained some cachet from Michael's arrival, as his father subsequently gave three speeches on campus.

Caputo, now a Citigroup executive, said she wasn't aware that Zucconi had any influence on admissions but suggested contacting him because he "was the only guy I knew in the Brown administrative structure. Dave was this big personality. Everybody knew him."

Although he embodied Brown to alumni and celebrities, Zucconi had many detractors within the university administration, who felt that the onetime Brown halfback specialized in end runs around their authority. Admissions officers, in particular, complained that his meddling added another level of caprice to an already arbitrary process. Zucconi, they noted, ran his own seminars for alumni children on how to get into Brown, and liberally dispensed advice and even his own admissions video to applicants he favored. Besides the usual list of candidates backed by the development office, Brown admissions officers often had to swallow a separate "Zucconi list." Much as they might have wanted to, they couldn't dismiss Zucconi's recommendations out of hand because of his wide contacts among alumni and his impressive track record as a fund-raiser.

Zucconi was a "giant gadfly," said Robert Reichley, the retired head of university relations. After starting his Brown career as an admissions officer, Zucconi worked for Reichley, overseeing alumni who interviewed Brown applicants. "I realized he had not stopped being an admissions officer. He was on his own submitting a list. . . . I didn't know I could get that angry." Reichley added, however, that Zucconi's influence was "not unchecked."

James Rogers, the former admissions director, said, "Every university needs a person like Zucconi to listen and work on behalf of its friends and alumni." Still, he said, Zucconi tried to "subvert the admissions process" by assuring alumni and celebrities that he could get their children in, and "seldom used as a criterion whether the student was qualified for Brown. He always used some inside information that he had as to what could advance this student. He wasn't necessarily working in Brown's best interest. He was trying to make the father and mother of the candidate feel good."

Former Brown president Vartan Gregorian said he discovered that trustees, alumni, and other notables used Zucconi as a back-channel advocate for their favored applicants. "I established a process that no case can go directly from Zucconi to admissions," Gregorian said. "They had to inform me. I have to know who's doing what. Zucconi didn't think anybody that applied to Brown should be turned down. I protected the admissions director. I never once called to overrule him. I never said, 'Zucconi has a great candidate.' " Gregorian added, "Zucconi was such a loveable man you couldn't get angry at him. He had one life—Brown."

Like a modern-day Othello, Zucconi loved Brown not wisely but too well, and his excessive zeal on its behalf was his downfall. Among other duties, he was executive director of—and raised millions of dollars for— the Brown University Sports Foundation, a booster club that helps finance the school's athletic teams. In 1999, he was caught offering Sports Foundation money to Brown sports recruits regardless of financial need, a violation of Ivy League rules. Ivy presidents imposed on Brown the harshest punishment ever meted out in the league's history—including ineligibility for the football championship in 2000—and specified that Zucconi could have no further contact with prospective athletes. He was reassigned to the development office.

The scandal exposed the long-simmering resentment within the admissions office over Zucconi's interference. In a letter to the *Brown Alumni Magazine* published early in 2001, former director James Rogers wrote, "I am amused that Zucconi has been barred indefinitely from 'providing any services to Brown student athletes.' This is a joke; Zucconi has made a career of disobeying direct orders from his superiors at Brown. Good luck to whoever must monitor his activities." The next edition published letters from eight alumni defending Zucconi, including one that accused Rogers of "jealousy" and "insensitivity to qualified sons and daughters of alumni."

On January 22, 2003, Zucconi died of cancer at the age of sixty-nine. On one of the coldest days of the year, two thousand people thronged the Cathedral of Saints Peter and Paul for his funeral. As his coffin was carried out, name tags of attendees were collected to be buried with him, and the organist softly played "Ever True to Brown."

At the funeral, Mario Zucconi recalled, "at least a dozen people said to me, 'If it wasn't for your brother, my son or daughter wouldn't have gotten into Brown.' "

———

THROUGH AN intermediary, Michael Ovitz let Brown president E. Gordon Gee know in 1998–99 that his son Christopher wanted to enroll there as a freshman. Although it's not certain, the go-between was most likely Dave Zucconi, on whom Gee relied for such sensitive missions. According to people familiar with the president's thinking, Gee was understandably enthused. Like Zucconi, Brown's new president had an aggressive, can-do attitude and a certain impatience for convention. Despite his propensity for bow ties, Gee was an outsider to the Ivy League, a Mormon who graduated from the University of Utah and arrived at Brown in 1998 after presiding over three public universities, most recently Ohio State. Eager to make a splash, he felt hamstrung by Brown's modest endowment and began planning a fund-raising campaign.

To Gee and his development staff, Ovitz's overture offered a rare opportunity not just to net one prize fish but to harvest a whole sea. Ovitz was a catch himself; he was famous, his income at Creative Artists Agency had reached $20–25 million a year in the early 1990s, and he had a track record of educational philanthropy, most notably a $25 million pledge in 1997 from his family foundation to the medical center at UCLA, his alma mater. (Ovitz has since suffered a number of financial reverses and fallen behind on fulfilling the pledge. From fiscal 1997 to fiscal 2004, the foundation gave UCLA less than $5 million, public records show. His lawyer, James Ellis, says the pledge was intended as a long-term commitment.) He was also generous on a smaller scale to his children's private schools, typically giving each of them between $5,000 and $30,000 a year. Even more significantly, he could open doors to a vast array of Hollywood talent and executives, what one former Brown administrator called the "high-end California market."

"Some people are rainmakers, some people are rain-givers," the former administrator added. Potentially, Ovitz was both. And while Brown officials did not spell out what they would expect of him, they didn't have to. Ovitz, the consummate deal maker, knew how to unlock doors at educational institutions; he once offered to help place the children of the *New York Times* Hollywood reporter, Bernard Weinraub, in private school, an offer Weinraub passed up.

"He was as enamored of having an affiliation with Brown as Brown was of him," one insider said. "This was mutually advantageous to both parties."

There was only one drawback: Chris Ovitz. By all accounts, his qualifications were well below Brown's usual stretch for development and celebrity cases. Classmates at Harvard-Westlake, the elite prep school in Los Angeles where he attended the seventh and eighth grades, say he did have one distinction: he carried a cell phone, then a rarity for a middle schooler. When a classmate in seventh grade grabbed his phone, he chased her into the school gym, picked up a baseball bat, and swung it—missing her but denting the wall. According to the girl's father, a Los Angeles real estate attorney, she was "terrified." He said the school suspended both students for "a couple of days," and afterward made sure they stayed away from each other. He added that his daughter also tore up Chris's prepaid lunch card—and that the Ovitzes later asked for reimbursement.

"He and my daughter received equal punishment—her for her mouth, him for his bat," the father said. "He should have been kicked out. But we were not in a position to do what the Ovitzes could do for the school. We sat down with the middle school headmistress, she talked about my daughter's mouth, how she provoked it."

Thomas Hudnut, Harvard-Westlake headmaster, said he remembers the incident "only dimly. It's much more sensational in the telling than it was at the time." Chris, he said, "was very socially mature, and got along well with adults. He was physically and academically immature. That's a very tough combination for a boy to have, particularly a boy who wants to be competitive and comes from a competitive family. He swam against the tide some. His father was in the paper every day. It was not easy being Chris Ovitz."

Hudnut said he encouraged the Ovitzes to send Chris to boarding school, where he would be under less of a microscope, but "they weren't ready to do that." Instead, Chris transferred after middle school to the Crossroads School for Arts and Sciences in Santa Monica, a progressive, arts-oriented school where students call teachers by their first names. (Hudnut said Crossroads called him before accepting Chris, and he assured

its headmaster that Chris was a "good kid," just "a little out of synch.")
Crossroads graduates include actress Kate Hudson (Goldie Hawn's daughter) and Robert Belushi, James's son, as well as Dustin Hoffman's sons Jake and Max and daughter Alexandra. Max and Alexandra Hoffman both enrolled at Brown.

Crossroads classmates and teachers say Chris was an average student who took few if any advanced placement courses, evinced little interest in learning, and did not excel in extracurricular activities. Chris "didn't have the drive to succeed," said a former Crossroads faculty member. He described Chris's attitude this way: "You don't really have to do anything because it's going to be taken care of for you."

Hudnut, the Harvard-Westlake headmaster, suggested that Chris may have aspired to Brown because Jessica Capshaw, Steven Spielberg's stepdaughter, had gone there. "The Spielbergs and the Ovitzes were tight," he said. "There's a well-trod path between Los Angeles and Providence."

But hardly anyone with Chris's academic record had trodden that path. Chris's test scores and grades were "egregiously uncompetitive," said a former Crossroads staffer. "Brown bent over backwards as far as any university could."

Of his five Crossroads classmates who would enroll at Brown, four were inducted into the Cum Laude Society, signifying that they ranked in the top 20 percent of their high school class. Chris was not inducted. One of those four classmates, Erin Durlesser, told me, "He definitely was not academic in my opinion. When he was admitted to Brown, the mood among some of the students was surprise and confusion. The ones who also applied to Brown felt it was inappropriate competition."

Brown passed over at least one Crossroads classmate who was a Cum Laude Society member: Arielle Reinstein. Wait-listed at Brown, she enrolled at Stanford, where she was named to Phi Beta Kappa and collected two degrees and a prize in essay writing. "I . . . hold no animosity towards Brown University," Arielle told me in an email. "While I don't agree with all of their admissions practices, I understand that a school's endowment is of great significance and money can buy some things I was surprised it could as a high school senior."

Michael Goldberger, then Brown director of admissions, balked at Chris's lack of credentials. According to people familiar with the internal conversations between admissions, development, and the president's office, he cautioned Gee that accepting Chris would damage the university's credibility with high schools in southern California. In admissions parlance, Chris Ovitz was so far out of "context" with other Ivy League applicants that his admission might upset counselors and parents of rejected students. But the president pressed the issue, and, understanding his boss's priorities, Goldberger compromised. Chris was admitted conditionally, as a nonmatriculating "special student" allowed to take classes at Brown. If he proved his mettle in those classes, he would be granted status as a regular student.

"The Ovitz case was a strange case," a person familiar with Brown admissions told me. "We all found it very trying. There were a lot of factors beyond his ability to do the work. There were issues of focus and motivation. The hope was that admission as a special student would jolt him into readjusting his perspective, and that he would do better out of his father's shadow."

"Special student" was an existing admissions category at Brown, but it was not intended as a loophole for low-achieving celebrity children, nor as a roundabout route to a Brown diploma. Every semester, Brown admits one or two students under this status who want to take a particularly esoteric course that isn't available elsewhere. Special students are not degree candidates, and if they later seek regular admission, they aren't supposed to be given any advantage over other applicants.

By designating Chris as a "special student" rather than a regular freshman, the admissions office preserved a shred of its integrity. But it also made Chris a one-of-a-kind case, and prep school counselors who heard about the arrangement wondered why Brown had singled him out instead of one of their students. "It's highly unusual," one complained. "I've never had that option granted to me."

Students, parents, and teachers at Harvard-Westlake and Crossroads were in the dark. As far as they knew, Chris Ovitz had gotten into Brown, and there could be only one reason why: his surname. "Brown did pay for it in this community," said a prep school administrator. "It reverberated here. People were horrified. Brown lost some credibility."

Michael Ovitz and his children declined comment for this book, as did Simmons, Goldberger, and former president Gee. James Ellis, a lawyer for Ovitz, defended Brown's admission of Chris Ovitz on the grounds that he contributed to the university's diversity. "If diversity in terms of background and experience that kids bring to a college campus has any meaning at all, having spent time with Chris and Kimberly . . . these kids have perspectives and experiences and backgrounds that I just think are tremendously valuable and unique and would be a benefit to any campus," Ellis said.

Whether due to his provisional status or not, Chris Ovitz kept a low profile at Brown. He was omitted from the freshman photo album, known as the "facebook" or "pig book." He left the university within a year and eventually enrolled at UCLA, his father's alma mater. "He thought Brown was boring, nobody knew how to party," a Brown classmate said. According to Harvard-Westlake headmaster Hudnut, Chris received his bachelor's from UCLA and became a graduate student in its film school. Gee soon departed Brown as well, becoming president of Vanderbilt University in 2000.

But the mutually beneficial relationship between Brown and the Ovitzes has outlasted them both, anointing the university with glamour and the family with prestige. Kimberly Ovitz followed Christopher to Brown in 2002, after one year at New York University. Fishman of the Creative Arts Council said Kimberly "didn't want help from her parents. She applied on her own." Brown's current president, Ruth Simmons, courts the onetime Hollywood kingmaker just as avidly as her predecessor did. As Ovitz told the spellbound throng on Parents' Weekend, Brown is truly an "amazing institution."

4

ENDURING

LEGACIES

Notre Dame's
Other Tradition

The University of Notre Dame's football team has tumbled in recent years from its traditional number-one spot. But the South Bend, Indiana, university, which has 8,300 undergraduates, does lead the nation in a more obscure category—legacies. Every year, between 21 and 24 percent of Notre Dame freshmen are alumni children, more than at any other major U.S. university, even though admission there has become increasingly competitive in recent decades.

Along with football, legacy preference is at the heart of Notre Dame's identity, helping to boost alumni donations and loyalty and preserve the university's Catholic culture. Notre Dame's legacy policies may be as responsible as its pigskin exploits for its rise from a little-known Catholic school in the middle of nowhere into one of the nation's premier universities. Its two traditions intersect in the 1993 movie *Rudy,* about a working-class underdog who fulfills his dream of playing for the Fighting Irish. While Rudy strives to make the squad, a teammate assured of a spot confides, "The only reason they keep me on here is 'cause I'm a legacy."

Yet as it solidifies its status in the top echelon, Notre Dame is grappling with the question of whether it has outgrown legacy preference—whether it can afford to turn away high-caliber applicants while accepting lesser candidates whose parents happen to be graduates. Its heavy reliance on the preference has also strained relations with alumni children whom it has rejected—and with cousins, nieces, nephews, grandchildren, and other extended family who resent that they are not considered eligible for the boost.

Alumni children are the biggest group receiving admissions preference at Notre Dame, outstripping African Americans (4 percent of the student body), Hispanics (8 percent), athletes (9 percent), international students (4 percent), and faculty and staff children (3 percent). While nearly one out of four Notre Dame freshmen is an alumni child, fewer than one out of ten comes from a family in which neither parent went to college.

At Notre Dame and other elite private universities, legacy preference provides affluent families with a form of insurance against a decline in educational status from one generation to the next, which might in turn lead to a decline in wealth and power. Just as English peers hold hereditary seats in the House of Lords, so the American nobility reserves slots at Harvard, Yale, Princeton, and other august universities. Based on pedigree rather than merit, legacy preference strikes at the heart of American notions of equal opportunity and upward mobility.

The power of legacy preference at Notre Dame is exemplified by its admissions decisions on two high school classmates, John Simmons and Kevin Desmond. Simmons and Notre Dame seemed like a match made in college admissions heaven.

John earned a straight-A average and was valedictorian of the 173-member class of 2004 at University of Detroit Jesuit High, a traditional Notre Dame feeder school. His test score on the ACT college entrance exam—31 out of a possible 36, equivalent to a 1360–1400 on the SAT—met the average for applicants admitted to Notre Dame, one of the nation's premier Catholic universities. Moreover, John's devout Catholicism and good works—he tutored other students, checked in surgical patients at a hospital, and distributed food to the homeless at a soup kitchen in downtown Detroit—appeared to suit a university where every dormitory has a chapel and four out of five students participate in community service. And the inability of his divorced parents—his mother is a preschool teacher, his father a hard-luck businessman—to afford Notre Dame's tuition, fees, and room and board, now $42,140 a year, would not deter a university that proclaims itself to be "need-blind."

By contrast, his high school classmate Kevin Desmond's credentials were borderline. Kevin was a good student at Jesuit High but not an outstanding one. His SAT score was 1290, about 90 points below the average for Notre Dame admits. He ranked in the top 15 percent of his high school class, while 84 percent of Notre Dame freshmen are in the top 10 percent. He played three sports—golf, lacrosse, and skiing—but none well enough to be a college recruit. He was wait-listed by another Catholic school, Boston College, which accepted John Simmons.

Notre Dame went the other way. It rejected John, while Kevin drove home from lacrosse practice one day to find an acceptance letter.

Kevin benefited from the preference for alumni children. His maternal grandfather, his father, his father's three brothers, and Kevin's five older siblings all graduated from Notre Dame. His father, Terry Desmond, owner of two funeral homes in the Detroit area, is past president of the Notre Dame Club of Detroit and is in the process of endowing a scholarship at the university.

Reinforcing these connections, Kevin referred to his family's close ties to Notre Dame in his college application essay. His maternal grandparents, parents, and two of his sisters were married on campus, his father's business has enlisted fellow "Domers" as clients, and Kevin has been going to Fighting Irish football games since he was a toddler.

"I don't know if I would have gotten into Notre Dame" without legacy preference, Kevin told me. "My family ties would have helped. I still had pretty good grades and test scores. I wasn't a lot below the Notre Dame average." He added that Notre Dame "was my first choice, partly because of my family. Up until I got the [acceptance] letter, there was a lot of anxiety," because he didn't want to let down his father and siblings.

Terry Desmond justified Notre Dame's admission of his six children on the grounds that they were all "top-notch" students, and that legacy preference bolsters school traditions and rewards alumni for financial contributions. "We didn't want one of them to be the first one turned down.

The two or three months waiting for the letter to come are the worst months to go through."

Both of John Simmons's parents went to Central Michigan University. Had he been a Notre Dame legacy, his stellar transcript would likely have gained him admission. But a relatively light load of advanced placement courses hindered him, and his test score fell short of the higher bar Notre Dame sets for unconnected applicants. The university's SAT average of 1394 for admitted students is artificially deflated by the lower scores of legacies, minorities, athletes, and other "special interests"; applicants without preference actually need a 1470 or so. "We don't jump at valedictorians" with SAT scores in the 1300s, said Daniel Saracino, Notre Dame's assistant provost for admissions.

John—who applied to six Catholic colleges and was admitted to all but Notre Dame—opted for John Carroll University in Ohio, which awarded him almost a full scholarship. As of March 2006, he was a sophomore psychology major with an A average. He said he bears no grudge against Notre Dame, but "if I was designing the system, I wouldn't do it that way." A degree from Notre Dame, he added, might have improved his chances of going to a top graduate school and embarking on a successful career in clinical practice. "As good as John Carroll is, it's not as well known," he said. "Everybody knows Notre Dame."

Scott Merchant, director of college counseling at University of Detroit Jesuit High, said, "Whether you get admitted to a hypercompetitive school has no bearing on what type of student you are. You have to have some kind of a hook to get in at schools like Notre Dame. For some kids, it's being the child of an alum.

"I still believe John deserved to get in there. The thing that impressed me about John—he wasn't only valedictorian of an extremely competitive academic school, he's also a tremendous human being. His outside interests and personal qualities are as high if not higher than his academic qualities. He could have gone anywhere and done well academically. He's also extremely religious and faith-oriented. He took the rejection a lot better than I would have."

Added John's mother, Kathy: "Notre Dame lost a great kid."

EDUCATIONAL INSTITUTIONS, including private universities, have been exempted from federal taxes since the income tax was introduced in 1913, and donations to them are tax-deductible. As tax-exempt institutions, they are prohibited from racial discrimination, and often profess to serve a greater social good by identifying and elevating students with leadership potential, regardless of race or income. Yet the legacies that so heavily populate their freshman classes are a singularly homogenous group—overwhelmingly white and rich. Only 7.6 percent of alumni child applicants whom Harvard admitted in 2002 were black, Hispanic, or Native American, compared with 17.8 percent of all successful applicants. One recent study found that 50 percent of legacy applicants to selective colleges boasted family incomes in the top 25 percent of American society, as against 39 percent of nonlegacy applicants. "Legacy preferences serve to reproduce the high-income/high-education/white profile that is characteristic of these schools," former Princeton president William Bowen and two coauthors concluded in their 2005 book, *Equity and Excellence in American Higher Education.*

Thus, legacies are more likely to afford private high schools, tutors, test prep courses, and other perquisites that usually translate into higher test scores. Also, because it is widely agreed that parental education is one of the best predictors of pupil achievement, alumni children should be high achievers; by definition, they start with the advantage of having at least one college-educated parent. To equalize opportunity for applicants from less enriched backgrounds, alumni children would need to be held to a *higher* standard, not a lower one.

Nearly all private universities in the United States and some state schools give a substantial admissions edge to legacies. At some liberal arts colleges, legacies are even more prevalent than at Notre Dame. Alumni children account for nearly 40 percent of students at Calvin College, a Christian school in Grand Rapids, Michigan, where President Bush gave the commencement address in 2005. At Ivy League and other elite schools, alumni sons and daughters typically make up 10 to 15 percent of the student body, often despite lesser academic credentials. Legacies are two to four times more likely to be accepted than other applicants, and many elite universities enroll more legacies than either African American or Hispanic students. Legacies, like minorities and recruited athletes, "have a decidedly better chance of being admitted, at any specified SAT level, than do other students," Bowen and his coauthors found.

To widen the pool of potential donors, some schools, like Wesleyan University in Middletown, Connecticut, give an edge to alumni grandchildren, siblings, nieces, and nephews. Davidson College, an elite liberal arts college in North Carolina, distinguishes between "direct legacies" (alumni children, stepchildren, and grandchildren) and "legacy-connected" applicants (siblings, cousins, nieces, and nephews). Other institutions, such as Stanford, broaden their definition of alumni to include anyone who holds a degree from its graduate or professional schools, not just its undergraduate college.

Legacies also catch a break since a high proportion of them apply to only one school—Mommy or Daddy's alma mater—under binding early decision programs. That's because they chose their college years before, or it was chosen for them, and they're too wealthy to have to worry about financial aid. (Applicants who commit early forfeit the chance to leverage one school's aid offer into more money from another.) Admission standards for early decision applicants are usually lower than for regular applicants because colleges sacrifice test-score points for the sake of raising their yield rates—the proportion of admitted students who enroll. The University of Pennsylvania explicitly links alumni child preference and early decision, urging alumni children and grandchildren to apply in the fall of their senior year for "maximum consideration for the legacy affiliation." Penn admissions dean Lee Stetson explained, "If we're going to give them a measure of preference, it should be when they're making a commitment to us."

Out-of-staters need SAT scores 30–35 points higher than Virginia residents to enter the University of Virginia, a premier public university—unless they happen to be alumni children. The university groups out-of-state alumni children with in-state applicants, and Virginia dean of admissions John Blackburn made no bones about the reasons for the preference. "Our private support particularly from alumni is crucial to maintaining the quality of the institution," he told me in 2003. "Legacy preference helps ensure that support by recognizing their financial contributions and their service on university committees and task forces." Out-of-state alumni contributed the majority of $1.4 billion raised in a university fund drive.

Alumni children enjoy special treatment at every stage of the admissions process, such as expert advice from college liaison offices, special tours and briefings from college administrators, reviews of applications by admissions directors, and, in the event that they're rejected, personal phone calls from university officials to ease the blow or recommend another school. The alumni office at Brown University has offered free college counseling for alumni children and grandchildren since 1994, while its counterpart at the University of Pennsylvania schedules and conducts admissions interviews for legacies. During homecoming weekend in November 2004, Amherst College provided an "overview of admission procedures" for alumni and their children.

Alumni are heavily involved in admissions—and they take care of their own. Not only do alumni volunteers interview applicants for many schools, but college admissions offices frequently hire alumni for staff positions. Sooner or later, these staffers encounter an application from the son or daughter of an old college classmate or roommate. Fairness would seem to demand that staffers confronted with such a candidate disqualify themselves on the grounds of personal bias, just as a judge won't hear a case brought by a friend or neighbor. But such recusals aren't part of the clubby college admissions culture.

To be sure, some alumni children have strong academic records that would warrant admission to a top university in any case. But the underqualified are avoiding a steep tumble. Unlike athletes, development cases, and celebrity children, legacies enjoy a hook at only one or two colleges—those their parents attended. Competition for slots at selective American universities has become so intense that subpar legacies rejected by their parent's Ivy League alma mater may slide down to a second- or third-tier college.

"With the legacy pool, those parents push the hardest, because it's the best shot they have," said Lloyd Peterson, a former Yale admissions officer. "If those legacies don't get into Yale, they aren't getting into Harvard or Princeton. They're going two steps down. If it isn't Yale, it's probably the University of Connecticut, not Wesleyan. The parent's thinking, 'I've got to go to the cocktail party Friday night and tell everybody my kid's going to UConn. That may cost me a contract.'"

For these lucky legacies, their undeserved college admission can be a passport to wealth, social status, and political power. According to *Who's Running America?*, an exhaustive study by Florida State University professor Thomas Dye, 54 percent of corporate leaders and 42 percent of governmental leaders hold degrees from twelve heavily endowed and prestigious private universities. By contrast, only 25 percent of the elite go to state universities.

"You do know the friends you make at Harvard are going to help you somewhere down the line," said Mary Anne Schwalbe, former associate director of admissions at Harvard. "The friends you make at Lewis and Clark College may not, although it's a perfectly good college."

No wonder that many alumni children feel a twinge of guilt over their admission to an elite college. "There's a self-doubt that creeps in," said Deborah Perlman, a psychologist who has counseled legacies at Georgetown University. "You find a parallel feeling among minorities" benefiting from affirmative action. Princeton's alumni weekly published a letter in 2002 from her and her father, Theodore Perlman—both legacies at the university—advocating an end to legacy preference. "The greater good is to be found in equality of treatment," they wrote.

"I think I might have been a borderline student coming in here," said Christopher Nanovic, a third-generation Notre Dame legacy whose family funded the Nanovic Institute for European Studies on campus. He and Kevin Desmond were living in the same dormitory, the aptly named

Alumni Hall. "Legacy definitely helps. It's kind of a question in my mind—if I would be here without legacy preference. I'd like to think I would be."

LEGACY PREFERENCE has long drawn criticism from populists and civil rights advocates who decry admissions breaks for an upper-class and almost exclusively white group. But the anti-legacy ranks are widening. Ivy League dissenters include William Bowen, president emeritus of Princeton, who called for "tight limits" on legacy preferences in his 2005 book. Massachusetts senator Edward M. Kennedy, a Harvard legacy himself, filed a bill in 2003 requiring colleges to divulge data on alumni child admissions.

Even some mainstream Republican opponents of affirmative action for minorities have reluctantly joined the attack, recognizing that to be consistent they have to oppose affirmative action for wealthy whites as well. Thus former CIA director Robert Gates, now president of Texas A&M University, abolished both affirmative action and legacy preference there. President George W. Bush, a third-generation legacy at Yale—his daughter Barbara represented the fourth Bush generation there—told an audience of black journalists during the 2004 campaign that admissions should be merit-based and there should be "no special exception for certain people." He was echoing popular sentiment; a May 2004 poll in the *Chronicle of Higher Education* found that 75 percent of Americans disagree with giving "extra consideration for admission" to alumni relatives.

So do many Europeans, even in class-conscious England. Just as the House of Lords has been stripped of power over the years, neither Oxford nor Cambridge asks applicants whether their parents are alumni, and any intimation of favoritism toward the upper classes prompts a storm of protest. Although Prime Minister Tony Blair graduated from Oxford, it turned down his son Euan in 2002, due to a C in French. He enrolled at the less prestigious Bristol University instead.

Yet, repudiating the popular will, not a single U.S. private college or university has dropped legacy preference. Colleges cling to the preference on the grounds that it is essential to their financial health. Alumni contributed $7.1 billion to higher education in 2005, representing 27.7 percent of all private giving to colleges, according to the Council for Aid to Education. Some of that money, no doubt, is given out of charity, with no concern for a son's or daughter's admission. But much is either donated in thanks for children already admitted to the alma mater, or in the expectation that a sizeable check will smooth a future acceptance.

"Without legacy preference, there would be a significant decrease in giving from a core body of traditional support—families in which at least a second generation has gone to the institution," said Sheldon Steinbach, vice president and general counsel of the American Council on Education, a Washington lobbying group.

Such dire predictions are highly debatable. There's no doubt that some alumni, counting on the admissions break, do fume when their children are turned down. On learning of his daughter's rejection by Princeton in 2002, R. J. Innerfield '67 composed an overwrought poem, entitled "WestCollegeioma," for the *Princeton Alumni Weekly:* "A cancer creeps insidiously here / Within our midst and masquerades about / Destroying as it does the very dear attachment / We can't bear to be without." Another Princeton graduate, Richard Hokin '62, stopped giving to his alma mater after it turned away two daughters several years ago. "I took it as a personal affront," said Hokin, chairman of Intermountain Industries Inc., an Idaho natural gas distributor.

Significantly, Hokin didn't stop donating to higher education. Instead, he redirected his giving to Brown and Northwestern, the institutions his daughters attended. Princeton's loss was their gain.

Hokin's behavior suggests that, contrary to the doomsayers' predictions, higher education would thrive even if legacy preference were abolished. If fewer legacies were admitted, alumni might give less money to their own alma maters—but more to their children's.

Plus, if legacy preference were eliminated, alumni such as Hokin might be less offended when their children are rejected. The exorbitant rates at which legacies are admitted raise parental hopes; alumni expect their children to be admitted, even with inferior academic qualifications. An end to legacy preference would mitigate both alumni expectations and their ensuing disappointment.

In any case, once their immediate anger over a child's rebuff subsides, alumni loyalty proves remarkably resilient. Mary Anne Schwalbe said one of her tasks at Harvard was to console alumni whose children were turned down. Nine out of ten times, she said, the parents would reply to her letters with reassurances that they weren't upset. One alumnus, whose family had given a building to Harvard, called her after his grandson had gotten the bad news and said, "I couldn't agree with you more."

LEGACY PREFERENCE at U.S. colleges is a relatively modern phenomenon. It emerged less than a century ago, largely for an unsavory reason: suppressing Jewish enrollment.

Before World War I, while the tradition of alumni donating to their alma mater was already established, their children did not require admissions preference. Even top colleges such as Harvard and Yale accepted all comers who could pass exams in Latin and other subjects—mainly affluent white Protestant students from private schools. By virtue of money and background, graduates of the most prestigious boarding schools ruled the colleges' social scene, dominating Princeton's upper-class eating clubs and Harvard's finals clubs, and cementing relationships that would buttress their subsequent careers in business or politics.

After the war, better transportation, improved public schools, and the impact of decades of European immigration combined to threaten this close-knit Yankee world. The number of applicants soared as more public school graduates began clamoring for Ivy educations and outperforming prep schoolers on newfangled standardized tests. Many such budding scholars were Jews—not only children of assimilated, wealthy German Jews but those of less educated, Yiddish-speaking peasants from Poland and Russia. The proportion of Jewish undergraduates at Harvard tripled from 7 percent in 1900 to 21.5 percent in 1922; at Columbia, Jewish enrollment neared 40 percent by 1918. As their numbers mounted, these Jewish students were often ostracized on campus, barred from athletic teams and extracurricular clubs.

In response to panic among alumni on whose wallets they depended, the universities considered three options. First, they could expand to accommodate all minimally qualified applicants, which was bound to dilute their cachet. Second, they could limit admissions to top students based on grades and test scores. But in that case brilliant Jews and other newcomers, many from impoverished circumstances and needing financial aid, would displace academically mediocre alumni children. "Aside from their disdain for socially undesirable Jewish applicants, alumni were concerned that their own children might not be accepted under tighter admissions standards," David O. Levine wrote in *The American College and the Culture of Aspiration, 1915–1940*.

Since both those strategies seemed unsatisfactory, the colleges devised a third: restricting admissions based on criteria that did not appear discriminatory but would have the effect of reducing Jewish enrollment. A prime example was Dartmouth College, which in 1922 developed admissions guidelines based not just on a candidate's academic potential but on such factors as character, athletic prowess, geographic distribution (designed to curb the number of students from New York City, where Jews and other immigrants were concentrated), and alumni status: "All properly qualified sons of Dartmouth alumni . . . shall be admitted." In another concession to alumni, they were allowed to interview applicants and weigh in on admissions decisions—a practice that remains widespread.

Presaging future debates, "critics asserted that the plan was a subterfuge to justify the selection of alumni children and athletes," Levine wrote.

Three years later, Yale's board of admissions voted that any limit on enrollment "shall not operate to exclude any son of a Yale graduate who has satisfied all the requirements for admission"—spurring a rapid increase in the proportion of Yale legacies to 21.4 percent in the class of 1931 and 29.6 percent in the class of 1936. Alumni children needed a 60 average on entrance examinations, compared with a 70 average for other candidates. The new preference for alumni children helped roll back Jewish enrollment at Yale from 13.3 percent in the class of 1927 to 8.2 percent in the class of 1934. Similarly, at Harvard, Jewish enrollment declined from more than 20 percent to between 10 and 16 percent in the late 1920s and 1930s.

Policies favoring legacies soon sprang up nationwide at both private and public universities and have prevailed ever since, withstanding occasional challenges from reformers. In the mid-1960s, Yale admissions dean R. Inslee Clark slashed legacy preference and turned down the son of Yale's largest donor. But a counterattack by alumni, led by conservative columnist William F. Buckley, forced Yale to backpedal by the early 1970s. "The only preference by inheritance which seems to deserve recognition is the Yale son," conceded Yale president Kingman Brewster.

Mindful of the Yale debacle, no other elite private university has sought since to roll back legacy preference. Yet the open door for alumni children has become harder to justify as elite universities lock out nearly everyone else. Harvard, America's oldest university, admitted 63 percent of its applicants in 1952. Half a century later, it admitted just 11 percent of applicants overall—but 40 percent of legacy candidates.

A 1990 review of Harvard admissions by the federal Office for Civil Rights, examining why Harvard was more likely to accept white students than Asian Americans with similar academic records, found that legacy status frequently determined an applicant's fate. Among comments written by admissions staff reviewing applicant files were: "Dad's . . . connections signify lineage of more than usual weight." Plus: "Two legacy legs to stand on." "Without lineage, there would be little case. With it, we will keep looking." "Not a great profile, but just strong enough numbers and grades to get the tip from lineage." Federal investigators concluded that preference for legacies, a "predominantly white" group, "can work to the advantage of an applicant by offsetting weaker credentials . . . There is also some evidence to suggest that certain alumni parents' status may be weighed more heavily than others."

UNLIKE THEIR blue-blooded counterparts at Harvard or Yale, most legacies at Notre Dame represent relatively new money. Their impoverished great-grandparents or grandparents emigrated to the United States in the last century and worked their way up, eventually saving enough to open shops or businesses and send a child to Notre Dame. Aided by legacy preference, the next generations then consolidate the family's prominence in business or the professions. A university-commissioned study of more than seven thousand alumni in 2004 found that slightly more than half had annual household incomes in excess of $100,000, including 18 percent above $200,000. Their most common work positions: manager, attorney, director, and vice president.

Legacies benefit from the Notre Dame name, which carries unmatched clout in the Catholic business community, particularly in the Midwest, and from one of the country's most active, tight-knit alumni networks. Of Notre Dame's 107,000 graduates, 70 percent belong to 214 Notre Dame clubs in the United States—plus 60 overseas. Clubs provide scholarships, religious services, and football "game watches," but their primary function is career advancement. They run panels on such topics as mentoring and sponsor golf outings to which legacies and other graduates bring clients and make contacts.

"If you come out here from Notre Dame and you don't have a job, somebody will find you a job," said James Ciapciak, an attorney and past president of the Notre Dame Club of Boston, after playing eighteen holes at a club-sponsored golf tournament. "If you've lost a job, we'll help you get back on your feet."

The Desmonds are a typical Notre Dame success story: Kevin's great-grandparents on his father's side were Italian immigrants. His paternal grandfather, Albert J. Desmond, founder of the funeral home business, didn't graduate from Notre Dame. But he was one of the "subway alums" devoted to Notre Dame, and his fondest hope was that his sons would study there. They fulfilled his dream, and now Kevin is carrying on the family tradition.

After Matthew Desmond, one of Kevin's older brothers and a 1991 alumnus, was hired as a trust manager at Fifth Third Bank, a midwestern bank, his supervisor told him that bank executives had been impressed by his Notre Dame degree. "I'm sure they were Catholic and grew up with a fondness for Notre Dame," Matthew said. "It did help open the door."

NOTRE DAME officials say that its abundance of alumni children is a product of self-selection—in other words, a large legacy applicant pool. Judging from the large membership in its alumni clubs, most Notre Dame graduates remember their college years fondly and pass on their affection for the university to their children by taking them to football games, class reunions, and other events. Imbued with the Fighting Irish mystique, some high-achieving alumni children do choose Notre Dame over the Ivy League. Of the legacies whom Notre Dame admits, 74 percent matriculate there, a substantially higher yield than the school's overall 57 percent rate. The higher alumni child yield probably reflects both the loyalty of excellent legacy applicants and the lack of other desirable options for some lesser lights.

Still, Notre Dame relaxes its standards for many legacies. The admission of Kevin Desmond over John Simmons is the rule rather than the exception. The university accepts half of its legacy applicants compared with one-fifth of applicants without any preferences. Although they are stronger academically than the minorities or athletes Notre Dame admits, legacy admits still average 80 points less on the SAT than students without preferences, most of whom are working-class and middle-class whites. At the same time, Notre Dame turns down 250 valedictorians a year, usually because their SAT scores, like John Simmons's, don't reach the elevated threshold for students without hooks. Daniel Saracino, assistant provost for admissions, told the *Chicago Tribune* in 2003 that half of the alumni children enrolled at Notre Dame would not have been admitted without special consideration.

Financially, legacy preference has paid off big-time for Notre Dame. In part because the Catholic school applies strict guidelines to corporate donors—for instance, it won't take money from manufacturers of contraceptives—it relies more than most universities on alumni giving. Their loyalty cemented by the admission of their children and grandchildren, grateful alumni have propelled Notre Dame's endowment from a modest $9 million in 1945 to $3.7 billion in 2005—the eighteenth largest endowment in the country, ahead of Ivy League schools Dartmouth and Brown, and biggest by far among Catholic colleges. Among major universities, Notre Dame consistently ranks in the top three in the proportion of alumni who donate. The theme of the university's 1994–2000 fund-raising campaign was "Generations"—a veiled reference to legacy preference. An astonishing 74 percent of alumni gave to that campaign, donating slightly more than half of the $1.06 billion it raised.

Notre Dame administrators defend legacy preference by pointing out that alumni donations underwrite financial aid for needy students and other worthy causes. They also cite a less tangible but real value to admitting students already familiar with the university's traditions, from lighting prayer candles at the Grotto to gyrating at Friday night pep rallies, and its distinctively old-fashioned rules: all dorms are same-sex, and people of the opposite gender may not stay overnight. Without so many legacies, they argue, the student body would chafe at such policies.

"I don't think anything but good comes out of giving alumni children a slight edge," said Saracino, a Notre Dame graduate whose three children attended the university.

A policy protecting the already advantaged does induce some moral qualms at Notre Dame, which prides itself on its social conscience. Saracino said 98 percent of alumni children at Notre Dame are white and that legacies from wealthy families with a record of substantial gifts to the university are given a particularly large edge. Even Notre Dame's head of fund-raising, Louis Nanni, expressed misgivings at the socioeconomic implications of favoring alumni children. "I would have a real problem" with legacy preference, said Nanni, who used to run a homeless center in South Bend, if the university were not also increasing minority enrollment.

Notre Dame's commitment to alumni children is also at odds with its academic aspirations. Widely considered one of the nation's top 25 universities, Notre Dame accepts only 29 percent of its applicants. As the university steadily increases standards for unconnected students, alumni children must improve as well. If they don't, either lagging legacies will drag down the university's overall stature or the university will have to admit fewer of them. Thomas Kane, a Notre Dame graduate and professor of public policy at the University of California at Los Angeles, said this is a huge issue for his alma mater. "It's hard to reconcile selectivity with alumni preference. Yet, if you don't recognize legacies, it's hard to sustain endowment. The alumni are a huge part of what they do. Given that, the trade-offs for Notre Dame have to be much more pressing—particularly given the rapid increase in selectivity over time."

Saracino said it was easy in the 1970s or 1980s to maintain legacy enrollment. But as Notre Dame has become more competitive, it's become harder to accommodate alumni. Every year, he said, "I deal with hundreds of alumni whose children have been denied. They run a gamut of emotions—hurt, angry, confused. If this is what the Notre Dame family means, what good is it?"

Such emotions ran high in the Desmond family when Notre Dame turned down Kevin's cousin Alison. Her father, Terry's younger brother John, is a 1967 alumnus and past president of the Notre Dame Club of Detroit. Although Alison Desmond was active in high school student government and captain of the swim team, John said, "even with legacy, her grades wouldn't get her in." Her rebuff, he added, "did diminish my affinity for Notre Dame a bit. Notre Dame lives by the creed of the Notre Dame family. They preach the family for their advantage—the loyalty of the alumni." John believes that "the legacy program should be expanded: the university should take care of its own first before it looks elsewhere for students."

In his autobiography, the late businessman and 1938 alumnus Edmond R. Haggar obliquely alluded to the conflict between academic goals and alumni interests. Haggar, a Notre Dame trustee and chairman of the university's fund-raising arm, was followed there by his son, nephew, and grandson, among other descendants. When he served on the university's Alumni Board, he recalled, "the raising of admission standards was discussed across the boardroom table time and again. . . . 'Let's be sure we don't get a bunch of eggheads who have no personality and can't get along with other people,' I told the board."

Like Haggar, vigilant alumni use their clout to maintain Notre Dame's legacy quotient. A slight decline in legacies from 23 percent of the freshman class in 2003 to 22 percent in 2004 triggered a "lot of concern" among alumni, says Mike Cottingham, class of '63. His father, also a graduate, helped raise money to build the Hesburgh Library on campus. "I know people who have given a lot to Notre Dame and their kids didn't get in."

One such complaint from an alumnus reached the university's Board of Fellows, a select group of trustees. In October 2004, Saracino received a late-night phone call asking him to appear the next day before the board and explain the slippage in legacies and in Catholics (from 84 percent to 82 percent of the student body). "I wore a nice dark funeral suit," said Saracino, who reassured the board that the year-to-year variations in alumni child enrollment were within the 21 to 24 percent range that Notre Dame had long maintained.

FOUNDED IN 1842, Notre Dame admitted every Catholic high school graduate who could afford tuition until the end of World War II. As it became selective after the war, it introduced legacy preference. Reverend Theodore Hesburgh, president from 1952 to 1987, says a policy evolved in the 1960s that alumni children should make up one-quarter of the student body. That target remains, although the proportion of legacies usually falls slightly short. In 1972, Notre Dame opened its doors to women, doubling the potential pool of legacy applicants and increasing pressure from alumni to maintain the numbers.

"We have always accepted a higher percentage of alumni children than most universities," Father Hesburgh said in an October 2004 interview in the university library that bears his name. "It's a family thing. They're at home an hour after they get here." He acknowledged that "it's going to be difficult to sustain" the 25 percent target as the university continues to raise standards, "but it's my judgment it's a core of our student body we have to pay special concern to."

That "special concern" starts with a college admissions video featured in the "Alumni" section of Notre Dame's website. On the DVD, Saracino explains that alumni children still have to meet stiff admission standards, and proffers advice on improving academic performance: turn off the TV, learn a second language, and the like. All legacy applicants receive a letter from Saracino informing them of the "special consideration" Notre Dame gives alumni children. "We hope that the daughters and sons of our graduates will constitute a quarter of the entering class," the letter reads. "To make our hope become a reality, we will admit the children of Notre Dame families at a rate significantly higher than the rate of admission for other applicants. In fact, we expect to admit at least half of the alumni children who apply." The letter continues with Saracino's pledge to review the applicant's admission folder personally, assuring "the most careful consideration our office can provide."

Once enrolled at Notre Dame, legacies are treated like everybody else—almost. Most housing assignments are random, but each dormitory rector does have discretion to choose a small number of residents. Alumni Hall, where Kevin Desmond lives, is a Gothic Revival–style dorm built in 1931, characterized by wide corridors and cramped double-occupancy rooms with transoms and bunk beds. Father George Rozum, the rector, said he gives priority to three groups: relatives of priests, sons of alumni who lived in the dorm, and siblings of current students there. (Kevin said he asked for Alumni Hall because a friend from home was living there, and his request was granted.)

Having received special treatment in admissions, legacies and their parents often expect the same favoritism when it comes to campus rules. In one instance, the late shopping mall magnate Edward DeBartolo, one of Notre Dame's richest alumni, sought to pressure Notre Dame to withdraw disciplinary sanctions against his son—and then retaliated financially when the university refused to bend.

After graduating from a parochial high school in Youngstown, Ohio, with what he described as "good but not great" grades, Edward "Eddie"

Debartolo Jr. enrolled in the early 1960s at Notre Dame, where his father was a trustee. Then he was caught driving onto the inner quadrangle of the campus—a grassy area closed to automobiles—and pilfering a book from the campus bookstore. The university president, Reverend Hesburgh, who had recently issued a directive warning of severe consequences for stealing, promptly expelled him for a semester. "As close as we were to Father Hesburgh, it was cut-and-dried," Eddie said. "Rules are rules. I was wrong." His father was so upset that he flew to campus the next morning and, according to two people familiar with the matter, threatened not to donate to Notre Dame unless Father Hesburgh relented. The president firmly replied that the university was not for sale, and Eddie spent a semester in exile at the University of Dayton. It was not until 1989, twenty-one years after Eddie's Notre Dame graduation and two years after Father Hesburgh retired, that the senior DeBartolo gave $33 million for a new performing arts center on campus. He died in 1994, a decade before the center opened in September 2004.

By then, Eddie had gained renown as owner of the San Francisco 49ers, five-time Super Bowl champions—and then lost the team to his sister after pleading guilty in 1998 to a felony charge of failing to notify authorities of an extortion scheme for a casino license in Louisiana. While none of his three daughters attended Notre Dame, Eddie says he remains devoted to his alma mater. Eddie, who was among the 2005 *Forbes* 400 with a fortune valued at $1.4 billion, attended the opening of the performing arts center and is negotiating a further family gift to Notre Dame. On a recent campus visit, he said, he bought Notre Dame garb for his one-year-old grandson at the university bookstore.

AT OTHER universities, fraternities, sororities, and social clubs such as Yale's Skull and Bones give membership preference to their own legacies, who by definition are alumni children. Notre Dame does not have a Greek system or exclusive clubs, but legacies there still gravitate to certain traditional rites.

Crisp and cloudless, October 9, 2004, was a perfect day for Notre

Dame football, and for the pregame gathering of the clans that have attended and supported the university for generations. John Desmond had not let disappointment over his daughter's rejection interfere with this cherished family ritual. At 7 a.m., he parked his brand-new silver Cadillac SRX in a choice, oak-shaded spot at the corner of the library lot nearest the football stadium, under the encouraging gaze of "Touchdown Jesus."

Until this season, the Desmond family had occupied even more desirable pregame real estate. For thirty years, ever since a close friend in the administration had granted them a pass, they had tailgated in Aero Field, just steps from the stadium. They had never missed a game. But this season, the construction on Aero Field of a science building—donated and built by another Desmond family friend and fellow alumnus—had exiled them to the library lot, where John worried that people would have trouble finding him. Thus the Caddy's rear tire anchored the pole of a blue-and-white flag emblazoned with an Old English *D*, a distinguishing landmark in what soon became a sea of green Notre Dame flags.

While steam from hundreds of grills wafted over the lot, John unfolded chairs and tables and laid out his family's feast: beer, soda, chicken, brownies, and chips and salsa piled high in a blue-and-gold football helmet. The strains of the "Notre Dame Victory March" blared through the Caddy's open front doors as dozens of relatives and friends, recognizing the flag, began showing up.

John's brother Greg, a Chicago real estate salesman and 1990 alumnus, commuted to the game from a cottage he bought on a nearby lake "so I could be only half an hour from this parking space." He was accompanied by his longtime partner, also a Notre Dame graduate. "I didn't marry a girl from Notre Dame," Greg said. "That's as close as I'll get."

Wearing jeans, sandals, and a green "We Are ND" T-shirt, Kevin Desmond joined the group. Slim and brown-haired, with an engaging smile, he said he hadn't slept much since the pep rally the night before. Alumni Hall was a "host dorm" at the rally, and Kevin was among its delegation that hooted and hollered every time a speaker mentioned the word *alumni,* which was often. Kevin introduced me to another Alumni Hall resident and third-generation legacy, Nick Cottingham—Mike's son. Nick, who went to high school in Wyoming, scored 1350 on his SATs. One of his high school friends, who was not a legacy, was "a little upset" about being rejected by Notre Dame while Nick got in, until Nick told him about the university's commitment to alumni children. "I definitely think he understood it," Nick said. "Legacy is great. Legacies grow up with a sense of tradition."

Nick said his older brother, who graduated in 2004, "got me into Alumni." Now, he and Kevin were planning to room together next year as sophomores. Legacies often become friends, he said, because they have "a little more in common."

As Notre Dame dynasties go, the Abowds reign supreme. The late Richard George Abowd Jr., a 1949 Notre Dame graduate and Ford Motor Company engineer who died in 1998, sired a dozen children. All twelve were admitted to Notre Dame, ten enrolled, and nine graduated, setting a one-generation record; there was an Abowd in the Notre Dame student body every year from 1969 to 1990—not counting other family branches stemming from Richard's brother and brother-in-law, both Notre Dame alumni as well. But now, as the next generation of Abowds begins to apply to college, legacy preference is dividing the family into haves and have-nots.

On the same October day that the Desmond family tailgated before the Notre Dame football game, the Abowds held a family reunion after it. It was attended by Richard's widow, Sara, five of their nine children with Notre Dame degrees, and numerous grandchildren. The reunion, in a hotel several miles from campus, was catered by Chili's, but Sara insisted on bringing her specialties—delectable Lebanese meat and spinach pies. She and her husband, both from Lebanese immigrant families, were not wealthy; they scrimped to send their children to Notre Dame with the help of scholarships. When their last child, Paula, graduated from Notre Dame in 1990, the university honored them at commencement. Asked what made her proudest, Sara wiped away a tear and said, "They all kept their faith."

Most of the twelve Abowd children had outstanding high school records. Eight were valedictorians. The eldest, John, was a National Merit Scholar; he edited the student newspaper at Notre Dame and is an economics professor at Cornell. John, whose wife and brother-in-law also graduated from Notre Dame, maintained that the university's abundance of alumni children "has nothing to do with scores. It's all about social networks, people self-selecting to go to a place where they feel comfortable. They could have gone to lots of places." Another brother, Gregory, was a Rhodes scholar and became a professor of computer science at Georgia Tech.

Still, two of their siblings at the reunion, Steven and Peter, said they likely needed the legacy boost. "I think legacy worked for me," said Peter, an engineer developing software for car radios. "I wasn't a valedictorian. I was a decent student." One of his accomplishments at Notre Dame, Peter recalled, was producing a blue-and-gold 45-rpm record, "100 Years," in 1987 commemorating a century of Notre Dame football. Peter composed and performed the song, which sold three hundred copies on campus and played for years on the jukebox in the Huddle, a student hangout.

Steven, the sixth to graduate from Notre Dame, confided that he was admitted off the waiting list. "I was lucky to get in, and I appreciate it," said Steven, a business analyst. He added that he had a B or B-minus average at Notre Dame. "They knew what they were doing when they put me on the wait list."

All twelve children likely would have enrolled at Notre Dame if not for their father's old-fashioned attitudes. Believing girls did not belong there, Richard refused to send his first two daughters, Elizabeth and Marypat, to Notre Dame, which had only recently become coeducational. They enrolled instead at Marygrove, a Catholic women's college in Michigan. Sara recalled that she wanted them to go to Notre Dame—and even sent in Elizabeth's deposit on her housing and obtained a room number for her— but Richard would not yield. He later relented, and their three younger sisters did graduate from Notre Dame.

Now, as Richard and Sara's thirty-four grandchildren start applying to college, his long-ago reservations about coeducation are coming back to haunt them, underscoring the capricious nature of legacy preference.

Notre Dame accepted John's daughter, Katherine, whose parents are both alumni. Katherine scored 1400 on the SAT—slightly above Notre Dame's overall average for admitted students but about 65 points below the average for unconnected students. "Perhaps what got me to stand out was the fact I was a legacy," said Katherine, a management information systems major. "I don't think that's necessarily bad. . . . Most legacies wonder why they got in. If I do poorly on a test, I think, 'I only got in because my parents went here.'"

Yet Notre Dame turned away two of Sara's other grandchildren, Katherine's cousins Sara and Mark Rockwell. Both Sara and Mark were strong enough academically to be admitted to Carnegie Mellon University in Pittsburgh, a top engineering school where both are undergraduates. Mark, in particular, had better credentials than many a legacy in the Notre Dame student body—including a 31 ACT score and 1360 SAT score—and badly wanted to go there, having attended his first Fighting Irish football game at the age of two. He applied to Notre Dame early, was deferred to the regular admissions process, and then put on the waiting list, where he languished for weeks before being told there was no slot for him. His grandmother, Sara, said she's "brokenhearted" at the rebuff. Added Steven: "We were all shocked when Sara and Mark didn't get in. I thought both were overqualified to be here."

In all likelihood, Mark was turned down because he didn't qualify as a legacy. When his grandfather steered his mother, Elizabeth, away from Notre Dame, he also deprived her children of admissions preference there. Notre Dame gives a break only to alumni children—not grandchildren, nieces, or nephews. Otherwise, more than 60 percent of the student body would be composed of alumni relatives, which "would not be healthy," Saracino said. "It would make Notre Dame an exclusive club."

The Rockwell family didn't attend the reunion. Elizabeth Abowd-Rockwell said in a phone interview that after Mark was deferred, she called admissions counselors to explain that he was descended from Notre Dame's most prolific paterfamilias. "It didn't matter to them," she said. "Legacy stops at the parents, it doesn't go beyond that." She said she had a "hard time with it" when Sara and Mark were rejected. "It did hurt when they didn't get in. I knew their cousin [Katherine] got in. In comparing her and Mark, they were similar." The experience has soured her on legacy preference: "I think I would eliminate legacy preference and go with each individual applicant and look at the person as much as possible."

Mark is majoring in mechanical engineering at Carnegie Mellon and is building a solar-powered boat. He has an A-minus average and wants to design roller coasters as a career. He and Sara bought Carnegie Mellon clothing for their uncle, Peter, who has a Carnegie Mellon graduate degree but more often wears Notre Dame garb.

Mark said he's enjoying Carnegie Mellon and likes Pittsburgh better than South Bend. "Even if I had gotten into Notre Dame, Carnegie Mellon would have been the better choice," he said. But the sting lingers. He and Katherine "were the same caliber student academically," he said. "We lined up everywhere. She's a business major, not as mathy as I was. She made up in social sciences and humanities what I have in math. She scored higher on the SAT, but overall we're about the same.

"I realized legacy was a problem when my sister didn't get in. They didn't consider me a legacy because my mother and father didn't go there. Still, if they're looking for genetics, the genes are obviously there.

"I was really bummed. Everyone's gone there. But I didn't want to get in because all these alumni were my uncles. Someone should get in for who they are, not who their parents are."

ON EITHER SIDE of the entryway to the Hessert Laboratory for Aerospace Research, a plaque and a framed poster pay homage to donor Thomas Hessert, a 1948 Notre Dame alumnus, former recipient of the university's Man of the Year Award, founder of a New Jersey construction firm, and "lifelong aeronautics enthusiast." But the university's biggest tribute to Hessert can be reckoned in a bit of folk wisdom that makes the rounds of Haddonfield, New Jersey, Memorial High School at college application time: if a Hessert is your classmate, don't expect to get into Notre Dame.

This local lore is rooted in bitter experience. For two straight years, Notre Dame spurned a high-ranking Haddonfield applicant and admitted one of Thomas Hessert's grandsons with lower grades but greater pull. The Hesserts' admissions success suggests that, to paraphrase George Orwell's dictum in *Animal Farm,* all legacies are equal, but some are more equal than others; those from wealthy families with a history of philanthropy to the university get a bigger admissions break.

At Notre Dame, assistant provost Saracino said, there's a strong "overlap" between legacies and development cases. Of the 5 percent of Notre Dame students given extra consideration for fund-raising reasons, three in five are alumni children.

Like the Hesserts, Michelle Lombardi appears to be an example of this double boost. Her father, Patrick J. Lombardi, a Notre Dame graduate and telecommunications executive, and his brother Paul endowed a scholarship at Notre Dame. In the fall of 2001, during Michelle's senior year in high school, her father arranged for her to meet William Sexton, then the university's head of fund-raising. Despite an ACT score of 28 out of 36—equivalent to an SAT score between 1240 and 1270, well below the Notre Dame average—she was admitted. Michelle said she often wonders whether her legacy status and the session with Sexton facilitated her acceptance. "That's always a question in the back of my head," she said. "If my dad hadn't gone here, would I have gotten in? I guess I'll never know."

Thomas Hessert's son William, also a Notre Dame graduate, has six sons of his own. The first four—William, Walter, Thomas, and Patrick—have all enrolled at Notre Dame. In 2002, Notre Dame chose Walter Hessert over Haddonfield salutatorian Kathleen D'Agati. Besides ranking second in the class with a grade point average of 98.96 out of 100, Kathleen was president of the student council, captain of the track team, and a member of the homecoming court; her community service included traveling to Mexico to build a public school kitchen and install water fountains in a park. The daughter of a mechanical engineer and a preschool teacher, she also found time to give her friend Walter Hessert a hand with his homework.

"Basically, I helped him get through school," she said. "He's so smart, but he's not the hardest worker. It was always like, 'Kathleen, did you do the questions?'"

They had something else in common—their college of choice. Walter wanted to go to Notre Dame because his older brother was there, Kathleen because of its academic prestige and school spirit, and both applied early. Since 83 percent of Notre Dame freshmen rank in the top tenth of their high school class, Kathleen's better grades seemed to give her the edge. She first sensed what she was up against at a briefing given at the high school for prospective students by a Notre Dame admissions representative, who turned out to be a friend of Walter's brother.

"It was definitely an element of the good old boys," Kathleen said. "Walter was like, 'Do you know so-and-so?' They really bonded."

Kathleen was deferred to the regular pool and then turned down, which she felt as such a devastating blow that she mentioned it in her baccalaureate address at Haddonfield's graduation ceremonies. "A few months ago, I was rejected from the college that I really wanted to go to," she told the assembled throng. "It was difficult for me because I had worked so hard to get in and they essentially told me I wasn't 'good enough.' I was upset, but I knew in my heart that I was 'good enough.' "

Kathleen settled instead for Clemson University, where as of March 2006 she was a senior with a 3.85 grade point average, expecting to graduate with honors in May. Walter, who was placed on the waiting list by less selective Fairfield and Bucknell universities, majored in political science and Spanish at Notre Dame. He also became friendly with top administrators and trustees, who succumbed to his gregarious charm—and, perhaps, his surname. As we lunched together at the Morris Inn on campus in the fall of 2004, a waitress interrupted us to say that two diners at a nearby table wanted to buy us dessert: former university executive vice president Timothy Scully and former Coca-Cola Corp. chief operating officer Donald Keough, an ex-chairman of Notre Dame's board of trustees. Walter waved to them and called to Father Scully, "Thanks, padre."

Over lunch Walter defended his Notre Dame credentials. Despite his B average in high school, he said, he had a much better SAT score (1470, including an 800 in math) than Kathleen D'Agati (1290). He was also an accomplished wrestler, recruited by Duke University and Davidson College. Notre Dame does not have a wrestling team. "Kathleen certainly was a very good student," he said. "As a friend, I felt awful she didn't get in. We were different types of applicants. Do I know if I would have gotten in if there was no legacy? I truly don't know. I was a strong applicant too."

The year after Walter graduated from Haddonfield High, Notre Dame's recruiter there again recognized one name among the prospective applicants. "You're a Hessert," he exclaimed to Walter's younger brother Thomas. Whereupon another hopeful, worried that the fix was in, asked if Notre Dame would only take one Haddonfield student a year. The representative denied it, but that's how it played out, much to Claire Campbell's dismay. She ranked third in her Haddonfield class, scored 1340 on her SATs, and played two sports. She applied to nine colleges, including Cornell in the Ivy League. All admitted her—except Notre Dame, which opted for Walter's younger brother Thomas.

Neither Thomas's grades nor his SAT score (1280) matched Claire's. "I'm sure legacy played a role," said Thomas, who made the dean's list at Notre Dame and became president of the student entrepreneur club. "I could have done worse than I did and still got in."

"If there's a building on campus that has your name on it, that's a good sign," said Jeffrey Holman, a Haddonfield High guidance counselor.

Thomas and Walter's father, William Hessert, who owns his own construction company, defended legacy preference on the grounds that it fosters "social cohesion," binding together children with long family histories of attending Notre Dame. He added: "I have no question that each one of my sons can match themselves at least equally with any member of the university. If being a legacy makes Notre Dame look at the application twice instead of once, I think it's a justifiable advantage."

Claire Campbell enrolled at Rice University in Houston. In March 2006, she was a junior majoring in biochemistry with a 3.68 grade point average and regularly spending time with an intellectually disabled woman through a university-sponsored buddy program. "Rice is definitely a better fit," she said. "Notre Dame is missing out on a lot of good students. If they're not accepting the better people, the whole school in general will be affected by that."

5

TITLE IX AND THE RISE

OF THE UPPER-CLASS

ATHLETE

Fencing, Crew, and Polo
Scholarships

Americans who watch college football and basketball on television see a lot of black faces and assume that most recruited athletes benefiting from lower admissions standards are minorities. That's a big misconception. Top universities also sponsor teams and give preference to athletes in a wide variety of patrician sports rarely played by minorities or low-income whites: squash, sailing, skiing, crew, water polo, fencing, equestrian events, and the like. Since few inner-city or rural public schools can afford the facilities, equipment, travel, and coaches' salaries, and few low-income parents are familiar with the fine points of these pastimes, only children from wealthy homes or attending suburban and private high schools are exposed to them. If these students show promise, their parents—fully aware of the potential return in college admissions—underwrite private lessons, club memberships, boats, horses, ergometers (machines that simulate rowing), or other expenses. This advantage for the rich raises the question of whether proficiency in squash or sailing or horseback riding should be considered a credential for a college education or just a token of social status.

Despite coming from prosperous families and solid high schools, Catelyn Coyle and Andria Haneman each scored well below the University of Virginia's 1370 average on the SATs for out-of-state students. But

Kevin Sauer was impressed by their results on a different test—the ERGs. Sauer, who coaches women's crew at Virginia, seeks prospects who can row 2,000 meters on the ergometer in seven and a half minutes or less. Because Catelyn and Andria met that standard, he offered them admissions slots set aside by the university for his recruits, and athletic scholarships to offset part of Virginia's $28,850-a-year out-of-state tuition, fees, and room and board.

Now, on the brisk Saturday morning of April 16, 2005, Catelyn and Andria faced another test. Virginia is usually one of the nation's best crew teams, but its top varsity boat had been performing below expectations. Tinkering with the lineup after a disappointing loss a week earlier to the University of California, Coach Sauer had elevated Catelyn and Andria to the first varsity eight for a contest against Oregon State University. It was being held on the Rivanna Reservoir, five miles from the UVA campus in Charlottesville. From the dock below the boathouse, teammates serenaded Catelyn, Andria, and the rest of the varsity eight with the traditional "Wahoo Wa" cheer as they lifted the shell over their heads, laid it in the water, and headed to the starting line.

For Catelyn—who, seated in the vital position of stroke, or rower nearest the coxswain, would dictate the shell's pace—the promotion culminated a college career sidetracked by hip and back injuries that had forced her to sit out one year and be less than full strength in other seasons. Because of the time she'd missed, she was still eligible to row for UVA even though she had graduated the year before with a B average and was now studying for a master's degree in education.

Catelyn's parents were both on hand for the race. Her father, Gary, a renowned chef, has presided over the kitchen at New York City's Tavern on the Green and other well-known restaurants. Her mother, Rena, is a successful author of children's cookbooks. Catelyn learned to row as a freshman at the Baldwin School, a girls' prep school in Bryn Mawr, Pennsylvania. "Basically, I wasn't really concerned with college for a long time in high school," Catelyn told me. "If I tried and when I tried, I was a good student. But my attitude was, 'I don't care, I can float along with trying a minuscule amount.' I didn't try that hard on my SATs either. I'm definitely more capable than my high school grades and board scores showed."

Nevertheless, top universities including Yale, Notre Dame, and the University of Michigan pursued Catelyn for her rowing prowess. "I went and looked at all the colleges the summer before my senior year," she said. "Virginia was the last school I went to. My year, Kevin would look at you if your ERG score was 7:30 and under. He puts a lot of faith in those scores. I was at 7:27 when I committed to UVA. And he looks at your height. I'm five-eleven. Being tall helps you with leverage in the boat, and in the length of your stroke.

"My college counselor at Baldwin said to me, 'Why don't you apply somewhere you could get into without a sport?' I said, 'I'm already slotted to UVA.' In-state, I would have been fine to get into UVA" on academic credentials alone. "Out of state, I would have been screwed."

Andria Haneman, sitting directly behind Catelyn, was the only freshman in the top varsity boat. Andria, whose father owns a waste removal company, had planned to focus on basketball at Holy Spirit High School in Absecon, New Jersey. But coaches there noticed her height (she's also five foot eleven) and steered her to rowing, which she grew to love. "They told me, 'It's hard to get into college for basketball. Try rowing, it's a growing sport,'" she said.

Andria said that one of her closest friends in high school, who had a similar academic record to hers but was not a recruited athlete, had been wait-listed by Virginia. Her friend wasn't resentful, she said, because he knew how much time and energy she had put into rowing. "You have to be intelligent to balance athletics and academics," she said. "It's a different kind of intelligence—time management."

Besides UVA, Duke and Syracuse recruited Andria. She could have rowed for an Ivy League school, she told me, "but I didn't want to take the SATs again. The Ivies wanted something closer to the 1300s. I could go to Virginia anyway, and it's the number one public university."

UNLIKE LEGACY and development preferences, athletic preference rewards applicants for their own accomplishments rather than their parents'. Still, it's debatable whether, and how much, colleges should value athletic prowess—particularly when opportunities to excel in sports are unevenly distributed in our society. Because fund-raising considerations influence colleges' choice of the sports they sponsor and the athletes they recruit, athletic preference, like legacy and development, favors the wealthy, the white, and the well-connected.

Currying favor with alumni and donors, elite colleges that profess to aspire to racial and socioeconomic diversity lower the bar for athletes in sports that are segregated by both race (white) and class (upper). The introduction of women's teams in country club sports under the gender-equity law Title IX has exacerbated this tendency. Coaches in all sports, meanwhile, have been known to reserve roster spots for borderline athletes whose parents have the capacity to endow a stadium or scholarship.

"Athletics is a major area where the playing field is tilting as we speak," said Harvard admissions dean William Fitzsimmons. "It's not just the sports you think of as upper-class sports. Even in my old sport, ice hockey, it would probably cost $2,000 to $3,000 to outfit a goaltender with all the latest high-tech stuff." Because of limited budgets, he added, urban public schools are eliminating varsity sports or charging participation fees. "That works against kids from the bottom half and bottom quarter of the income range. It's also true for music and dance. People who are middle-class and above now have a much bigger edge when it comes not just to academic opportunity but athletic and extracurricular opportunities."

No wonder that, contrary to the stereotype, varsity athletes at elite colleges are more homogenous, both racially and socioeconomically, than the student bodies as a whole. Counterbalancing the diversity of football and basketball teams is an array of segregated sports: men's golf (87.6 percent white, 2.0 percent black, 1.4 percent Hispanic, 5.2 percent international students), men's lacrosse (90.9 percent white, 1.8 percent black, 1 percent Hispanic), women's lacrosse (91.0 percent white, 2.2 percent black, 0.9 percent Hispanic), women's horseback riding (92.8 percent white, 0.9 percent

Hispanic, 0.2 percent black, 0.8 percent Asian American), and women's crew (84.1 percent white, 3.2 percent Asian American, 2.3 percent Hispanic, 1.8 percent international, and 1.7 percent black). Other overwhelmingly white sports: men's skiing (90.4 percent white, 6.1 percent international, 0.8 percent Asian American, 0.2 percent Hispanic, 0.2 percent black), women's skiing (89.2 percent white, 5.1 percent international, 0.8 percent Asian, 0.2 percent Hispanic, 0.0 percent black), and women's water polo (78.8 percent white, 5.4 percent Hispanic, 3.8 percent Asian American, 2.9 percent international, 0.8 percent black).

At Middlebury College in Vermont, a faculty committee found in 2002 that 26 percent of athletes had family incomes over $200,000—compared with 21 percent of nonathletes. Similarly, a recent study of nineteen Ivy League universities and liberal arts colleges found that only 6 percent of recruited athletes came from the poorest one-fourth of American families, versus 12 percent of nonathletes. "Recruited athletes as a group do not contribute to racial or socioeconomic diversity," the study concluded.

As a taxpayer-supported state institution, the University of Virginia's primary mission is to provide a high-quality, affordable education to bright young Virginians—and, by so doing, to give a leg up to promising low-income graduates of public elementary and secondary schools. Yet the women's crew team at the university illustrates how athletic preference helps the already advantaged. Like college squads in many sports that are rarely seen on television or covered by the national media, the women's rowing team (Virginia has no men's varsity rowing team) is virtually all white and predominantly affluent.

Although 68 percent of the student body as a whole comes from Virginia, the women's crew team is mainly composed of out-of-state private school graduates (from such upper-class bastions as Noble and Greenough in Massachusetts, Exeter in New Hampshire, Lawrenceville in New Jersey, and Sidwell Friends in Washington, D.C.) and international students. Few of its sixty athletes would have made the grade at the elite university on academics alone. Yet they are not only admitted but also encouraged to enroll with athletic grants-in-aid—usually called "scholarships," a misnomer because scholarly attainment is irrelevant to the awards—on the basis of skill in a sport that's inaccessible to or prohibitively expensive for most Americans.

The Virginia women's crew team is given twelve admissions slots each year, more than any other sport except football. To fill those slots, Coach Sauer submits transcripts and test scores of fifty recruits to the admissions office for preapproval, prioritizing them in three categories: worthy of a full athletic scholarship, partial scholarship, or none. The office approves about forty, whom he may then offer a slot and scholarship; their actual applications for admission, submitted later, are a formality. If the office has denied a top rower, he may prod her to retake the SATs or boost her grades so he can resend her name to the admissions office. Since other universities pursue the same rowers, most enroll elsewhere, but he lands his dozen.

"Most of the kids we recruit need help to get in," Coach Sauer said.

FOR MOST high school athletes, participation in sports is at best a marginal boost to their college admission chances. But for those skilled enough to make the list of recruits that each college coach sends to the admissions office, athletic preference is becoming a bigger factor than ever in getting into elite colleges.

The number of student athletes at a typical college increased from 332 in 1992–93 to 366 a decade later, reflecting a rise in female athletes prompted by Title IX. Moreover, a higher proportion of varsity athletes enter elite colleges through the sports door than they used to. In the old days, walk-ons—well-rounded undergraduates who tried out for a team because they enjoyed competitive sports—made up the lion's share of college squads. As a professional, win-at-all-costs mentality has pervaded college sports, walk-ons have largely been supplanted by more proficient recruits receiving admissions priority.

Although big state universities dominate high-profile sports such as football and basketball, recruited athletes make up a higher proportion of students at elite private institutions. That's because the typical Ivy League school fields teams in at least thirty sports—double the collegiate average. Also, because they don't offer athletic scholarships, Ivy League schools often recruit more players than they need to fill rosters, anticipating that, without a financial incentive to play, some will quit their sport.

Private high schools that traditionally send their graduates to the Ivy League profit from the admissions power of aristocratic sports. Consider, for example, the contrast in varsity sports sponsored by two Massachusetts high schools twenty-five miles apart: East Boston High and Phillips Academy at Andover. East Boston High, with an enrollment of 1,435, is a typical urban public school: nearly three-quarters of the students are minorities, 68.4 percent are low-income, and graduates rarely go to four-year colleges. Eastie offers football, basketball, baseball, softball, hockey (a boys' team shared with four other high schools), swimming, track, volleyball, and soccer; students may also join a citywide cross-country team.

Andover, enrollment 1,087, is a premier private school that charges $31,160 tuition to boarding students. It has teams in all the sports that East Boston does, plus tennis, field hockey, golf, lacrosse, crew, squash, diving, water polo, girls' hockey, wrestling, cycling, and skiing. Eighty of its 2004 graduates matriculated at Ivy League universities that (like other top colleges) give an admissions edge to athletes in such sports. Thus Andover students can get into college as recruits in a dozen sports that Eastie students never have a chance to play in high school.

"If you ever looked at all the sports at Harvard, we don't have a clue about most of those sports," said Kenneth Still, senior program director for athletics in the Boston public schools. "It reflects what moneys are put into the athletic program here as opposed to private schools. If you're going to Andover or Exeter, one thing they have on their ticket to college admissions is that you have to play sports. They put sports on the same level as they put academics."

IN 2002–2003, a Notre Dame coach recruited high school standout Patrick Ghattas, hoping he would help the university win another national championship in a sport it had dominated for decades. There was one stumbling block: his SATs. Although he comes from a well-off family (he described his Lebanese immigrant father as a "savvy investor") and maintained a B average at prestigious Oregon Episcopal School in Portland, Oregon, Patrick scored only 970 out of 1600—400 points below the university average. While they wanted to accommodate the coach, Notre Dame admissions officials told Patrick they couldn't take him unless he raised his score. On his second try, Patrick nudged his score above 1000. Although it was still more than 300 points under Notre Dame's average, he was admitted and awarded a full athletic scholarship. "That's as low as we'd go" on the SATs, said Daniel Saracino, Notre Dame assistant provost for admissions.

One might expect Notre Dame, with its glorious football tradition, to dip that far for a quarterback or a linebacker. But Patrick Ghattas is a fencer. He makes passes not with a football but a saber.

"I always wasn't too good at standardized tests," he told me in the spring of 2005, when he was a Notre Dame sophomore majoring in political science with a 2.4 grade point average—between a B and a C. "Fencing definitely helped a lot." Patrick said his high school academic record would have been more impressive if he hadn't missed so many classes to travel to fencing tournaments.

Patrick's SATs "were much higher than the average athlete in many universities," said Notre Dame fencing coach Janusz Bednarski. "Test results are not everything. I know who is a hard worker. I am always talking with the coaches. If his coach tells me he is a very serious, goal-oriented kid, I pass my opinion to admissions. We will help him too, with academic services."

Football, basketball, and ice hockey—major sports that generate revenue and television exposure—generally command the most deference from college admissions officers. But even in blue-blooded sports, many recruits benefit from significant admissions edges. *Reclaiming the Game,* a 2003 study of selective colleges by William G. Bowen and Sarah A. Levin, found SAT scores of recruited athletes lagging behind those of other students in such affluent sports as men's squash (a 67-point gap at Ivy League universities) and men's golf (66 points). "The more selective the school, the greater the admissions advantage enjoyed by its recruited athletes," they concluded. Premier recruits such as Patrick Ghattas enjoy a bigger advantage than borderline candidates.

Once in college, Bowen and Levin found, recruited athletes in golf, fencing, crew, squash, and other upper-class sports often sink to the bottom half of their classes academically and are less likely than classmates to earn honors or be elected to Phi Beta Kappa. "Troubling issues of academic performance are not limited to the high-profile sports," they found.

Why do these colleges compromise their admissions standards for athletes in marginal sports that don't enhance racial or economic diversity and rarely generate revenue or media buzz? The kindest explanation is that great universities pursue excellence in all their endeavors. In sports, excellence equals winning, winning demands talented athletes, and those athletes need admissions help. The desire to win in all sports great or small is reinforced by the coveted Sears Directors' Cup, given annually since 1994 to the university (usually Stanford) with the best record in athletics across the board, and by bureaucratic pressures to give all sports their due; both the athletic and admissions staffs would balk at denying coaches in minor sports their recruits while giving carte blanche to football. As coaches in any sport win consistently, they gain more credibility and clout with admissions.

"It's evident that football and basketball have lower standards, but the colleges' attitude is, 'We'll do something for all the other sports. If we're going to have those sports, let's give them the tools to be successful,' " said Virginia rowing coach Kevin Sauer. "Otherwise what's the point to having a team? If you're restricted to the overall academic criteria at your school, the schools that are easier to get into would have a huge advantage. If the tougher schools loosen their criteria a little bit, that levels the playing field."

The first-year grade point average for women rowers at the University of Virginia in the fall of 2003 (3.0) trailed the university median (3.18). Still, Sauer contended that athletes contribute intellectually. "It's not just about having the best and brightest students," he said. "You should have academic diversity as well. If you have kids who have to struggle, it brings a good mix. That kid may ask a more common-sense question."

Many of the minor sports are played in the Olympics, drawing media coverage (and patriotic fervor) once every four years. Notre Dame fencer Mariel Zagunis, for instance, cast glory on the university by winning a gold medal in women's saber in 2004. The daughter of an investment broker, Mariel grew up in Portland, Oregon, and attended a Catholic high school there. "You'd have to say, fencing is for the fairly well-off," she told me. "If you want to get serious, you have to have the money, you have to buy expensive equipment, you have to travel nationally and internationally and pay tournament fees and hotels."

Like Patrick Ghattas, Mariel trained at the Oregon Fencing Alliance club under the tutelage of Ed Korfanty, the U.S. national coach in women's saber, who has close ties to Notre Dame. A former Notre Dame assistant coach, Korfanty has been friends with Notre Dame coach Janusz Bednarski ever since they fenced against each other many years ago in Poland; later, Korfanty was a member of Poland's Olympic fencing team, which Bednarski coached.

Mariel, who received a full athletic scholarship, told me that Coach Korfanty steered her to Notre Dame along with three other fencers from his club, including Patrick. "I think my coach pulled some strings," she said. "He got us all into Notre Dame on a package deal. It was always a given I'd be going to Notre Dame and only Notre Dame." She acknowledged that academics were not her strong suit at Valley Catholic High in Portland. "I missed a lot of school during high school. That affected my overall grades. Honestly, based on my grades alone, I don't think I would have been what Notre Dame was looking for." Her SAT score, she added, was "not so good. I was practically out of town for every test date. I could only get into the very last test date. I never had time to take preparatory classes."

To prepare for the Olympics, Mariel delayed enrolling at Notre Dame until 2004. In the spring of her freshman year, she told me she was "doing okay" academically and liked her classes. Bednarski, the Notre Dame coach, told me Mariel is "close to the level of the best students" at the university.

Asked why Notre Dame bends standards for fencers, Saracino told me, "We give special consideration for maybe five, six, seven fencers every year. That's not a significant number." The assistant provost said that fencing builds geographic diversity by attracting international students and that Notre Dame has won more national championships in the sport than any other university.

"It's a tradition, much like football," Saracino said. "Does it get the same attention? No. What you find is, Olympic sports like fencing appeal to academically solid students who have a real talent they're bringing to the university. Even if we don't find thousands of individuals who go out and cheer them on as they're fencing, it still is a sport that does get some attention nationally and does draw to the university students who do really excel."

Still, there's another reason why elite universities go to such lengths for upper-class sports—money. While almost invisible to the nation at large, these sports are important to wealthy alumni and donors who played them in college or enjoy them as leisure activities. For instance, several major donors on Harvard's Committee on University Resources rowed for the school, including former Olympians Richard Cashin and Franklin Hobbs IV, and A. Clinton Allen III, the stroke on Harvard's undefeated 1966 team. The late COUR chairman Robert Stone captained Harvard's heavyweight crew in 1947 and endowed the men's heavyweight crew coach's position in 2001. Those four ex-rowers alone have had eight children enroll at Harvard—including Frances Cashin, R. Gregg Stone III, and Jennifer P. Stone, who followed their parents on Harvard crew. Fellow committee member Finn M. W. Caspersen, a big giver to Harvard Law School and Brown University, is a devotee of rowing and horseback riding and has supported both sports financially.

In 1995, former Williams College squash star Greg Zaff founded Squashbusters, a nonprofit program that teaches middle-school and high-school minority students from inner-city Boston to play squash, while also providing mentoring, academic enrichment, and college counseling.

"Make no mistake about it: squash is a meal ticket into these top schools if you're good enough at it and you've got some academic firepower," Zaff said. Asked why elite colleges care about squash success, he said, "The squash world is a moneyed world. The alumni have deep pockets. There's disproportionate power in the squash world, so it's good to have a great team. You attract the attention of powerful rich people, and the money of powerful rich people."

Perhaps no sport attracts powerful rich people as much as polo, a game in which mallet-wielding horseback riders wearing helmets, white pants, and boots try to whack a small ball into a goal. Known as the sport of kings, a favorite recreation of Prince Charles and other members of England's royal family, polo is played at only a handful of U.S. high schools and hasn't been an Olympic sport since 1936. Yet top prospects enjoy admissions preference from at least two elite colleges, Cornell and the University of Virginia, which annually duke it out for the national title.

Polo is a club sport at Virginia, which means that it is funded not by the university but by member dues of $500 a year and alumni gifts. Fortunately, Virginia polo players and alumni can well afford the expense. According to club coach Lou Lopez, alumni paid for the seventy-five-acre Virginia Polo Center, considered the best college polo facility in the United States, with irrigated outdoor fields, an indoor arena, and stabling and paddocks for ponies. Alumni also underwrote the purchase of seventy ponies for between $2,500 and $60,000 apiece. The club honors top recruits with the prestigious, privately funded Raymond Nicoll Polo Scholarship, named after a late Virginia polo player and endowed by his friends.

Coach Lopez said the polo club has enhanced the state university's geographic diversity by drawing players from Malaysia, Colombia, England, and Hawaii. "Some polo alumni have become major donors to Virginia," the coach added. "They not only have supported the polo program over the years, but they support the football and basketball teams."

Unlike varsity teams, the polo club isn't formally allotted slots in the freshman class. Coach Lopez was coy about his influence, saying, "We try to talk to admissions, as much as they'll listen. We're at their mercy." (He was also reticent about the Nicoll Scholarship; when I asked about it, he pleaded with me not to mention it in this book, without explaining why.) "I know Virginia has that ability on their side to get admissions help," said Cornell coach David Eldredge, who submits his own short list of preferred applicants to Cornell admissions.

Nina Marks, formerly the longtime college counselor at the National Cathedral School in Washington, D.C., said UVA admissions dean John Blackburn personally reads the applications of all polo recruits, because they and their families are regarded as potential donors. "He takes a strong interest in polo recruits," she said. "Good polo ponies" are expensive. "If you have a string of polo ponies, that makes colleges sit up and pay attention."

Carol Wood, a spokeswoman for the university, told me, "While Dean Blackburn's attention is brought to student applicants who play polo, he and his staff review them as they would any other application. . . . Their polo-playing ability is taken into consideration when their applications are reviewed, just as a student's ability to play for the University's marching band is taken into consideration. It would just be one of a long list of qualities and achievements that our admission office looks at when evaluating each applicant." She added that students who play polo "are not looked at as potential donors; they are looked at as high-achieving academic students who also bring an interesting athletic talent that adds to the diversity of the student body."

Molly Muedeking, club president and a top player, told me that Virginia admissions gives special consideration each year to two male and two female polo recruits, who also receive the Nicoll Scholarship. "It was obvious polo helped me get into school," said Molly, a lawyer's daughter and Nicoll Scholarship recipient. Molly described herself as a good student with SAT scores in the 1300s but said she didn't rank in the top tenth of her class at Garrison Forest School in Maryland.

Garrison Forest, one of only two girls' schools in the United States to offer the sport, regularly supplies polo players to Virginia. Its head polo coach, Lissa Green, also starred at Virginia and received the Nicoll Scholarship. "I used polo to help me get in," said Green, who graduated from a private high school in 1999 with SAT scores in the 1200s. "Getting into UVA out of state is very difficult. I had average grades and didn't participate in student government. Most of my extracurricular activities centered on riding. That little extra push really helped."

ALTHOUGH COLLEGES justify a wide variety of admissions preferences under the mantle of diversity, preferences advancing one sort of diversity frequently detract from another. In these conflicts, socioeconomic diversity generally takes a backseat. For instance, Notre Dame and Virginia officials defend the edge given to international fencers and polo players on the grounds of geographic diversity, but this influx of wealthy athletes also reinforces the upper-income tilt of their student bodies.

By the same token, Title IX, the federal law banning sex discrimination, has increased gender diversity in college sports while decreasing socioeconomic diversity on athletic teams and campuses as a whole. Although Title IX helped popularize racially integrated and economically diverse sports such as women's basketball in the 1970s, more recently colleges have responded to the law's pressure for equal athletic representation of the sexes by fielding women's teams with large rosters in racially segregated upper-crust sports such as crew and horseback riding. In effect, Title IX has evolved into an admissions giveaway to rich women.

Passed in 1972, Title IX acquired teeth in 1979, when the federal government adopted a controversial three-part test for college sports. To comply with Title IX, the relative proportions of men and women among varsity athletes must mirror the student body as a whole, the athletic program must fulfill the interests and abilities of female students, or the school must make progress toward equal athletic opportunities for women. In 1984, a Supreme Court decision exempted most college athletic programs from Title IX, but Congress broadened the law four years later, overruling the decision.

The key fight over Title IX's tripartite test began in 1992, when members of Brown University's women's gymnastics and volleyball teams—which had lost their funding the previous year during a budget crunch, along with two men's teams—sued the university. Brown, under president

Vartan Gregorian, argued that the proportionality test amounted to an unfair quota because women are less interested in athletics than men. In 1995, a federal district court found for the women athletes, and two years later the U.S. Supreme Court let the ruling stand. In 1998, Brown agreed to a compliance plan that included making women's water polo a varsity sport.

As the Brown case made its way through the courts, the NCAA in 1994 endorsed nine "emerging sports" for women that nervous colleges could sponsor to show progress under Title IX: crew, synchronized swimming, ice hockey, team handball, water polo, archery, badminton, squash, and bowling. (The NCAA added equestrian events to the list in 1998 and rugby in 2001.) Of these, crew was the quickest fix because of its roster size; each shell required eight (or sometimes four) women, and one team could float a lot of boats at various levels of competition, from novice to varsity. Also, there was an abundance of affluent ex-rowers to fund crew scholarships.

Dubbed "women's football" because it helped counterbalance the biggest men's sport, crew became such a widespread immunization against Title IX violations that the NCAA authorized a national championship in women's rowing in 1996 and made it a full-fledged sport a year later; even heartland schools such as the University of Kansas introduced the traditionally coastal sport. The NCAA also allowed colleges to provide a maximum of twenty full scholarships or the equivalent in women's crew, more than any sport except football. Because few high schools nationwide had girls' crew teams, colleges began awarding scholarships to tall, strong women without any rowing experience. From 1992–93 to 2002–3, the number of varsity women rowers in college more than quadrupled, from 1,555 to 6,690, the greatest percentage increase of any sport. Also reflecting the impact of Title IX, the typical women's crew team over the same span grew from 31 to 47 members, while the average men's squad fell from 39 to 30 participants. The University of Wisconsin women's crew team boasts as many as 150 rowers, including its lightweight squad. Unlike heavyweight crews, which are mostly recruits, lightweight teams often rely on walk-ons.

After the boathouses came the stables. Equestrian events, another upper-crust sport with an expandable roster, were soon second only to crew in Title IX–inspired popularity. From 1998–99 to 2002–3, the number of varsity riders nearly doubled from 633 to 1,175, and average squad size rose from fifteen to twenty-seven. Brown, the University of Georgia, and Texas A&M University are among schools that galloped into the equestrian arena and began giving admissions preference—and in some cases scholarships—to horseback riders. Many of the riders come from the suburban or rural gentry and bring their own horses to college.

"The reason we exist is to balance out the football team," Collins Daye, assistant coach on the Georgia equestrian team, told me. The team was given varsity status in 2002 and now has sixty-five members, who divvy up the fifteen full scholarships allowed by the NCAA. Ms. Daye said that Georgia has admitted riders with a 1050 SAT score, 150 points below its average. "Like anybody that functions within athletics, we can generally pull in students that are lower than the school standards," she said. "They aren't dumb kids, they still have a 3.5 GPA."

Texas A&M, another selective public university, has seventy women on its equestrian team, which started in 1999. In addition to facilitating admission of her top recruits, Coach Tana Rawson told me, she also has the power to reverse rejections of less sought-after applicants who might fit into her team. "There's a handful of girls we talk to every year, they don't get into A&M," she said. "Then we'll either go watch them ride, or get some more videos and assess their riding ability as best we can and decide, 'Are they right for our program?' " If they are, she continued, "we can write a letter to admissions and just state that they will be on the equestrian team and ask that they can be reconsidered to be admitted again. That's not a problem. The admissions office will bend a fair bit if they will be valuable on an athletic team or if we decide to give them a scholarship."

Title IX has fostered yet another high-toned sport—women's squash. To "advance its commitment to gender equity" and improve "financial aid opportunities for women," Stanford University announced in 2005 that it would field the first varsity women's squash team on the West Coast.

As colleges added genteel women's sports, they also grappled with Title IX's proportionality test by discontinuing working-class men's sports that lacked wealthy patrons. For instance, Southern Methodist University in Texas started a women's crew team in 1999 and an equestrian team in 2003. The following year, it eliminated a racially and economically integrated men's track and field program that consistently ranked in the top ten nationwide and had produced forty-seven individual national champions. The men's golf team at SMU was left unscathed.

The most frequent target of cutbacks was wrestling. Although public high schools nationwide compete in wrestling, a sport with a long tradition and small cost, colleges pinned it to the mat. According to NCAA statistics, 130 colleges dropped men's wrestling teams between 1988–89 and 2002–3 while only 23 added them, by far the biggest net loss of any sport. The National Wrestling Coaches Association sued the U.S. Department of Education, seeking to void the proportionality standard, but the case was dismissed in 2003. Nor did the NCAA identify women's wrestling as an "emerging sport," even though it was a plausible candidate.

"Title IX has reduced socioeconomic diversity," said Lloyd Peterson, a former admissions officer at Yale, which eliminated varsity wrestling. "At the end of the day, you start whacking off some of the blue-collar sports. Most of the country club sports have small numbers. All Yale needed was two fencers to win a national championship. You hang on to those sports, the NCAA is happy, the alumni are happy. The alumni's kids all play squash. So we gave up wrestling. Who's upset about that? Kids from Pittsburgh. They're not going to make any noise."

At one private university, an affluent ex-wrestler did save his sport— but the price wasn't cheap. Bucknell University in Lewisburg, Pennsylvania, cut its fifty-seven-year-old varsity wrestling program in 2001–2 even though a former wrestling team captain, insurance broker William Graham, offered $500,000 to promote gender equity. The university rejected his gift, saying it wasn't enough to underwrite two women's sports needed to offset wrestling under Title IX. Three years later, Bucknell restored wrestling after Graham raised his donation to $5.6 million, enough to expand the women's crew team and support other women's sports.

The University of Virginia did not discard any men's sports. Instead, to comply with Title IX, it added women's crew in 1995 and women's golf in 2003, reinforcing the largely white profile of its female athletes. University data show that two women's teams, basketball and track, have substantial minority representation. In 1998–99, 9 of 23 track athletes and 7 of 14 basketball players were African American. But of 142 varsity athletes in other women's sports that year, 134 (94 percent) were white; the other 8 consisted of 2 each of blacks, Hispanics, Asian Americans, and international students. All 9 members of the women's golf team in 2004–5 were white.

Although Title IX is intended to ensure gender equity, the elevation of women's crew to a varsity sport also led to what some male rowers considered reverse sexual discrimination. Since both men's and women's crew had previously been on equal footing as club sports, the change subordinated the men's club to second-class status, without official admissions slots, athletic scholarships, or university support. The Virginia men's rowing club rents the boathouse, which it owns, to the women's team; it also raises money through donations, raffles, and rowers doing yard work and other manual labor for Charlottesville residents.

"The fact that we can't recruit and have to raise all that money puts us at a disadvantage," said Chad Richard Ellis, cocaptain of the rowing club. "I really don't think it's fair to us that we have to go out and compete against varsity crews." While the UVA women's crew competes in California regattas, he said, the men's club only goes as far west as Ohio. "Our accommodations are quite different" on the road, he continued. "We're pretty big guys, and we end up having four guys to a room. That means two guys, each six-four and two hundred pounds, sleeping in a double bed. I'm sure the women at most have three to a room."

The university introduced women's golf after receiving $1.4 million for golf scholarships from a private donor. In light of the gift, adding women's golf "makes financial sense in UVA's continuing effort to comply with Title IX," a university report concluded. UVA hasn't been shy about exploiting the affinity of the rich for golf. At a 2004 fund-raiser sponsored by the Virginia Athletics Foundation to benefit the golf programs, alumni paid $250 apiece to play a round with the men's and women's golf teams.

Team parents have also contributed to a planned facility for putting and chipping practice.

As a top recruit on the inaugural women's golf team, also sought after by Notre Dame, Wake Forest, and other schools, Leah Wigger received a full athletic scholarship to UVA. A dentist's daughter who learned the game at Audubon Country Club in Louisville, Kentucky—"My parents are fortunate enough to belong; I was able to go out there anytime I wanted"—Leah hopes to play on the professional tour. As a freshman and sophomore, she was UVA's top female golfer and was named to the all-conference team. Leah, who attended a Catholic high school, told me she had strong grades but a disappointing SAT score, which she declined to disclose. "I would say I'm not a very good standardized-test taker. My academic talent is a little better than what the test shows. I do feel I wouldn't have got into UVA without golf."

AFTER MORE than thirty college coaches tried to recruit Ty Grisham, he accepted a baseball scholarship at the University of Virginia in 2001. The school got more than an outfielder. Ty's father, John Grisham, best-selling author of *The Firm* and other legal thrillers, had often donated money to help renovate the scruffy ballparks where his son played ball. Sure enough, once his son was on the team, he stepped up to the plate with more than $1 million to renovate the university's decrepit stadium.

But the coach who had ardently pursued the novelist's son soon cooled on the freshman. Ty batted only ten times in a little more than two seasons and finally quit the team in 2004. His son's experience has left the elder Grisham wondering why his son was wooed by the Virginia coach in the first place. "There were some schools that wanted my son, and there were a handful that wanted me," said the elder Grisham. "It's no secret I've given a lot of money to youth baseball."

In college athletics, money doesn't just influence a school's choice of which sports to sponsor or eliminate. It also intrudes on a realm usually considered a bastion of meritocracy—the selection of players. Not only do rich students have access to more sports than lower-income applicants, and thus more opportunity to leverage athletic skill into college admissions, but they also have a better chance than other athletes of equal ability to be recruited or picked for the varsity team.

While coaches pursue top players based on their abilities, some borderline candidates are helped by factors other than physical prowess. Children of wealthy alumni and donors sometimes are given slots on teams even if they're out of their league athletically, in the hope that their parents will renovate a locker room or a sprinkler system. In some ways, the recruitment process is akin to a sandlot baseball game where two children choose sides. Hoping to win, the captains pick the best players first. But, after divvying up the good players, they'll give an edge to the kid who brought the bat and the ball.

For some privileged players, who are marginal academically as well as athletically, a coach's interest may tip the scale with the admissions office. Others likely would have been accepted anyway but still divert roster slots and sometimes scholarship money from equally skilled players. Although they often are frustrated with their lack of playing time, they benefit from the prestige, networking, and career opportunities that come with a spot on a college sports team.

Parents "pull strings or they donate so they can call their kid a student-athlete even though the kid's not actually out there performing," Curtis Brown told me. He's a former college baseball coach who works for the Baseball Factory in Columbia, Maryland, which links high school prospects with college teams. "They're able to tell somebody, 'My kid plays baseball at the university.' That person they're talking to has no clue that the kid is the seventh option in the outfield."

College basketball fans can't help but notice that many teams with African American stars have white players who rarely get into the game unless their team is ahead or behind by a large margin. Basketball coaches—a predominantly white group—sometimes use the last few seats on the bench as patronage plums for the children of donors, ex-players, and others with connections.

College basketball teams often hold open tryouts on campus that draw as many as one hundred hopefuls. But the nonscholarship slots they vie for may be taken by insiders instead. Every year, on the first day of practice, St. Joseph's University men's basketball coach Phil Martelli holds such a tryout. But in 1999 Coach Martelli exempted one candidate, who had averaged only two points a game as a high school senior, from the competition. His name: Phil Martelli Jr.

Coach Martelli told me that Phil junior was "average at best." But he said that his son aspired to be a coach and having him on the team was the best way to teach him. The younger Martelli, who graduated in 2003 and is now an assistant basketball coach at Manhattan College, recalled that crowds in opponents' arenas used to hurl "Daddy's boy" and other taunts at him.

Similarly, Jared Sichting didn't participate in Marquette University's open basketball tryout in 2002. The five-foot-eleven guard secured his spot on the powerhouse team through a Marquette assistant coach who had worked for the National Basketball Association's Minnesota Timberwolves, where Jared's father, former NBA star Jerry Sichting, has been an assistant coach. Jared, who averaged about 10 points a game in high school, told me he was recruited by several colleges with lower-level basketball programs and hadn't considered Marquette. But in April of his senior year in high school, the Marquette assistant coach called Jerry Sichting, said the team could use an extra player, and asked if Jared was interested. Jared agreed, in part because he aspired to a coaching career. Although the deadline for applying to Marquette had passed, the coaching staff arranged his admission.

"If he's interested in coaching, it's a way to get a foot in the door, something to put on your resume," Jerry Sichting told me.

The younger Sichting received plenty of perks at Marquette. He got top-of-the-line gear that Nike gave the Marquette team for reaching the Final Four in the 2003 NCAA tournament; when he and his teammates played at Madison Square Garden, they were feted at a banquet on an aircraft carrier museum docked on the Hudson River. But he had misgivings about his limited role on the team. He played a total of nine minutes in five games in the 2003–4 season and did not score. The next year he quit the team. "Whenever I use one of my dad's connections to help me out, I feel a little guilty," Jared told me. "It didn't take much time for me to realize how much better the other players were at certain things. It's hard to sit on the bench and know you're not going to play when you've played all your life."

Duke University nonscholarship basketball player Joe Pagliuca also has a well-placed father, Stephen Pagliuca, managing director of Boston buyout firm Bain Capital Inc., and part owner of the Boston Celtics. The elder Pagliuca played on Duke's freshman basketball team and has given more than a million dollars to the university. He chaired the undergraduate school's board of visitors in 2004–5.

A strong student and a good outside shooter, Joe averaged 17 points a game as a senior cocaptain at Belmont Hill School, a Boston-area private school, but was not recruited by big-time college basketball programs. Bob Gibbons, who publishes a newsletter that evaluates high school players, told me he did not rank Joe Pagliuca on his list of the country's top eight hundred college prospects in 2003.

Early in Joe's senior year in high school, his father called Steve Wojciechowski, an assistant coach at Duke, one of the nation's premier basketball teams. Wojciechowski told me he was familiar with Pagliuca as a successful businessman and Duke alumnus and spent "the better part of a day" escorting the Pagliucas around Duke's athletic facilities in Durham, North Carolina, and advising Joe on how to improve his game. He said he and Pagliuca kept in touch afterward. "We're lucky here—the culture of the university is that all Duke people look out for each other," Wojciechowski said. "If one needs a helping hand, another is there to provide it."

After Joe enrolled in 2003, Duke coaches invited him to scrimmage with the team, which doesn't hold an open tryout. According to Wojciechowski, "our guys said he was a good player, a really good guy," and Joe walked on to the team. He rarely played and didn't score a point in his freshman, sophomore, and junior seasons. The *Boston Globe* reported in April 2004 that the younger Pagliuca "readily admits he made full use of his father's position" to make the team. But in a later telephone interview with me, Joe downplayed his father's role, saying he believes it was "mostly" his own doing. "It's a great experience to be on a team with such high-caliber coaches and players," he said.

"I call tell you definitely nobody has ever been chosen because of who his father was," Duke head coach Mike Krzyzewski told me. He says he picked Joe as much for his "strength of character" as for his basketball skills. While Duke is a top Division I program, Joe "should probably have been a Division II or III player," he said. "He's not going to have a role where we're counting on him in our rotation."

Another Duke basketball benchwarmer, Andy Means, who graduated in 2004, told me that his father, aunt, and several other relatives attended the university, and his grandmother was an old friend of Coach Krzyzewski. (The coach acknowledged this relationship but said he has a lot of friends.) "My grandma knew Coach K a long time ago," Andy told me. "They knew my name. I don't know if that had anything to do" with being picked for the team. He said the basketball coaches didn't push for his admission to Duke but that he benefited instead from legacy preference. "My SATs weren't as good as other people's," he said.

Country club teams such as golf and crew, which reap little revenue from ticket sales or television contracts, often carry more players than they need, padding their rosters with kids from families wealthy enough to pitch in. Although a college can send only five golfers to a tournament, the Georgetown University men's team in 2003–4 had fifteen members, all of whom enjoyed the pleasure of practicing at a Professional Golf Association tour course, the Tournament Players Club at Avenel in Potomac, Maryland. When I asked Georgetown coach Thomas Hunter whether colleges seek golfers whose parents can afford to donate, he said, "There's a bit of that." He added, "I'm not going to do just anything for the sake of adding a person to the program. The player has to have some talent."

Although the Grishams live only twenty miles from the University of Virginia campus, Ty hadn't seriously considered going to the elite state university because, as a B student with average SAT scores, he was unlikely to get in on his academic credentials. But when Dennis Womack, then the UVA baseball coach, surprised the family by offering a $4,000 partial scholarship, the prospects changed, not because the Grishams needed the money but because scholarship recruits are generally given a substantial admissions boost as well as a fair chance at playing time. "Suddenly with the offer of a scholarship, which meant guaranteed admission, he had a chance to go to a wonderful academic school and compete in the ACC [Atlantic Coast Conference], which is a very good baseball conference," John Grisham says. "There's an old saying in college baseball: if you give a kid money, you've got to give him a chance to play."

In Division I college baseball, teams typically have thirty-five players, and the NCAA limits them to the equivalent of 11.7 full scholarships. They generally spread that money among twenty or so players by doling out partial scholarships. Some coaches who recruited Ty Grisham, who had been a standout player at a small Virginia prep school, did not consider him good enough for a scholarship in a top league. They thought he was fast but needed to improve his batting to play in Division I. "He was a decent ballplayer," said Ron Atkins, University of Richmond coach. "For us, he was not a scholarship player." But Atkins says that if he'd known that Ty's father would finance a stadium, "he would have been a scholarship player."

Virginia's baseball team had been in the middle of the pack for years in the ACC, partly because its obsolete stadium made it hard to lure top talent. At the time, John Grisham said, he was persuaded that Virginia recruiters "had nothing but the purest of motives. They wanted my son as a baseball player." Now, he added, "you've just got to wonder." He recalled being skeptical of several recruiters from other colleges, whom he declined to identify: "I was just very suspicious of a coach who would show us his stadium and say he wanted to build this or that, expand here or there, put in lights." He said Ty did not want to be interviewed but is "as confused as I am."

Womack, now an assistant athletic director at UVA, acknowledged that the potential financial benefit to his struggling baseball program of having Ty on the team did cross his mind. "It would make sense," he said. "It's public knowledge that Mr. Grisham is a very generous person with baseball." But he said the hope of a refurbished stadium was not why he gave Ty a scholarship. "First and foremost, the kid's got to be able to play," he said. "He had a chance; that's why we signed him. Some pan out, some don't." Craig Littlepage, now Virginia's athletic director and then senior associate athletic director, said a gift from Grisham was never discussed and that the baseball program at the time was concentrating on in-staters such as Ty.

After his son signed with Virginia in fall 2000, Grisham promised his wife he wouldn't build a stadium for the university. "We knew it wasn't the right thing to do with our son involved in the program," he told me. Then in April 2001, a university task force recommended eliminating baseball scholarships and limiting the team to regional travel to avoid a budget deficit and comply with Title IX by narrowing the spending gap between men's and women's sports. Alarmed that the program his son was about to join would be gutted, Grisham successfully lobbied the school's governing board to reject the program—and then volunteered to put UVA baseball on a sounder footing by upgrading the stadium himself. Although his gift was anonymous, he told me he was the largest donor to the $5 million renovation and also helped with fund-raising. In hindsight, he said, his gift was a "huge mistake to do when I did it," because it put "tremendous internal pressure" on Ty to "prove he belonged. I beat myself up every day."

After missing his freshman season with a foot injury, Ty barely played in 2003. Womack said Ty saw little action—in the stadium his father built—because he was "a young guy behind a veteran outfield." John Grisham retorted, "He was not sitting on the bench behind a bunch of all-Americans, I can promise you that." Teammate Matt Street, also an outfielder, told me Ty was "a little raw" when he arrived at Virginia. "He kind of got pushed down to the bottom and they forgot about him," Matt said.

In 2004, under new coach Brian O'Connor, Ty quit the team after ten games. Matt Street said Ty's patience ran out when a freshman started ahead of him against a "cupcake" opponent that Virginia defeated 15–2.

Because baseball was so time-consuming, "Ty thought he was missing so much of the college experience," his father said. "It's very frustrating to sit on the bench day after day when you know you can compete with the people on the field. That's what ate him alive." He said Ty told him after quitting, "When I drove away from the stadium, it was the happiest day of my life."

When I interviewed Grisham in the summer of 2004, he told me that he and Womack had not spoken in more than a year. "There's some real strain there," he said, adding that he also stopped supporting the program financially. "Once Ty walked away, so did I," he said. "I have no involvement with the program now and don't want any. I don't go to games, don't go to that beautiful stadium over there."

WHILE VIRGINIA'S first varsity crew had faltered, the second varsity eight had dominated its competition leading up to the Oregon State meet, earning Catelyn Coyle and Andria Haneman promotions to the first boat. Without those two stalwarts, Katie Yrazabal, Kerry Maher, and the other second varsity rowers would race their Oregon State counterpart, hoping to maintain the JV's undefeated record, before the universities' top eights battled.

Katie grew up in San Francisco in an upper-middle-class family; her father is a real estate agent, her mother a gate agent for American Airlines. They sent her to St. Ignatius College Prep, a Jesuit school that happened to be the only San Francisco high school with its own crew team, and Katie began rowing as a freshman. Her team flourished on the water, and even more in college admissions; aided by athletic preference, two teammates enrolled at Yale and one each at Brown, Wisconsin, and the University of California. Katie, with an SAT score of "1260 or 1270" and an impressive ERG score, was slotted at Virginia. "Our college advisers at St. Ignatius were like, 'Have backup schools ready,'" she told me. "They didn't believe it."

Kerry Maher was one of five Canadian rowers on the Virginia roster, including four from the province of Ontario. Because rowing is a favorite pastime for working-class families in English-speaking Canada, unlike this country, the Canadians on the Virginia team tend to come from humbler backgrounds than the Americans. Kerry's father was a maintenance worker, and her mother was laid off from a nursing job; she attended a public high school and learned to row at a boathouse shared by all the schools in the area. She also rowed for a local club, and Virginia offered her a scholarship after her boat won the Canadian Henley championship. The UVA rowing team "is full of a lot of wealthy kids," Kerry told me. "Most of the Canadians are coming from families who either have farms or large families that can barely afford to get by. You can tell the difference sometimes. Sometimes I feel like, 'Oh, man, I wish my parents could just buy me that.'"

The working-class Canadian rowers have to adjust not only to the affluent atmosphere but to the academic rigor of an elite university. Kerry, who had been a good student in high school and scored "just under 1200" on the SAT, was placed on academic probation after her freshman year; she had to take summer courses, attend study hall, and go through an appeals process to stay on the team. As a sophomore, she improved to a 3.0 average, "just from learning how to do things properly."

Another Canadian rower, Amanda Kennedy, also had a rough transition academically. Over bagels at a crowded Charlottesville, Virginia, breakfast spot, Amanda told me that her father and mother—a General Motors plant supervisor and a billing clerk—didn't go to college, and that she had needed donations from Ontario service clubs to rent a single scull. At a regatta in her high school senior year, somebody handed out almanacs that listed U.S. colleges with rowing teams; she picked thirty-two of them and sent them her athletic resume. "My phone didn't stop ringing," she recalled. Because American colleges required the SATs, she took them, "did horrible," tried again, and raised her score to "1000 or 1100. The colleges said, 'We can work with that.'"

She ruled out the Ivy League because they didn't offer athletic scholarships; as an international student, she didn't qualify for federally funded need-based aid. She ended up visiting four colleges: Boston University, Miami, Temple, and Virginia. Although she says she didn't realize that Virginia was viewed as a top school, she enjoyed the small-town ambience and accepted Coach Sauer's offer of a partial scholarship, supplementing it with Ontario student loans.

As a freshman, she said, "I screwed off, I just rowed and partied." This regimen caught up to her when she was suspended from the team for the first semester of her sophomore year. She told me that Coach Sauer threatened to withdraw her scholarship, but he eventually relented, and she boosted her grades. "The work wasn't hard, you just had to go to class," Amanda said. She graduated in 2003 and now works for a local business.

Despite a brisk wind that whipped up waves on the Ravenna Reservoir course, Katie, Kerry, and the second varsity trounced the Oregon State JV by fourteen seconds. Next came the revamped first eight's turn, with Catelyn Coyle quarterbacking the boat at stroke and Andria Haneman in the next seat. Parents peering from a nearby churchyard or from a motorized barge shouted, "Pick it up, UVA!" "Let's go!" and other encouragement as Virginia's orange oars cut crisply through the water, scattering ducks right and left. Team boatman Roger Payne, steering the barge, timed the race and announced the strokes per minute: "UVA is at thirty-four, Oregon State thirty-four and a half." Steadily widening their lead until open water could be seen between the two boats, the varsity defeated Oregon State by nearly eight seconds. As the first eight crossed the finish line, Catelyn thrust her arms in the air and shouted to Roger, "Nine for nine, Roger"—a reference to her undefeated racing record for the year.

After carrying their shells to the boathouse, the rowers repaired to a nearby lawn where parents had prepared a gourmet repast. Over grilled chicken sausages and bow-tie pasta with feta cheese, Coach Sauer shrugged off my suggestion of socioeconomic and academic disparities between American and Canadian rowers. He told me that he had grown up on a farm himself and had attended Purdue, a state university in Indiana, where he hoped to play football. "I got my bell rung" and switched to rowing, he said. "People go, 'It's an elitist sport.' If it is, I didn't know about it. I sure as hell don't come from that."

Nevertheless, Coach Sauer acknowledged he was concerned about the team's lack of racial diversity—so much so that he had recently made an exception to his cherished ERG rule of thumb for recruits. In the summer of 2004, Amanda Fulwood had been touring colleges and made an appointment to meet him. Amanda, who is African American, was then entering her senior year at Shaker Heights High School in a well-to-do Cleveland suburb. Her family had moved there from suburban Maryland in 2000 so that she could attend the highly regarded public school; her father, Samuel Fulwood, had become a columnist for the *Cleveland Plain Dealer*. He had encouraged his daughter to play basketball, but Amanda took up rowing instead because many girls in her honors classes belonged to the crew club, which has since attained varsity status, one of the few public school girls' crew teams.

"I began to love it," Amanda told me. "Then I noticed I was the only black person at the meets." Her father said, "We went to the first regatta and there weren't many black families at all. In the whole crowd of four hundred people, maybe five were black, including me, my wife, and my daughter." Still, he said, his daughter found her social niche with the rowers, who, like herself, were tall, athletic, and conscientious about their studies. Amanda was in the top quarter of her high school class but needed athletics for admission to an elite college.

Amanda was a good rower but not a prime prospect; her ERG score before her senior year was 7:48, well above Virginia's 7:30 threshold. Still, when she talked to Coach Sauer, he saw that she had the build and the determination to be a college rower. He told her flatly that he had never recruited an African American rower and wanted an integrated team. His directness impressed her. "Most coaches talk about diversity on the campus but not on their team," Amanda told me. "If you talk about diversity on a crew team, you talk about having Protestants and Catholics together, not about racial diversity," because it's an overwhelmingly white sport. Coach Sauer "acknowledged the team had faults," she continued. "He had had black women on the team as walk-ons but they weren't comfortable."

Still, one barrier remained—the all-important ERG. Coach Sauer promised Amanda that if she could improve her time of 7:48 on the 2,000-meter test by the following March, he would give her a slot. Back home in Shaker Heights, she worked out diligently, toning up and losing weight, and shaved her time to 7:37. It was still above the cutoff, but her dramatic improvement persuaded the coach to offer her a slot and a partial scholarship, and Amanda became the team's first black recruit and a national anomaly; as of the most recent figures, only 130 black women were rowing for colleges.

As a freshman at Virginia in 2005–6, Amanda was placed on the novice team. Although white teammates welcomed her, she told me, "socially, it's been a very hard transition. I spend so much time rowing that I haven't had the opportunity to explore the black community here."

6

A **BREAK** FOR

FACULTY BRATS

Free and Easy Entry for the
Children of Professors

Professors often complain that the admissions boost for athletes diminishes the intellectual caliber of their campuses. But they rarely criticize a preference for another group with questionable credentials—their own children.

Free or reduced tuition for faculty children, originally intended as a financial fringe benefit, has morphed into an admissions break at Notre Dame and many other elite universities. To avoid the humiliation of a rebuff and the expense of paying tuition elsewhere, faculty members aren't shy about using their clout and connections to wangle their children's admission. Since most universities have faculty committees overseeing undergraduate admissions, and since it's easier to replace an administrator than a professor with lifetime tenure, the last thing any admissions staff wants is to alienate faculty. Saving themselves grief, admissions deans at many universities have lowered standards to the point where faculty children often receive an edge bigger than that given to alumni offspring.

Peter Cavadini, for example, would almost certainly not have applied—or been admitted—to Notre Dame were it not for his father's influence. With a 1240 SAT score, 150 points below the university's average, Peter worried that he "wasn't cut out for Notre Dame academically." Although he did well in most subjects in high school, "I was really terrible in math, and still am," he told me. Peter, who graduated from a public school in South Bend, also found Notre Dame students snobbish and thought he would fit in better at Indiana University.

Notre Dame had its doubts about Peter too. Daniel Saracino, assistant provost for admissions, advised Peter's father to consider sending him to a two-year college, where he could improve his study habits, and then have him transfer to Notre Dame. Saracino also told Peter that he would have to work harder at Notre Dame than he had in high school.

Nevertheless, John Cavadini was determined his son would go to Notre Dame, not only because of the university's academic excellence but also because of its employee benefits. Tuition—$31,540 in 2005–6—is free for faculty and staff children. Parents pay only for room and board—and faculty children often live at home anyway. If they enroll anywhere else, Notre Dame pays only one-third of their tuition.

Cavadini, who chairs Notre Dame's theology department, was well aware that "the admissions criteria are different for faculty and staff children," he told me. "It's, 'Can the person do the work? Will they succeed?' As opposed to, 'Where do they fall in the pool of competitive applicants?' " He said he "gave a counterargument" to Saracino, and promised to keep an eye on his son and furnish Peter with tutors as needed.

Deferring to the chairman, Saracino admitted Peter, who enrolled in 2001. "We bend like crazy for faculty children," Saracino said, even more than for alumni children, and the numbers bear him out. Notre Dame accepts 19 percent of its applicants who enjoy no preferences at all, half of legacy applicants, and 70 percent of faculty and staff children. The median SAT score for faculty and staff children admitted to Notre Dame runs 90 points below the median for legacies, 100 points below the median for all admitted students, and 175 points below the typical unhooked admit.

Their pedigree, Saracino added, is no guarantee that faculty children will measure up. Their SAT scores range widely: "You've got 1500s and 1100s," he said. "I'm trying to change the culture of entitlement among the faculty. They feel if their child can do the work, he or she should be admitted. Everyone has to take it up a notch."

Cavadini has seven children, and the five oldest, including Peter, have enrolled at Notre Dame. (One received a partial athletic scholarship as a swimmer.) Depending on where they would have gone otherwise, Cavadini has probably saved several hundred thousand dollars, particularly as the tuition waiver doesn't count as income for federal tax purposes.

He defended Notre Dame's admission of his son as a reward for his own hard work teaching other students there. "I exert so much effort thinking about the education of other people's kids—I'm treating them in the same way I treat my own kid," Cavadini said. "I got accepted into medical school; I could be making a lot more money. I'm not, I'm doing this, I'm happy I'm doing this.

"If you're part of a community of teaching, and you're spending all this time, and you come home and talk about these kinds of educational ideals, you want to believe your own kid could benefit from that energy you're investing in other people," he continued. "If I were a doctor, my kid would get free medical care from someone else's parents. It's a kind of professional courtesy."

THE NOTION of professional courtesy seems reasonable on the face of it, but in practice it means that faculty children displace better-qualified regular applicants—just as professional courtesy in medicine often means that a doctor treats a colleague's child ahead of a sicker patient. Financially the preference for faculty children is even more inequitable. While gifts from alumni and other donors often fund scholarships for low-income students, reduced tuition for faculty children indirectly increases the financial burden on their classmates. Also, since tuition benefits for faculty children are tax-free, their educations are subsidized by other American taxpayers, including parents of regular applicants. Thus faculty members, who might otherwise become a natural constituency for fighting skyrocketing college tuitions, are insulated from the rising cost of higher education.

Lured by the combination of economic incentive and easy admissions, faculty and staff children make up 2 to 3 percent of undergraduates at Notre Dame and some other major universities, an astonishing total given the small pool of potential applicants. The large majority are children of faculty or highly paid administrators. Although universities typically offer the same tuition benefits to all employees, children of janitors and other low-income staff are less likely to enroll. They might not meet even reduced admissions standards, and their parents lack the institutional clout to intimidate the admissions office.

According to data gathered by two Vanderbilt University economists, John Siegfried and Malcolm Getz, nearly one-third of children of faculty at research universities and one-fifth of children of faculty at liberal arts colleges attend the parent's institution if it offers them a financial incentive to do so. If the parental institution pays the same share of tuition no matter where its faculty children enroll—Vanderbilt and the University of Chicago, among others, provide fully "portable," or transferable, plans— the proportion of children staying home drops substantially. Only 13.3 percent of children of university faculty and 5.1 percent of children of liberal arts college faculty attend the parental institution if there is no tuition advantage.

Boston University's plan isn't portable. If children enroll at BU and their parents have been employed there since 1996, it pays 100 percent of tuition, worth about $30,000 tax-free; if their parents were hired after 1996, it pays 90 percent. If they go to another university, BU pays nothing.

To ensure employees every opportunity to attain such a valuable benefit, BU sponsors a twice-yearly seminar starting when faculty and staff children are in middle school, walking the families through case studies of BU applicants and spelling out grades and scores needed to get in. Once children apply, BU executive director of admissions Kelly Walter writes to the parents to say that she is aware of their applications and will give them special attention. A senior admissions officer is designated as a faculty/staff liaison to read files and counsel families. No one is rejected without a final review from Walter. "I may agree with the committee recommendation, or I may ask them to go back for additional information," she said. "I may say, 'I know the family, I know the brother, I think this student can make it, let's give him or her a chance.' "

This hand-holding translates into a massive admissions edge. BU, which admits about half of all candidates, accepted 160 out of 176 faculty and staff children—91 percent—in 2003. Only about half of them enroll, usually the weaker admits; in the case of high-achieving children also accepted at Harvard or Princeton, faculty and staff parents often decide that an Ivy League education is worth the price difference.

Of forty-two faculty and staff children who applied early decision to enroll in the fall of 2005, BU took 79 percent and deferred the rest to the regular pool. Not one was rejected. A faculty or staff child "would have to be extraordinarily weak academically for us to deny them early decision," Kelly Walter said. "Waiting for senior grades or perhaps even additional standardized testing is part of that special attention or plus factor that we would extend to this population."

Columbia University pays full tuition for faculty and staff children who enroll there, half if they enroll elsewhere. Of Columbia's 5,493 undergraduates in 2004–5, 157, or 2.9 percent, were children of faculty or staff. Among them was Timothy Stanley, stepson of English professor Michael Seidel. With a 1300 SAT score and a B average, Timothy didn't meet Columbia's academic profile, although he did boast one unusual credential: despite being white, he ran the black and Hispanic student union at his Manhattan prep school.

"I don't think I could have gotten in" without being a faculty child, Timothy told me. "It wasn't a sure thing." An early decision candidate, he was deferred to the regular review. "I had to work my ass off for a month or two. I did that."

Professor Seidel described his stepson as a "smart kid. His grades and scores were decent. I don't feel Columbia bent over backwards in any way." Still, he continued, "anything helps. If you've got nothing, your scores have to be truly superb, your recommendations have to be off the charts. Having a faculty member as a parent is a help." Seidel added that he and Timothy's mother, a former Columbia administrator, "both know people here. If you've got a good candidate, being known at a place is an advantage. There's no such thing as a completely even playing field. The world doesn't work that way, nor do job applications work that way, nor does college work that way. Columbia will enroll twelve hundred students a year. A certain percentage is development cases. A certain percentage is athletes. The term is *juice*. You see it's not all of a piece. It's not an even tapestry."

Two other Ivy League universities don't give a special tuition edge to faculty and staff children who stay put but do bend admissions standards for them. At Harvard, which admits eight to sixteen faculty children each year, professors are eligible for ten-year, no-interest loans for their children's room, board, and tuition. Harvard's admissions preference for faculty children is at least as large as the tip given to legacies; it justifies this boost on the grounds that the faculty's "commitment and dedication are critical to the University's smooth functioning." Princeton University, which pays half the tuition at any accredited institution for children of employees with more than five years' service, considers having a faculty or staff parent a "plus factor" in admissions. This preference helps explain why Princeton takes a lot of applicants from Princeton High School, which many faculty and staff children attend. From 2001 through 2004, fifty-two graduates of the local high school enrolled at Princeton, compared with twelve at Yale, eight at Columbia, and six at Harvard.

In 1998, twenty-five of Princeton High School's 209 seniors graduated with honors. Although Rebecca Tilghman was not among that top 12 percent, the daughter of Professor Shirley Tilghman, a renowned molecular biologist and then chair of Princeton's Council on Science and Technology, was admitted to Princeton. While 95 percent of Princeton students graduate in four years, the art and archaeology major took five years to obtain her degree, graduating without honors in 2003. She and her mother, who ascended to the presidency of Princeton in 2001, declined comment.

HAVING EARNED their own eminence through intelligence and scholarly dedication, professors tend to be strong advocates of meritocracy; they grade tests and papers and vote on hires, tenure cases, dissertations, and the like based on quality of work, not wealth or parentage. Still, to maneuver their own children into college, many faculty members rely on an admissions edge benefiting a group that needs help the least. After all, faculty children grow up surrounded by books and intellectual conversation, familiar with the ways of academia. Their parents have excelled academically at the highest educational levels, which is one of the strongest predictors of children's scholastic success. While not superrich, most professors are comfortably well-off, particularly at elite universities, and can generally afford homes in districts with good school systems. The average salary of a full professor at a private research university in 2004–5 was $127,214, not counting supplemental income from books, speaking fees, consulting gigs, and housing subsidies. Yet their children enjoy free tuition while many colleges can't cover the financial need of low-income applicants.

Faculty families that take advantage of the admissions break are violating their own beliefs in meritocracy and equal opportunity not only to save on tuition but also to secure their position in America's upper echelons. By attending elite universities where their parents teach, faculty children can network with well-placed classmates for lucrative jobs, translating their parents' educational attainments into their own wealth and status. (Due to their free tuition, they aren't saddled with student loans.) As alumni, they qualify their own children for legacy preference— an advantage to be handed down for generations to come.

Yet the break for faculty children makes their parents' jobs more difficult. To make room for lesser lights who are faculty children, a university turns away more promising applicants—sapping the vitality of classroom discussion, diminishing the quality of student work, perhaps even eroding the reputation of the institution.

Moreover, some experts believe that faculty children often underperform academically at their parents' universities—particularly if they would rather have left home but yielded to family pressure to save tuition. Vanderbilt University used to pay 94 percent of faculty child tuition there and nothing elsewhere but switched to a fully portable system in the late 1980s, in part because so many professors' children were unhappy. "Faculty kids had way lower grades than nonfaculty kids," recalled Vanderbilt economics professor John Siegfried. "That's because they had this discussion with their parents: 'I don't want to go to Vanderbilt.' 'You've got to go because it's cheaper.' So they go, and it doesn't work out. The kid sits there and does nothing until he flunks out and goes somewhere else. If the kid says it's not going to work out, it's not going to work out. The whole idea when we revised the tuition plan was to reduce the number of faculty brats. They were a problem for the student body."

Siegfried added that Vanderbilt's earlier system had a bizarre twist. It would pay 94 percent of tuition for a faculty child at any other institution under one condition: Vanderbilt had to reject the student first. The concept was that a faculty child who aspired to Vanderbilt should not be penalized financially for being turned down, but in practice it offered a perverse incentive to fail. Brilliant Vanderbilt offspring used to contrive ways of being rebuffed so they could go to Harvard or Yale on Vanderbilt's dime. According to legend, top students who couldn't play a note would apply to Vanderbilt's music program, which required an audition. One such conniver showed up purporting to be proficient at the oboe, then surveyed an array of wind instruments before allegedly asking, "Which one is the oboe?"

When it comes to college, Stewart Schwab's children don't have a choice. Schwab, the dean of Cornell University Law School, said Cornell's tuition benefit is a "great deal." Children of Schwab and other longtime faculty receive free tuition; those of more recent hires get half off. If faculty children enroll elsewhere, Cornell pays 30 percent. Cornell also gives admissions preference to faculty and staff children, as reflected in their 58 percent admit rate in 2004, double the university's overall rate of 29 percent. That year, Cornell accepted 57 students from nearby Ithaca High School (of 101 applicants), including many faculty and staff children. Other Ivy League universities admitted only 14 of 87 applicants from Ithaca High.

Of Schwab's eight children, the three oldest, all Ithaca High graduates, have enrolled at Cornell under his prodding. Free tuition "puts a lot of pressure on the family," he said. "Cornell is such a fine school. You'd better have a darn good reason for going somewhere else beyond just, 'Dad, I'm sick of being here in Ithaca and want to leave town.'"

Schwab's first child, a son, did want to leave Ithaca. Using Cornell as his safety school, he applied to four other elite universities—and was rejected or wait-listed at all of them. "He had the most difficult time adjusting to the fact he was going to his hometown school," the dean said. "He wishes he had applied more widely, even though we would have strongly pressured him to go to Cornell anyway. The hometown kids—I joke if they lived fifty miles away, they'd be really excited to get into an Ivy League school like Cornell. They know the faculty as their friends' parents; there's a little less luster to the place."

The lesson Schwab drew from his son's disappointment was not to let his other children go wherever they wanted but rather to dispel any illusions of escaping home by pushing them to apply to Cornell under binding early decision. His third child, a daughter, took that advice. "Everyone in every walk of life wonders about paths not taken," he said. "But she was eager enough to go to Cornell, and certainly acquiesced." With her younger siblings, he added, "We're really pushing Cornell."

IN ANALYSES of college admissions, preferences for children of alumni and faculty are sometimes paired. The *New York Times*, for instance, described faculty children as "the other legacies" in a January 2005 headline. Both preferences do involve universities taking care of their own, but there's an important distinction between them. Legacy preference is a fund-raising tool; its primary purpose is to separate alumni from their bankrolls. But the admissions edge for faculty children loses money, at least on the surface, because it's tied to a tuition benefit. Each faculty child that enrolls for free replaces a potentially full-paying customer. The cost to universities is considerable—$9 million a year at Boston University, for example.

Why do universities maintain such an expensive tuition and admission package? One explanation is historical: tuition benefits for faculty children date back to an era when college education was cheaper and admissions were less competitive than they are today. Already available at some universities in the nineteenth century, discounted tuition for faculty children became widespread during the Great Depression, when colleges couldn't afford a decent wage for professors but had plenty of empty seats in their classrooms.

Later, fully portable plans that allowed faculty children to go anywhere at reduced cost became commonplace. Tuition exchange consortia sprung up, in which liberal arts colleges traded slots, admitting each other's employee dependents for free. But in recent years the soaring cost of tuition has prompted some universities to curb tuition subsidies for faculty children going to other schools. According to a 2004 survey of 354 schools by the College and University Professional Association for Human Resources in Knoxville, Tennessee, 58.1 percent pay full tuition for employee children attending their own institution, while only 19 percent pay it elsewhere. Another 23.5 percent of the institutions surveyed pay at least half of tuition at their own institution, versus another 9.5 percent that do so elsewhere. This tuition differential has increased pressure on universities to admit their own faculty children.

Also, while expensive for universities, discounted tuition for faculty children is still cheaper than one possible alternative—raising salaries so faculty could more easily afford their children's college tuition. Such a salary hike would likely have to be across the board, as it would be politically impossible to increase salaries only for professors with college-age children. Since a tuition waiver, on the other hand, is targeted to those professors, it indirectly enables universities to maintain lower salaries for other faculty members who don't have children or whose children are already adults.

In addition, at most universities, professors qualifying for the benefit don't have to pay taxes on the tuition money they save. Under federal law, the perk is tax-free as long as it is also provided to low-paid employees such as custodians. The tax-free status means that the U.S. taxpayer shares the burden with the university of paying the faculty child's tuition.

Since there is no obvious reason why U.S. taxpayers should subsidize college tuitions of faculty children, the Internal Revenue Service has repeatedly proposed taxing the benefit. Each time, the well-organized higher education lobby has fended off the attack. Cornell's Schwab recalled writing to his senators and congressmen to defend the tax-free status: "I managed to dream up all kinds of high-flown justifications for it," he joked.

The issue reemerged in January 2005, when Congress's joint taxation committee recommended doing away with tax-free tuition benefits for faculty and staff children, which it estimated would reap $1.9 billion over 10 years. The committee report described the tax exclusion as raising "fairness concerns" because "it is not available to individuals working in fields other than education and, within the education field, may be available primarily to those working for educational institutions which have the greatest resources."

"This will be the fourth time I've fought the repeal," sighed Sheldon Steinbach, vice president and general counsel of the American Council on Education. "This baby just will not go away. . . . We've been able to defend it as a very traditional faculty fringe benefit. It's been around for a very long time. People have made career decisions based on it. To upset it midstream would be grossly inequitable." As on the previous occasions, the committee's proposal failed to gain traction.

A generous tuition and admissions package for faculty children also helps universities hang on to—and recruit—star professors, reducing the financial and prestige hits of unwanted turnover. "Every time I think about leaving Notre Dame, I think about that tuition benefit, and how many of my kids haven't gone through here yet," said Cavadini. "I practically signed my life away." The tuition benefit, the theology chairman added, is a "great selling point for recruitment. I use this to recruit people all the time," such as Gary Anderson, a tenured Harvard professor who joined Notre Dame's faculty in 2003. Anderson's son, then entering his senior year in high school, wanted to go to a Catholic university, and his first choice was Notre Dame. Although Notre Dame faculty members generally become eligible for the tuition benefit after three years of service, Anderson negotiated a one-year vesting period so his son would qualify for free tuition as a freshman. The youth subsequently was admitted and enrolled at Notre Dame.

Without the faculty child edge, Anderson said, "it's hard to know" whether his son would have been accepted. "Notre Dame is extraordinarily competitive. If you looked at his scores, he was right in the thick of things."

While his son's free education at a top 25 university was a "nice benefit," Anderson added, he moved chiefly because he's grown weary of secular academia and believes in Notre Dame's "overall ethos and goal." He's there "for the long haul," he said, not just until his son graduates.

A HIGHLY competitive school with growing prestige, Tufts University has attracted more and better applicants in recent years. In 2005, candidates for Tufts averaged 1344 out of 1600 on the SAT, up from 1313 in 2001. Tufts, which admits one out of every four applicants, has raised its bar accordingly, with accepted students averaging 1410 in 2004, up from 1360 in 2001.

Tufts professors are delighted with the improvement in the student body—except when it doesn't leave room for their own children. Because Tufts pays full tuition for faculty and staff children enrolled there, and nothing elsewhere, its rejections of several underqualified faculty children have prompted grumbling by professors forced to pony up tuition at other universities. Professors who profit from Tufts' increasing selectivity every day in their own classrooms nevertheless argue that faculty children should be exempt from the higher standards.

"We shouldn't allow this benefit to float higher or lower depending on what the demand is in a particular year of getting into Tufts," said Sheldon Krimsky, president of the Tufts chapter of the American Association of University Professors. "It should be based upon principles, such as 'Has this faculty child met the minimum requirements?' 'Can the faculty child do the work?' 'Will they succeed at the university?' Rather than, based on the whims of demand, 'Will there be enough space for them this year?' "

To save money and boost student quality, most selective universities have sought at one time or another to trim either the tuition subsidy or the number of faculty child admits. But distinguished academics protest any rollback of this cherished perk with the ferocity of professional athletes fighting a salary cap. Stanford University and the University of Pennsylvania, among others, have scaled back proposed cuts in tuition benefits rather than antagonize faculty. (A Stanford spokeswoman said the benefit was retained for its value as a recruiting tool. She added that Stanford has conducted workshops on applying to college for faculty and staff, and that being a faculty or staff child "can be a plus factor.")

Daniel Saracino, Notre Dame's assistant provost for admissions, said few professors respond meekly to his warnings that their children don't measure up academically and might not be admitted. Typically, he said, the faculty member will complain that Notre Dame admits football players with worse grades and test scores than his child. Who's more important to the university, the football team or the faculty? a disgruntled faculty member might ask.

At Tufts, where the average full professor was paid $109,000 in 2004–5, favored treatment for faculty children has been a long-standing source of contention. About one hundred undergraduates, or 2 percent of the student body, are offspring of faculty and staff. Tufts used to provide free tuition for faculty children but had a less generous plan for staff dependents. But the university began reexamining that policy after a 1984 federal law specified that only tuition benefits provided to both highly paid and low-salaried employees would be considered tax-free. In 1991, Tufts capped the benefit for faculty children at its current level of tuition, then $16,750.

The faculty reaction was fearsome: 90 percent signed a petition protesting the cap. "We got more response than we've ever gotten from faculty in terms of signatures." Professor Krimsky said. The Tufts administration backed down in 1992, not only restoring free tuition for faculty children but extending it to staff children as well to preserve the tax-free benefit. "As a practical matter, these benefits are very difficult to change," observed Laurence Bacow, Tufts president since 2001. "Expectations have been created among the faculty."

One of the administrators who crafted the cap, Steven Manos, later benefited from its demise. Although Manos, Tufts' executive vice president for finance, was paid $294,210 in salary in 2002–3, plus $83,767 in contributions to employee benefit plans and $6,064 in expenses, his son Alan qualified for free tuition when he enrolled at Tufts in 2003. Both Manoses declined comment.

Having preserved the tuition benefit, faculty members assumed Tufts' admissions office would go along by accepting their children. But that premise, solid in the 1990s, became shaky in the next decade under Bacow and a new admissions dean who had big ambitions for Tufts. While the administration still gave an edge to faculty children, it didn't want the gap between them and other students to widen. As admissions standards soared overall, faculty children needed to improve too.

Driving home this lesson, Tufts rejected the daughter of history professor Gary Leupp in 2004. "It was a very unpleasant surprise," said Leupp. "We have very few perks. The faculty think, 'At least my kid will go to this school.' I assumed, as did several of my colleagues, that our kids would get in. When they didn't get in, we felt irked. We don't make that much money; how are we going to pay for our children's college?"

Leupp told me that his daughter would have been a stronger candidate for Tufts had he been able to afford private schooling or SAT coaching. "If a kid's parents aren't wealthy and are obliged to put their kid through a local public school where the teachers might not even be competent, and whose A's, B's, and C's don't necessarily mean a whole lot," then her grades aren't a reflection of her intelligence, he said.

"It looks good for a university to boast that its admitted freshman class has an ever higher SAT cutoff," Leupp added. "Paradoxically, the better a reputation a university gets (which is primarily a result of the work of the faculty), the higher this very dubious bar gets placed, and the more difficult it becomes for institutions to respect their implied commitment to provide admission to faculty kids. That's really frustrating to the faculty parent."

At a Tufts faculty meeting in February 2005, a colleague of Leupp in the history department asked university president Laurence Bacow to clarify the policy on faculty child admissions. President Bacow replied that while Tufts was committed to preference for faculty children, admissions standards were rising for all applicants. "It's gotten more competitive for everyone, not just the faculty kid," President Bacow told me. "The faculty kid who would have gotten in five or ten years ago now has a lower probability."

Lee Coffin, dean of undergraduate admissions at Tufts, told me that the university admits faculty children at similar rates to other preferred groups, including athletes, legacies, and Medford residents. "What we're saying to the faculty is that in this applicant pool, which is increasingly national and international and powerful, we'll give your children a special look," he said. "We're not guaranteeing all faculty children a place in the freshman class. I think there's some sense among the faculty that this is what they expect. All things being equal, or a little less than equal, we can" admit a faculty child, he continued. "But we only have so many slots. At some point you have to ask the question, 'Who's not getting in?' "

Coffin answered his own question at the next faculty meeting, where he gave a presentation entitled "The Case for Need-Blind Admissions at Tufts." Unlike most premier universities, including those in the Ivy League, Tufts is "need-sensitive" rather than "need-blind" in admissions jargon; in other words, it factors an applicant's financial status into its admissions decisions. Thus, even as Tufts subsidizes faculty children with marginal credentials, it spurns top-notch candidates whose only flaw is their low income.

In 2004, Coffin moved 193 low-income candidates, who would have required an average of more than $25,000 a year in grants, from Tufts' pool of admitted students into its rejected pile to avoid exceeding the university's $7.8 million aid budget for freshmen. "In a need-blind universe, we would have taken them all, and you would be teaching them," Coffin told the faculty. The about-face, Coffin added, "made me sick." The last-minute discarding of the 193 applicants made the Tufts student body wealthier, whiter, and academically weaker than it would have been otherwise, Coffin said. Despite growing up in poverty, 52 percent of students jettisoned for financial reasons ranked in the top tenth of their high school classes, and nearly half surpassed Tufts' median SAT scores.

Although whites make up more than three-quarters of the Tufts student body, they constituted only 52 percent of the 193 students turned away. Instead, a disproportionate number of those cast aside—24 percent—were Asian American. (The Tufts student body is 14 percent Asian American.) While he had sought to preserve racial diversity, Coffin explained to the faculty, relatively few white applicants came from low-income families, while affirmative action for underrepresented groups protected blacks and Hispanics, leaving disadvantaged Asians vulnerable, including immigrants and first-generation college students. President Bacow said in March 2006 that Tufts' "top priority" in its next capital campaign is rasing $200 million for financial aid to enable the university to admit students regardless of their ability to pay.

Leupp's daughter, meanwhile, still ended up at Tufts. After she was turned down, Leupp complained to his two deans, saying he would find it hard to "go about my work with my wonted energy and enthusiasm." A dean then made inquiries and suggested that the professor's daughter, who had enrolled at Clark University in Worcester, Massachusetts, reapply as a transfer student. She was accepted and enrolled at Tufts for her sophomore year in the fall of 2005.

PETER CAVADINI still thinks some Notre Dame students are stuck-up, but he doesn't regret going there. After some initial trepidation, he realized in a freshman literature seminar that he could hold his own with classmates. Although a late switch of majors from philosophy to anthropology postponed his graduation until the spring of 2006, he compiled a respectable 3.2 grade point average, took a catechism course from his father, and, most important, found a calling. Substituting for his father (sidelined by eye surgery) at a conference in Nigeria, he encountered firsthand the poverty and disease afflicting Africa and hopes to return there after Notre Dame and teach high school.

Peter made up his mind on another question too: admissions breaks for faculty children such as himself. "Although I'm really glad I came here, I believe the preference for faculty children is unfair," he said. "Some kid worked really hard in high school and got beat by a kid whose father happens to work there. That's wrong."

7

THE

NEW JEWS

Asian Americans
Need Not Apply

Henry Park and Stanley Park grew up on opposite coasts, but they had a lot in common: surnames, Korean American heritage, stellar test scores, and a misplaced faith that elite universities accept students on merit.

Henry ranked 14th out of 79 members of the class of 1998 at the Groton School, a supercompetitive prep school in Groton, Massachusetts. He got a perfect 800 on the math SAT for a combined score of 1560 out of 1600, placing him in the top one-quarter of 1 percent of college-bound students across the nation. On the SAT II subject tests, he scored another perfect 800 on the harder of the two math exams offered, along with 760 out of 800 in Latin and 740 in physics. He played violin and competed on the cross-country team, and a respected math journal published a paper he coauthored with two classmates. And as the son of hardworking, middle-class Korean immigrants who dreamed of a better life for their children and scrimped to pay Groton's tuition, Henry seemed to embody the up-by-his-bootstraps American saga that is supposed to appeal to college admissions officers.

Henry thought his record gave him a good shot at an elite college, particularly as classmates with lower grades and SAT scores seemed confident about their chances at Harvard, Yale, and other premier schools.

What he failed to realize was that these classmates—legacies, development cases, rowers, underrepresented minorities—compensated for any academic shortcomings with admissions preferences that had little to do with brainpower. Unlike these students, Henry couldn't rely on any hook. As an Asian American, he did not qualify for affirmative action, which colleges generally limit to blacks, Hispanics, and Native Americans. His parents had gone to college in Korea, ruling out legacy preference for their son in the United States, and they couldn't afford to donate to a university; in fact, Henry applied for financial aid to pay his college tuition.

His Groton guidance counselor knew the score. She discouraged Henry from applying to the Ivy League, telling him it was a long shot at best, and advised him to lower his expectations to second- and third-tier schools. When Henry disregarded her advice, he was spurned by four Ivies—Harvard, Yale, Brown, and Columbia—as well as Stanford University and Massachusetts Institute of Technology. While they rejected Henry, Ivy League universities admitted thirty-four of his Groton classmates. Brown accepted the daughter of a best-selling author; Harvard, the grandson of one of its biggest donors; Columbia, an African American candidate; and Stanford, the daughter of an oil tycoon who chaired the university's board.

"When the decisions came out, and all these other people started getting in, I was a little upset," Henry told me. "I feel I have to hold myself to a higher standard." Added his mother, Suki Park, "I was naive. I thought college admissions had something to do with academics."

Unlike Henry, Stanley Park seemed to have a special hook to bolster his academic credentials, which included a 1500 SAT score. Stanley was born and raised in California, where voters abolished affirmative action in public university admissions in 1996. In the wake of that ban, the University of California, Los Angeles, revamped its admissions criteria to favor students who had conquered "life challenges," such as family illness, being raised by a single parent, or being the first in the family to go to college.

Stanley, who graduated from University High in Irvine in 2002, had overcome more than his share of adversity. After his parents—immigrants of modest means with only high school educations and little English—

divorced in 1999, he lived with his mother. When she was diagnosed with breast cancer a year later, he began tutoring children to help pay the rent.

"All the money he earned tutoring was donated to his family," his high school guidance counselor wrote in Stanley's college recommendation. "In the time I have known Stanley I have been impressed with his incredible balance. It's easy to view him as a top mathematics student, but there is so much more to this complex young man that makes him interesting. For the past three years, he has gone to the Bethel Korean Church at 6:30 a.m. every Sunday morning. Once there, he loads vans with food, and with other church members distributes food to the homeless."

Stanley's own college application essay movingly recounted how his mother's illness had inspired him. "I have the most loving and caring mother anyone can ever have," he wrote. "I admire her so much because she works hard even after her divorce last year. She sacrificed her youth and free time so that I might have a promising future. She went as far as to giving up her whole Christmas bonus to pay for an SAT class. Then something unfair happened to my mother; she was diagnosed with breast cancer. When my mother had her breasts removed, I could visibly see the pain and shame on her face. Although I am very grateful that she is alive, I could not bear to see my mom in that kind of pain. Now that she can't work as hard as she used to, I do not want to let all my mom's past sacrifices for me to be in vain. I slowly realized that the only thing I can do to help out was to make her happy by showing her the fruits of her sacrifices. I began to study harder in school and take my volunteer work . . . more seriously."

Nevertheless, UCLA and the state university's other elite campus, Berkeley, rejected Stanley while admitting black and Hispanic applicants with far lower scores. Stanley learned the hard way that the "life challenge" preference at his state university was a back-door substitute for affirmative action. It was never meant for him or other Asian Americans at all.

ASIAN AMERICANS are the new Jews, inheriting the mantle of the most disenfranchised group in college admissions. The nonacademic admissions criteria established to exclude Jews, from alumni child status to leadership qualities, are now used to deny Asians. "Historically, at the Ivies, the situation of the Asian minorities parallels very closely the situation of the Jewish minorities a half a century earlier," said former Princeton provost Jeremiah Ostriker.

Once ostracized, Jewish students are now widely coveted for their intellectual prowess. Today, many Jewish applicants have admissions hooks, often as children of alumni, donors, or faculty. Having apologized profusely for restricting Jewish enrollment in the past, selective universities now vie to provide the best kosher meals, build the biggest Jewish cultural centers, and offer the most complete array of Judaic studies courses.

Vanderbilt University in Nashville, Tennessee, for instance, not only built a Jewish center but also hired a rabbi to recruit students as part of what chancellor Gordon Gee called an "elite strategy" to lift the university to Ivy League status. "Yes, we're targeting Jewish students," Gee told a March 17, 2002, board meeting of the Vanderbilt affiliate of Hillel, the national Jewish campus organization. "There's nothing wrong with that. That's not affirmative action. That's smart thinking." The proportion of Jews among Vanderbilt freshmen soared from less than 5 percent in 2000 to nearly 13 percent in 2004, according to a university survey.

Few universities apply the same "smart thinking" to pursuing another academically proficient group: Asian Americans. Instead, just as they constrained Jewish enrollment before 1950, they now set a higher bar for Asian American applicants, freezing out students who would be considered scholastic superstars if they hailed from a different heritage. To be sure, working-class and middle-class white students—such as John Simmons, the high school valedictorian rejected by Notre Dame—also face a rough go in college admissions. But overall, Asian Americans are the odd group out, lacking racial preferences enjoyed by other minorities and the advantages of wealth and lineage mostly accrued by upper-class whites. This second-class status stymies Asian aspirations to join the country's inner circle of political, economic, and social leaders; limits that leadership circle's exposure to bright minds with fresh ideas; and breeds cynicism among Asian students and parents who emigrated here in search of opportunity. Meanwhile, by rejecting top applicants, elite universities damage their own educational quality—and inadvertently boost the academic status of second-tier schools that, in hopes of joining the first rank, welcome high-achieving Asian students.

Like Jews during the quota era, Asian Americans are overrepresented at selective colleges compared with their U.S. population (which is why they don't qualify for affirmative action as an underrepresented minority) but are shortchanged relative to their academic performance. Legacy preference, initiated to keep out Jews, has become academia's justification for excluding Asian Americans. Similarly, geographic preference for applicants from rural states, popularized to squelch Jewish applicants from New York City, now hurts Asian students concentrated in metropolitan areas, particularly Los Angeles.

Now as then, a lack of preferences can be a convenient guise for racism. Much as college administrators justified anti-Jewish policies with ethnic stereotypes—one Yale dean in 1918 termed the typical Jewish student a "greasy grind"—so Asians are typecast in college admissions offices as quasi-robots programmed by their parents to ace math and science tests. Asked why Vanderbilt poured resources into recruiting Jews instead of Asians, a former administrator told me, "Asians are very good students, but they don't provide the kind of intellectual environment that Jewish students provide."

Similarly, MIT dean of admissions Marilee Jones rationalized the institute's rejection of Henry Park by resorting to stereotypes. Although she wasn't able to look up his application because records for his year had been destroyed, "it's possible that Henry Park looked like a thousand other Korean kids with the exact same profile of grades and activities and temperament," she emailed me in 2003. "My guess is that he just wasn't involved or interesting enough to surface to the top." She added that she could understand why a university would take a celebrity child, legacy, or development admit over "yet another textureless math grind." College administrators who made such remarks about black or Jewish students might soon find themselves higher education outcasts.

———

"ASIAN AMERICAN" is not an identity deeply rooted in history or tradition. Chinese and Japanese students popularized the term in the 1970s in
an effort to be included in affirmative action programs. In 1977, the federal government (which had previously counted immigrants from China,
Japan, Korea, and so forth by their countries of origin) introduced "Asian
or Pacific Islander" as a data collection category—defined as "a person
having origins in any of the original peoples of the Far East, Southeast
Asia, the Indian subcontinent, or the Pacific Islands."

The strategy worked almost too well. Soaring Asian enrollment
soon provoked a backlash. In 1984, with Asian Americans accounting for
more than a quarter of its freshman class, the University of California at
Berkeley declared they would no longer qualify for affirmative action as
an underrepresented group. Five years later, under pressure from a federal
investigation into allegations of Asian quotas at Berkeley and UCLA,
Berkeley's chancellor publicly apologized for a decline in Asian admissions. In 1990, federal investigators concluded that UCLA's graduate department in mathematics had discriminated against Asian applicants.

Also in 1990, a report by the U.S. Department of Education's Office
for Civil Rights documented that Harvard admitted Asian American applicants "at a significantly lower rate than white applicants" despite their
"slightly stronger" SAT scores and grades. From 1979 to 1988, it concluded,
Harvard admitted only 13.2 percent of Asian Americans, compared with
17.4 percent of whites. Applicants from California and those intending
to study biology—two disproportionately Asian American groups—had
lower admission rates as well. Accounting for most of the admissions gap
between white and Asian applicants, federal investigators concluded, was
"preference given to legacies and recruited athletes—groups that are predominantly white." Asian Americans accounted for 15.7 percent of all Harvard applicants but only 3.5 percent of alumni children and 4.1 percent of
recruited athletes.

Federal investigators also turned up stereotyping by Harvard admissions evaluators. Possibly reflecting a lack of cultural understanding,
Harvard evaluators ranked Asian American candidates on average below
whites in "personal qualities." In comments written in applicants' files,

Harvard admissions staff repeatedly described Asian Americans as "being quiet/shy, science/math oriented, and hard workers," the report found. One reader summed up an Asian applicant this way: "He's quiet and, of course, wants to be a doctor." Another wrote that an applicant's "scores and application seem so typical of other Asian applications I've read: extraordinarily gifted in math with the opposite extreme in English."

Nevertheless, the Office for Civil Rights concluded that Harvard did not violate federal antidiscrimination statutes. Although legacy and athletic preferences "adversely affected" Asian Americans, it said, the hooks were "legitimate and not a pretext for discrimination." As for the stereotyping, it "could not be shown" to have hurt the chances of Asian applicants.

Federal investigators also found no evidence of a quota on Asian enrollment because the proportion of Asian Americans among entering freshmen had increased from 5.5 percent in 1979 to 19.7 percent in 1990. Since the federal reprieve, that growth has stalled. In the past decade, the percentage of Asians among Harvard's admitted students has fluctuated between 14 and 20 percent. By comparison, Harvard's Jewish quota in the 1930s was slightly lower—between 10 and 16 percent.

Given free rein by the federal decision, most elite universities have maintained a triple standard in college admissions, setting the bar highest for Asians, next for whites, and lowest for blacks and Hispanics. According to a 2004 study by three Princeton researchers, an Asian American applicant needs to score 50 points higher on the SAT than other applicants just to have the same chance of admission to an elite university. (Being an alumni child, by contrast, confers a 160-point advantage.) Yale records show that entering Asian American freshmen averaged a 1493 SAT score in 1999–2000, 1496 in 2000–1, and 1482 in 2001–2. For the same three years, the average for white freshmen was about 40 points lower. Black and Hispanic freshmen lagged another 100–125 points below whites. A Yale spokesman attributed the Asian-white gap to more whites being recruited athletes, and said Asians and whites are held to the same academic standards.

At Notre Dame, average SAT scores for Asian American freshmen are 19 points higher than for whites. "The scores are identical between the two ethnic groups when you take out athletes, alumni children, development admits, etc.," said Daniel Saracino, assistant provost for admissions.

The higher expectations for Asian students may be most damaging to low-performing ethnic groups trapped under the Asian American umbrella. Students from Chinese, Korean, Indian, and Japanese families drive the high enrollments and SAT scores of Asian Americans at Yale and other elite universities. Those from countries such as Laos, Cambodia, and the Philippines, as well as the Pacific Islands, come from poorer, less-educated families, have lower scores, and are underrepresented in colleges compared with their population. If they were considered as separate groups, they might qualify for affirmative action.

As a result, both Southeast Asians and Pacific Islanders have lobbied to secede from the Asian label. Pacific Islanders gained a victory in 1997 when the U.S. Office of Management and Budget, noting that only 11.9 percent of Hawaiians obtain college degrees compared with 37.7 percent of Asians, designated "Native Hawaiian or other Pacific Islander" as a separate group. They were counted separately in the 2000 federal census. The common application form used by many colleges now contains a check box for "Native Hawaiian, Pacific Islander." But as of January 2005, the College Board, which oversees the SAT and other standardized tests, still grouped all Asian Americans together. And Southeast Asians haven't been able to shed the Asian American label.

"Southeast Asians are at the very bottom of the Asian American population, with poverty rates several times higher than the national average. Some Southeast Asian communities have higher welfare defendencies than any other groups, including blacks and Latinos," said Paul Ong, a professor of public policy at UCLA. "Talking to people about college admissions and recruitment, there's a growing acknowledgment there are groups of Asian Americans and Pacific Islanders that are disadvantaged. They need to factor that somehow into screening and admissions."

DISCONTENT AMONG Asian Americans over college admissions has long simmered at Princeton, where Asian enrollment (12.8 percent of 2004 freshmen) lags behind rivals Yale (18 percent), Harvard (19.7 percent), and MIT (26 percent). In the late 1980s, an internal Princeton study found that admission rates for Asians, as at Harvard, were lower than for whites; the gap was similarly traced to a scarcity of Asian legacies and athletes. But this explanation did not satisfy the late Chang-Lin Tien, the first Asian American chancellor of the University of California at Berkeley and a Princeton trustee. Every year, upon receiving enrollment figures, Tien would demand an explanation from Princeton's admissions dean as to the relatively low number of Asians.

Princeton economist Uwe Reinhardt was one of a group of professors who raised the issue with the university administration a decade ago. "I tend to feel in my gut that there is an anti-Asian policy," said Reinhardt, whose wife is Chinese. "There are many non-Asians with lower SAT scores admitted to the Ivy League. A lot of Asians have been rejected with far higher SATs than non-Asians who have been accepted. Within the Asian community, of which I'm a part, there's this feeling that, for you to get into Harvard or Princeton, you've got to be better than everybody else.

"We had several frank discussions with the administration. It was kind of a standoff. We told them, 'We're really conscious of it.' But there was nothing we could do. They would say that academic criteria aren't the only thing they use, and it's useful to have different cultures represented here. You wouldn't want half the campus to be Chinese. Well, why not?" He added that the stereotype of the quiet Asian student is "really a strange notion. My Asian American students are very lively. They take leadership positions. They're not at all shy or reticent."

Reinhardt, a German immigrant, told me that the selection of white legacies over Asian scholars reflects a disturbing trend in American society. "When I got to the USA in the early 1960s, this country had become, by virtue of the GI Bill, pretty much a meritocracy," he said. "The GI Bill showed how much talent had been wasted in the generation when the Ivy League was a gentleman's club. We've never had a corporate aristocracy like the one that was started in the mid-eighties. You look at some of the worst losers in corporate America, who walk away with half a billion dollars, and where their kids go to college. I do worry about the future of

America in connection with these legacies. I don't think we ever had as huge or as monied an aristocracy as we are building now."

Kai Chan, a Princeton doctoral student in economics and the son of Chinese immigrants, has been another campus voice appealing for equity for Asian applicants. In a November 29, 2004, column in the student newspaper, the *Daily Princetonian,* Chan wrote, "Is it fair in the name of (skin-deep) diversity to hold back qualified students from admission to the Ivies because of their race? After all, it is a fact that Asians need higher academic achievements than their peers to get admitted to the same school . . . Besides, aren't programs such as legacy admissions just another form of 'affirmative action' that also works against Asians? . . . The misguided approach of programs like affirmative action can be seen through my experience. I am the son of poor, non-English speaking parents, neither of whom attended high school. They never read to me as a child. They never attended my graduations. I went to some terrible high schools. (Altogether, I attended five high schools, one of which was known locally as "last chance high.") I worked practically full-time while attending high school and college. But I've never gotten the benefit of the doubt anytime in my life. If anything, I've had to be better than my peers." In a follow-up column, Kai urged Princeton to promote socioeconomic diversity by including more people from low-income backgrounds in admissions decisions: "A more diverse admissions committee would see the merits of an applicant who waited on tables to support her family."

A Princeton spokesman said that the university does not discriminate against Asian American applicants. "We consider each applicant as an individual and take into account everything we know about the applicant—including not only grades, scores, and activities, but recommendations, the application itself, and anything else that helps us develop as full an understanding of the applicant as possible," the spokesman wrote in an email. "No candidate is 'typecast.' When we make admission decisions, we are limited by the size of the entering class, and the overall quality of the applicant pool is so high that many truly excellent candidates cannot be admitted."

Asian American students who are admitted to Princeton, Chan said, often feel socially excluded there. In particular, they rarely join its five invitation-only "bicker" clubs, which have about six hundred to nine hundred members in the junior and senior classes, predominantly from white, affluent backgrounds. While Princeton's six "sign-in" eating clubs pick members by lottery, candidates for bickers undergo two days of interviews and games, sometimes with an element of hazing. But the humiliation—and $6,500-a-year membership fee—often pays off with postgraduation jobs and advancement from bicker alumni and parents.

"If you get a chance to actually join one of these clubs, it helps a lot with your professional career," Chan said. "You have a whole social network to fall back upon." Without such connections, he added, Asians bump into a glass ceiling; employers "want an Asian as a quant person. They're not expecting someone to take a leadership position but to work in a back office, printing numbers."

Why few Asians apply to the bickers is hotly debated on campus. In 2003, a South Asian student who worked as a minority affairs adviser caused a furor with an online posting on a Princeton search engine that mocked other Asian Americans for "self-segregation" in Spelman dorm, which he characterized as an "internment camp." Spelman provides housing with kitchen facilities for students who don't belong to eating clubs.

J. W. Victor, a senior in 2004–5 and president of the Princeton Inter-Club Council, acknowledged the scarcity of Asians in the bicker clubs but said they aren't intentionally ostracized. He noted that the bicker process is much like college admissions, giving preference to children of alumni and donors. "I don't think it's malevolent," he said. "It's who your friends are." Quadrangle, a sign-in club of which J. W. is president, promoted inclusion by cosponsoring parties with black and Asian student groups in the spring and fall of 2004. The parties, billed as "Rush Hour 3" and "Rush Hour 4" in reference to the popular *Rush Hour* movies costarring Jackie Chan and Chris Tucker, "made a loud statement," J. W. said.

THE HIGH test scores and humble backgrounds of many Asian American applicants have created a political quandary for the University of California, the nation's premier public university system.

In 1996, California voters adopted an initiative prohibiting the university from practicing affirmative action. Nevertheless, university administrators are under heavy pressure from Hispanic legislators to have student demographics conform more closely to the California population. Hispanics make up a third of the state population but only an eighth of the university's 150,000 undergraduates; Asians are 11 percent of the population but almost 40 percent of the undergraduates.

To redress that imbalance, Berkeley and UCLA first considered replacing race-based affirmative action with a preference for low-income applicants. But officials vetoed the idea when they realized that it would mostly elevate Asian Americans such as Stanley Park, who combined poverty with academic achievement, rather than low-income blacks and Hispanics, relatively few of whom could qualify for Berkeley even with a boost. "We found that using poverty yields a lot of poor white kids and poor Asian kids," said former Latino legislative leader Marco Firebaugh. Socioeconomic diversity was a "pie-in-the-sky solution," Robert Laird, who was then Berkeley's admissions director, told me. "That was never going to work in California."

The UCLA School of Law did test Laird's conclusion. In 1997, it adopted a formula to select 40 percent of its first-year class that gave preference to students from families and communities with low incomes and limited education. As Laird would have predicted, the main beneficiaries were working-class and lower-middle-class white and Asian students with solid academic credentials. Asian enrollment rose to eighty-two students in 1997 from forty-eight the year before, while black enrollment fell to ten from nineteen. Disappointed by the failure of the formula to boost Hispanics and blacks, UCLA law phased it out and initiated a program with lower entrance standards called Critical Race Studies, which was intended to appeal to minority students.

Instead of an income-based preference, the University of California accommodated Firebaugh and other Latino legislators by adopting an undergraduate admissions system known as comprehensive review, which awards extra credit for surmounting a wide range of personal, economic, economic, family, or psychological obstacles—"life challenges," in UCLA's words. "Applicants with extraordinary academic performance, alone, are not offered admission at UCLA," declared the campus website. University officials say comprehensive review gives preference to educationally disadvantaged students, not to any particular minority, and can identify diamonds in the rough. But the rules seem to count more for some groups than others, and to penalize low-income families, many of them Asian, that have sacrificed to move to districts where their children can attend better schools.

Like Stanley Park, Blanca Martinez grew up in a working-class immigrant family, and helped support it when her mother had breast cancer. Although her SAT score was 390 points below Stanley's, both Berkeley and UCLA admitted her. Blanca, the daughter of a blue-collar worker from Mexico, attended 99 percent Hispanic South Gate High, an overcrowded facility near Los Angeles with temporary classrooms and few advanced courses, and got extra points under comprehensive review for participating in a university outreach program to low-performing schools. Berkeley admitted sixteen South Gate seniors in 2002, compared with six in 2000, while UCLA took thirty-six, up from fourteen in 2000.

South Gate's Susana Pena, daughter of a construction worker and another outreach participant, was admitted to UCLA with a 940 SAT score, 560 points below Stanley Park's. "People should understand it's harder for us," she told me when I visited Southgate in 2002. "Once in a while, they should give us a little break so we can catch up to them."

At another mainly Hispanic high school near Los Angeles, Belmont, UCLA student and outreach worker Alex Paredes helped Rosaura Novelo edit her application essay, which appeared tailored to fit the "life challenge" criterion. "It has been difficult for my parents, Mexican immigrants who did not even get to third grade in school, to raise a family of seven," Rosaura's essay began. "My father is the only person in the family who works, getting only minimum wage. . . . Our situation has taught me to appreciate education, learn how to overcome challenges that I have been faced with, and to take advantage of the benefits that come from all my hard work. . . . Taking advantage of the opportunities my parents have provided me with has sometimes been difficult because of all the challenges I have had to overcome. . . . Things have not been handed to me on a silver platter, which makes it challenging for me. . . . My community has also been an obstacle: gangs and violence are an everyday occurrence." UCLA—which took twenty-four Belmont seniors in 2002, tripling the previous year's number—admitted Rosaura despite an SAT score of 980, 520 points below Stanley Park's.

When I dropped by University High in Irvine on the same trip, I found that its admissions to Berkeley and UCLA were plummeting. University High is one of the best public schools in California, with a mean SAT score of 1247 in 2003–4 compared with a state average of 1015. It's also 45 percent Asian American. UCLA admits from University High dropped from 112 in 1998 to 65 in 2004, and Berkeley admits from 91 to 46 over the same period, relegating more University High graduates to less selective campuses such as Riverside and Santa Cruz. As a highly ranked school, University High didn't qualify for University of California outreach, hurting its students' prospects under comprehensive review. In other words, Stanley Park's mother had moved to a cramped Irvine apartment she could barely afford to provide him a better education—and may thereby have thwarted his admission to Berkeley and UCLA.

I chatted with Stanley and several Asian American classmates who had also been rebuffed by the two elite UC campuses. Hyejin Jae thought she had hurt her chances by soft-pedaling family hardships. But "I didn't want too much of a pity party," said Hyejin, who scored 1410 on her SATs and is the daughter of a struggling Korean-immigrant pastor. "No matter how bad your situation is, someone has it worse."

Asian applicants to Berkeley or UCLA who hadn't confronted a life challenge soon rued this gap in their resumes. Albert Shin, another University High student and the son of an engineer, scored 1540 on his SAT, had a 3.9 grade point average, and could read English, Korean, and Latin. Both Berkeley and UCLA turned him down. "It would be okay to look at social disadvantage a little bit, but judging it more than academics would be wrong," Albert told me. He, Stanley Park, and Hyejin Jae enrolled at the university's San Diego campus. As of March 2006, Stanley Park was a senior bioengineering major with a 3.5 grade point average, and "pretty worried" about admission to medical school. Financial aid and a job as a nuclear medicine assistant at a San Diego hospital had helped pay his tuition.

By 2003, parental complaints that comprehensive review meant rejecting top Asian and white students caught the attention of John Moores, then chairman of the university's board of regents. Studying Berkeley's admissions records, he found that in 2002—the year Albert, Stanley and Hyejin were rebuffed—Berkeley turned down 1,421 Californians with SAT scores above 1,400, including 662 Asian Americans. Of the 359 students accepted with SAT scores of 1,000 or less, 231 were black, Hispanic, or Native American.

The regents chairman accused his flagship campus of "blatantly" discriminating against Asian Americans and denounced comprehensive review as "fuzzy . . . It's silly to pretend that very low scoring applicants should be admitted to one of America's premier universities with the expectation that somehow these students will learn material that they missed in K–12." University officials disputed Moores's contention, noting that SAT scores are an imperfect measure of academic ability. Still, in April 2004, a university study group compared a statistical model of how the UC admissions process was supposed to work with actual cases. Buried deep inside its report was the finding that "somewhat fewer Asian students, and more African American and Chicano/Latino students (and, in some cases, White students) were admitted" on most campuses than would have been expected. One possible explanation: "small but real racial or ethnic effects on admissions decisions."

LESS THAN two weeks before Christmas 2004, a festive mood prevailed in the lobby of Hunter College High School, a mammoth brick fortress on the corner of 94th Street and Park Avenue on Manhattan's East Side. Serenaded by the mellow warbling of a nearby flute lesson, beaming students lined up to buy fifty-cent "candy grams"—holiday cards designed by ninth graders with a choice of candy canes, lollipops, or chocolate inside.

Four floors up, cheer yielded to anxiety as seniors, many of them Asian Americans, drifted in and out of the college counseling office with little to do but wait and hope. It was early decision week, when most Hunter seniors learn whether they have been accepted, rejected, or deferred to the regular pool by their first choices. One of the country's best public high schools, with an average SAT score of 1430, Hunter sends one-third of its graduates to the Ivy League. Nevertheless, its Asian American students face an uphill battle against legacies, development cases, and athletes.

"All the schools basically say, 'We don't discriminate,'" observed Iris Wang, a Hunter senior who arrived in the United States from Beijing at the age of eight, not knowing a word of English. Her father is a chemist, her mother a postal worker. With a 1520 SAT score and top grades, she applied early to MIT, which deferred her. "But I went to the Columbia session and they said they value a multicultural community. If they want to be multicultural, there's only so many of one culture they can take." Asked whether legacy preference is justified, she added: "If you're going to accept a kid with a 1230 SAT score, you don't know he's going to accomplish anything, just because his parents did something great."

Iris would hear more bad news the following spring. Despite her stellar credentials, she was turned down by Harvard and Yale and wait-listed by MIT, Columbia, and Johns Hopkins. She was accepted by only one private school, New York University, and two public campuses, the State University of New York at Binghamton and at Stony Brook. She enrolled at NYU as a presidential honors scholar—a designation signifying that she was in the top 5 percent of the entering class.

For Asian students such as Iris, the subjective, nonacademic criteria for college admissions—wealth, legacy, athletic prowess, personal qualities—stand in stark contrast to the process that got them into Hunter. Put simply, Hunter's mission is to find and educate New York City's most intellectually gifted students. Even to qualify for its entrance exam, public school students must score above the 90th percentile in both math and reading on the city's fifth-grade test; private schoolers must display equivalent proficiency. Then, through tests in math and language arts plus an essay, Hunter winnows three thousand candidates to an entering class of two hundred seventh-graders. Other than giving a small edge to applicants from poor families—the income cutoff is whether they qualify for a subsidized school lunch—Hunter picks the best students. No preference is given to legacies, athletes, or underrepresented minorities. (An additional thirty students, who were identified as gifted in kindergarten but did not surpass the cutoff on the Hunter exam, come from a feeder elementary school run by Hunter in the same building.)

This system produces a student body that is nearly 40 percent Asian American, including many first-generation students. They flourish at Hunter High, often achieving exceptional grades and test scores. But as they begin to think about college, Hunter advisers drum into their minds that they need more than academic excellence to distinguish themselves from the pack—and from each other. Like Opal Mehta, heroine of a novel by Harvard student Kaavya Viswanathan, they have to overcome the stereotype.

Although *How Opal Mehta Got Kissed, Got Wild, and Got a Life* was recalled by its publisher in 2006 for plagiarism, its story rings true to anyone familiar with the college-application experience of Hunter's Asian Americans. A Harvard admissions interviewer advises Opal, a brilliant Indian American teenager, that it isn't enough for her to excel in science and be fluent in four languages, she also needs a rambunctious social life.

Beverly Lenny, then Hunter's director of college counseling, said admissions officers at elite universities often complain that Asian American applicants all look the same on paper. "When Harvard calls us back and gives us a brief synopsis of why certain kids didn't make it, they'll say, 'There were so many kids in the pool that looked just like this kid.'" Lenny said she understands their viewpoint, but it makes her job harder. "We run Hunter more like a meritocracy," she said. "That's what you have to do for gifted education. Harvard isn't necessarily a meritocracy. They're trying to build a community.

"We have five counselors doing the college process. We draw lots and assign groups by alphabet. What is the most difficult group to get? *K-L*, the Kim-Lee group. That group is the hardest to write recommendations for. Part of what makes that group survive is the exact same thing that works against them in college admissions. The way they survive is more of a group mode. Their community is very strong for them. They make kids the same. They want to be like everybody else. You get a group of them. Every single child has had music lessons. Every single child succeeds well in math. Every single child has done community service in a hospital. Every child has done Chinese or Korean studies on Saturdays and is fluent in that language. You're writing the same letter" again and again.

Lenny acknowledged that the failure of college admissions staffs and high school counselors to probe below these superficial similarities and get to know Asian American students as individuals may reflect unconscious racism. As a "white melting-pot woman," she said, it may be harder for her to communicate with Asian students than it would be for an Asian counselor. At the time of my visit, none of Hunter's counselors were Asian American.

At Lenny's request, half a dozen Asian American seniors chatted with me in a conference room adjoining her office. I soon understood why she described them as "outstanding survival kids." All knew the uphill challenge they faced in college admissions, yet they weren't bitter. Instead, they adapted as best they could, trying to counteract the stereotypes by expressing individuality in their activities and essays. These valiant efforts apparently made little headway with admissions offices. Although all of the group would end up at prestigious colleges, only one was accepted by his first choice; none of the others were judged worthy of the Ivy League.

When Senna Ye emigrated from China at the age of seven with her divorced mother, she knew two words of English: *apple* and *pear*. A decade later, she scored 1460 on her SATs, including a 720 verbal score, and was a mainstay of the Hunter math team. Yet despite this remarkable progress, she feared that Columbia, her first choice, where she would qualify for free tuition as a staff child because her mother worked as a medical researcher there, would dismiss her as just another Asian science whiz. So in her application essay, she adopted a humorous tone toward her research into

Legionella pneumophila bacteria: "Oh LEGs, LEGs, where are you? Are you trying to elude me on purpose? With my trusty pipetmen [tubes used to transfer liquid], I'll be as meticulous as Sherlock Holmes and as unstoppable as Superman." The verdict was still out on this strategy; Columbia had deferred her. Months later, all four Ivies to which she applied—Columbia, Penn, Brown, and Cornell—would reject her. She would enroll at the University of Maryland.

Shirley Shaw, the daughter of Chinese immigrants, acknowledged her college admissions predicament: "I'm the stereotypical Asian, more into math and science. I don't particularly like writing and social science." With a 3.85 grade point average and a 1540 SAT score, including a perfect 800 in math, plus choir and bowling for outside activities, she applied to MIT and was deferred. She later enrolled at Johns Hopkins.

Thomas Lee, a Korean American senior, learned from the cautionary tale of his older brother, David. Despite scoring 1590 out of a possible 1600 on the SATs, David was rejected by MIT, Cornell, Columbia, and the University of Chicago, and enrolled at the University of Michigan. Realizing that his brother "didn't present himself as well-rounded," Thomas was "more open" to school activities and "took every opportunity that came my way," including captaining the track team, and still notched a 1560 SAT score. He was accepted at an Ivy League school, the University of Pennsylvania. In a subsequent email to me, David Lee theorized that a slump in his junior-year grades had sunk his Ivy prospects. "I do wish perhaps that I'd have concentrated more deeply on my extra-curriculars," he added. "But I wasn't much of a believer in doing things to 'look good for college,' and I don't really regret it.'"

Another Asian American senior in the group, Elizabeth Wai, had the opposite problem. She had bent over backward so much to distinguish herself from the Asian stereotype and demonstrate leadership, particularly in community service efforts to prevent teen pregnancy, that she had neglected her studies, she told me. She settled for a 3.7 grade-point-average and a 1530 SAT score, which she jokingly termed an "Asian fail." She feared that an "Asian fail"—which she also defined as "getting a 95 on a test"—would undermine her aspirations to her dream school, Yale.

Her worries proved well founded. The next day, she learned that Yale had rejected her. Elizabeth enrolled at Georgetown.

Asian Americans aren't the only unconnected group confronting especially imposing odds in college admissions. Also bypassed in colleges' pursuit of the rich and famous is another set of applicants even more distant from the American establishment: international students who need financial aid.

Admissions directors from the humblest community colleges to the Ivy League these days aspire to international diversity. They go on overseas recruiting junkets, pontificate about spreading American values and competing in the global marketplace, and boast about how many countries are represented in their student bodies. What they neglect to mention is that their foreign students don't just offer diverse backgrounds and viewpoints; they also offer ready cash.

Most foreign students enrolled at U.S. universities come from wealthy families and pay full tuition. Many of them graduated from exclusive boarding schools or international schools overseas that cater to children of businessmen, diplomats, and upper-class families and charge hefty tuitions. They commute to campus in their BMWs and Mercedes-Benzes, and jet off to Paris for the weekend.

Foreign applicants from lower social tiers learn a painful lesson about the economic limits of American goodwill. They aren't eligible for federal financial aid and are often charged out-of-state tuition at public universities. (Undocumented students living in the United States in violation of immigration laws are in similar straits.) Only a few U.S. universities, notably Harvard, Yale, and Princeton, evaluate foreign candidates on a need-blind basis. Whatever pittance other colleges provide usually takes the form of merit scholarships—which often reward affluent students who don't need the money—rather than income-based assistance. According to a 2004 Institute of International Education survey, 81.8 percent of foreign undergraduates listed their primary source of funds as "personal and family," compared with only 10.1 percent citing "U.S. college or university." Most of the others were sponsored by their home government or private companies. By contrast, 63 percent of all undergraduates in 2003–4—and 83 percent of students at private four-year colleges—received financial aid from federal, state, institutional, employer, or other sources.

American colleges are looking overseas for what one admissions dean described as a "trifecta": students who have high test scores, don't need financial aid, and are children of potential donors. Colleges "talk about international diversity, but if you look more closely, you'll often see they're admitting a foreign national who brings less of a diverse perspective because of time spent in America, or schools attended in America," this person told me.

Even for the cream of foreign undergraduates, poverty can be a barrier. Amherst College ranks applicants on a 1–7 scale from best to worst, and admits 85 percent of the 1s. Who makes up the rejected 15 percent? Often, it's international applicants seeking financial aid. Neither the University of Southern California nor New York University, which boast among the largest foreign-student enrollments in the United States, offers need-based aid. Barbara Hall, NYU's associate provost for enrollment, pointed to "limited dollars" and difficulty verifying need: "You get the financial statement and the bank has certified that the family has two cows and three goats. How do you put a dollar value on that?"

Although college administrators lament that increased security and visa delays in response to the September 11 attacks, as well as increased competition from Canada and Australia, have slowed foreign enrollment, they haven't compensated by seeking a broader socioeconomic spectrum of foreign students. In 2003–4, Kasia Szalecka was an exchange student at the high school in Barrington, Rhode Island. While her SAT score was unexceptional, the teenager from Warsaw, Poland, ranked in the top 10 percent of her senior class with a 3.8 grade point average and was named to the National Honor Society. "She was a very serious academic kid," said her great-uncle, Bill Malinowski, a *Providence Journal* reporter. "She had to tell me to turn the music down." She also joined Barrington High's archery club, volunteered as a "junior keeper" and translator at a nearby zoo, and earned money babysitting.

Savoring her first taste of America, Kasia decided to go to college here. Believing all the rhetoric from American higher education leaders about their commitment to global diversity, she figured she would have little trouble getting into a good school. Dipping into her babysitting savings, she paid a $130 fee to take the Test of English as a Foreign Language (TOEFL), which most U.S. colleges require for international students, and scored a strong 260 out of 300. Overall, she spent nearly $1,000 in test and application fees.

But Kasia soon discovered that her intelligence and dedication meant little without wealth. Because her father, a doctor, only earned about $20,000 a year, Kasia was dependent on aid—and little was available. Foreign students don't qualify for federal financial aid, and as much as colleges espouse global diversity, most are loath to spend scarce scholarship dollars in its name.

At first, Kasia wanted to attend nearby Providence College, and she scheduled an interview there. The interviewer was "very interested," Kasia later told me, until she confessed she would need financial aid, whereupon he "sounded very surprised" and told her not to expect any. She next tried the University of Rhode Island, only to find the state school was no bargain for foreigners; according to its website, "minimum costs" for international undergraduates are nearly $30,000 a year. Kasia and her Barrington High guidance counselor, Steve Rotondo, then scoured websites and polled colleges until they identified a handful of schools offering assistance to international students. "Most of my friends were applying to a handful of schools, having so-called 'sure shots,' 'safety options,' 'high reach,' etc.," she emailed me. "Unfortunately I could only apply to a few of the best schools in the U.S., because they were the only ones to provide any financial aid." Princeton, Wellesley, Bates, and Connecticut College all turned her down—as did less selective St. Anselm College in New Hampshire. St. Anselm's scholarship money for non–U.S. citizens is so limited that it prohibits international students who need financial aid from applying there under its binding early decision program.

"No college ever told me, 'We don't want foreign students,'" Rotondo said. "They all brag about geographic diversity." But financial aid "is not a top priority."

Kasia applied early to her first choice, Middlebury College, one of the most generous U.S. colleges in giving financial aid to foreign students, which deferred her to the regular pool and then placed her on its waiting list. "I know Middlebury would be the place for me," she wrote its admissions office. "Many people in the United States take equality for granted, but I know, coming from a country like Poland, how precious it really is. Throughout my life, I saw my father, a physician, work endless hours for meager pay. I watched my mother, who is well educated, grow increasingly frustrated with her inability to get a job because she is a woman and a mother. . . . I came to the United States with the hope of a better future. I want to continue my education here where the opportunities for a woman are boundless. I know that Middlebury is a place where I can receive an excellent education, develop as a person, and strive for a better life.

"My friends in Poland have doubts that a young woman from Warsaw can actually get into a top college in the United States. They are just teenagers, but they have abandoned their dream. I want to show them that we can all dare to dream." Despite her appeal, Middlebury did not make room for her. Kim Downs, director of student financial services, said the decision was based solely on academic merit and her financial need was not considered.

Stymied in her pursuit of a U.S. education, Kasia enrolled at less expensive Dalhousie University in Nova Scotia, Canada, where she plans a double major in sociology and social anthropology. After college, she hopes to become a photographer for *National Geographic* or *Discovery* magazine, preserving the world's cultures and religions with her camera.

But the money culture of American college admissions is one she'd prefer to forget. "It was horrible," she said. "I didn't know that I could go to Dalhousie, and I was at the point of thinking that probably I would not go to college. I was there in high school, and all my friends around me who had better or worse grades than I did, they got in somewhere. I was trying so hard, and there was nothing I could do, because of finances."

———

WHEN I arrived at the luncheonette in the Johns Hopkins student center one afternoon in March 2003, Henry Park emerged from the kitchen to greet me. I waited while he cooked the last order of his work-study shift. Then he changed out of his chef's coat and we walked to an off-campus restaurant. His mother, who had driven to Baltimore from the family's New Jersey home, soon joined us for coffee.

She told me that her husband used to own a string of small clothing stores in the New York area, enabling the Parks to send Henry to Horace Mann, a Manhattan private school, through ninth grade. But several of the outlets failed in the mid-1990s, forcing his mother to work full time teaching Korean. Concerned that she couldn't spare enough time to drive Henry to Horace Mann and his extracurricular activities, she decided to send him to boarding school for grades 10 through 12. After visiting several schools, she chose Groton for its small enrollment, "homey" campus, and notable Ivy League placement record. To pay Groton's $30,000-a-year tuition and room and board, she sold her only investment property, an apartment building in Hoboken, New Jersey. "I thought, the most important thing is really my child's future," she told me.

Founded in 1884, located on a graceful Gothic Revival campus 40 miles northwest of Boston, Groton has long been regarded as a bastion of the elite. It borrows heavily from the English "public school" model and vocabulary: grade years are known as "forms," student leaders are called "prefects," and students attend chapel each morning. Distinguished alumni who fulfilled its call-to-duty credo—"To serve is to reign"—include Franklin Roosevelt, Dean Acheson, Averell Harriman, and McGeorge Bundy. The class of 1998, among its roster of illustrious or wealthy families, boasted Stanford-bound Margaret Bass, daughter of oil baron Robert Bass; Julia Halberstam, the daughter of best-selling author David Halberstam, destined for Brown; and Elbridge Colby, grandson of the late CIA director William Colby, who was headed for Harvard.

Academically, Henry more than held his own in this company, excelling in German, Latin, and especially math. But as one of only three Asian American students in his form, he felt ill at ease socially, except for one party where he loosened up and demonstrated his proficiency at "liquid dancing"—dancing with a glow stick. In 1997, when England's Princess Diana was killed in a car accident, three-quarters of the Groton student body—many of them from America's royal families—closely followed the news, and 15 percent bought tribute magazines. But the House of Windsor's travails didn't interest Henry Park, who preferred listening to Korean music and studying martial arts at an academy off campus. "I don't think I really fit in," Henry told me. "I just felt it was a very homogenous population."

Classmates admired his intelligence but resented his aloofness. In a retaliatory snub, they voted him most likely to "never be heard from again." One said, "I wish I knew him better. He was just not a part of the Groton community." Neither was his mother. Busy with teaching, she didn't become friendly with Groton faculty or administrators. Nor could she elevate Henry's status there by donating to the school.

Most students at Groton, as at other prep schools, feel intense pressure to get into a top college. Those who come from generations of Ivy League old money want to maintain their families' status and avoid social disgrace and economic decline. Those from middle-class backgrounds want to lift their families into the upper echelon and prove that their parents' hard-earned tuition money wasn't wasted. Scholarship students from humble beginnings carry their parents' dreams for a better life for their children.

"It's a high-pressure environment," recalled Eric Cohen, a 1995 graduate who attended Williams College. "You had made it to Groton, and everything seemed to turn on the next step. Would you make it to Harvard, Princeton, Amherst, Williams?"

For many in the class of 1998, preferences eased the transition. Affirmative action lifted Groton's minority students. Lakia Washington, an African American who grew up in the Bronx, attended Groton on a scholarship. She was admitted to Columbia, where her father worked as a student loan representative, despite ranking 60th in her class and scoring 1110 on the SAT. She said affirmative action gave her a "great opportunity." But, she added, preferential treatment for children of alumni and donors "amounts to exactly the same thing. That's what upsets me the most about criticism of affirmative action."

At Groton, Lakia outpaced another African American scholarship student, Latoya Massey, who had a 1080 SAT score and ranked 64th in the class. Wesleyan University in Middletown, Connecticut, a top liberal arts college where three-fourths of freshmen in 2003 scored at least 1290 on the SATs, admitted Latoya. "I was competing with children who had been in private school," said Massey, who was the first in her family to go to college and who attended New York City public schools through eighth grade. Her father, an immigrant from Trinidad, is a Brooklyn hairstylist. "I worked every summer and babysat on weekends for extra cash. Most Groton students didn't have to do that. It's a white male world."

One white male at Groton had a record strikingly similar to Henry Park's but fared much better in the college-admissions process. John Roberts was tenth in his class—four spots ahead of Henry—but had a slightly lower SAT score, 1530. They were two of three Groton seniors enrolled in the school's most advanced math course, and their research for an article titled "Mapping the Hypercube" was published in a math journal for high school teachers and students. In addition, both students were on the Groton cross-country team.

But John, unlike Henry, had a significant Harvard hook. His grandfather and uncle, Albert H. and Albert F. Gordon, both alumni, gave Harvard an indoor track and tennis center and a professorship, among other donations. John says that when he was applying to Harvard, his family arranged for him to meet with William Fitzsimmons, the admissions dean, and Jeremy Knowles, then dean of arts and sciences. John's relatives also linked him up with Harvard's track coach and team members in the hope that he would be given preferential treatment as an athletic recruit. Harvard accepted him.

As noted in Chapter 1, Fitzsimmons unofficially interviews about one hundred applicants a year, many of them well connected. Knowles said he occasionally saw alumni or friends "with their offspring in tow" but never contacted the admissions office afterward.

John Roberts said Henry Park was a "tremendous" math student. "If Henry had some kind of legacy connection, that would have helped him" get into Harvard, he added. "In my case, I had the scores. The family connection took out the added doubt."

Overall, Harvard admitted a dozen members of the 1998 class at Groton—more than any other Ivy League university. At least five of those accepted by Harvard were alumni children, including Matthew Burr—son of seven-figure Harvard donor Craig Burr—and Forbes Reynolds McPherson. McPherson, known as "Renny," traces his lineage all the way back to Increase Mather, a seventeenth-century Harvard president; he's also the son and grandson of Harvard graduates. He had a solid 1480 SAT score but ranked in the bottom half of his Groton class. Applying in 1998, he was initially wait-listed at Harvard; the other top-tier universities to which he applied rejected him. After his grades improved in his final semester of high school, Harvard placed Renny on its "Z-list" of students admitted on condition that they delay enrolling for a year. Fitzsimmons says the university offered deferred admission to forty-eight applicants in 1998. Of those, seventeen students, or 35 percent, were children of alumni.

"I didn't have the best grades, but I knew I could handle the work at Harvard," said Renny, who graduated in 2003 and joined the U.S. Marines. He said his grades in college were better than in prep school. He was also editor in chief of a campus poetry review and a staffer on the *Harvard Crimson* newspaper.

Henry Park's mother said a school counselor, echoing the Asian American stereotype, warned her that Henry wouldn't stand out from Harvard's other applicants. Since the counseling office typically writes a school's letter of recommendation, which can carry a good deal of weight, the implicit message was that Groton didn't consider him worth fighting for. Henry said his counselor, Johanna Boynton, recommended applying to "a lot of schools I hadn't heard of. My parents weren't too happy."

Marilee Jones, the MIT admissions dean, also suggested that Groton didn't put its weight behind Henry. "If the school was really plugging for him, he would've gotten into at least one" of the six elite schools that rebuffed him, she wrote me. "I'd bet my next month's paycheck that the school just wasn't supporting him as strongly" as other students.

William Polk, then Groton headmaster, said in a written statement, "It is always disappointing when a student doesn't get into his/her college of choice, but we understand that a student's academic record is only one of many different factors that colleges consider."

Rejected by his top half-dozen choices, Henry was admitted to two universities in the next tier: Carnegie Mellon and Johns Hopkins. He attended Carnegie Mellon for a year before enrolling at Johns Hopkins, where he majored in neuroscience and was on the dean's list. He is now in medical school at the University of Kansas.

The psychological scars—and lessons—of his college admissions setbacks have lingered for Henry and his family. "I have thought many, many times why Henry failed," his mother said, "It was just devastating. He just failed like a falling leaf. . . . Korean Americans have to do a lot better than Caucasians to get admitted, and it's probably the same for other Asians. It's very, very tough. Presently, yes, there is discrimination."

8

THE **LEGACY**

ESTABLISHMENT

Taking On Congress and the
Higher Education Lobby

In the late summer of 2001, Michael Dannenberg proposed a provocative strategy to his boss, Massachusetts Senator Edward Kennedy, for rallying public and media support behind the besieged cause of minority preference in college admissions. The lanky, boyish Dannenberg, who had recently joined the senator's staff as senior education counsel, made his suggestion as affirmative action was reeling from one judicial setback after another. Federal courts had struck down race-conscious admissions policies at state universities in Texas, Michigan, and, just the week before, Georgia. No longer could universities take shelter under Supreme Court Justice Lewis Powell's concurring opinion in *University of California Regents v. Bakke* (1978) that the value of having a diverse student body justified special treatment for minority applicants. The state of the law was increasingly unsettled, and the Supreme Court was widely expected to take up the Michigan case in its 2002–3 term.

Dannenberg's brainstorm was that Kennedy, then chairman and now ranking minority member of the Senate education committee, should counter conservative opposition to affirmative action by attacking the preference for alumni children. Because it isn't racially discriminatory on its face, the preference for alumni children is less vulnerable than affirmative action to legal challenge, but a legislative assault on it would likely have grassroots appeal. And since the Supreme Court's consideration of Michigan would likely coincide with debate over reauthorizing the Higher Education Act, Kennedy could package an anti-legacy provision in the Democratic version of the bill.

This idea struck some of Kennedy's other staffers as politically naive. Edward Kennedy was the last legislator one would expect to assail legacy preference. The senator belonged to one of the country's best-known Harvard families; he, his father, his three older brothers, and several nieces and nephews had all gone there. The reception room of his Senate office proudly displayed a framed photograph of the senator as a young man scoring a touchdown for the Crimson against Yale.

Moreover, private higher education—not only Harvard, but also MIT, Boston University, Boston College, Tufts, and many other schools—was one of the biggest businesses in Massachusetts, the senator's home state. Senator Kennedy had served on the boards of Boston University and Boston College; his daughter Kara graduated from Tufts. Private colleges had supported him for decades; their lobbyists had raised money for his campaigns and worked side by side with him to increase financial aid for low-income students; now they were allies again in defense of affirmative action. These colleges all gave legacy preference to alumni children and would oppose any initiative to restrict it. Small wonder that one savvy colleague warned Dannenberg that an anti-legacy initiative might be good policy but would never get off the ground.

Still, Dannenberg was determined to explore this uncharted terrain. Three-fourths of Americans agreed with Dannenberg that legacy status should have no bearing on college admissions, according to a 2004 poll by the *Chronicle of Higher Education*. A 2003 poll of Michigan voters found that 61 percent opposed "extra admission points that are added to a student's application if one or both of that applicant's parents or grandparents attended the school"; only 27 percent favored the legacy boost, with 12 percent undecided.

Yet no one had ever filed, much less succeeded in passing, legislation to curb legacy preference. No one had even made a serious effort to muster the outrage of ordinary Americans, who wanted their own children to achieve the college degrees and white-collar careers that had eluded them, at this emblem of upper-class privilege. The issue had languished for decades as an occasional rhetorical target for affirmative action support-ers. As the advent of minority preference in the late 1960s triggered out-cries of reverse discrimination and lawsuits from white applicants who had been passed over, liberals responded that wealthy whites enjoyed their own preferences.

"It is somewhat ironic to have us so deeply disturbed over a program where race is an element of consciousness," Justice Harry Blackmun wrote in *Bakke*, "and yet to be aware of the fact, as we are, that institutions of higher learning . . . have given conceded preferences up to a point to those possessed of athletic skills, to the children of alumni, to the affluent who may bestow their largess on the institutions, and those having connections with celebrities, the famous, and the powerful."

Avoiding the inconsistency that Justice Blackmun mocked, a few conservatives have opposed both affirmative action and alumni child pref-erences. Notable among these anti-legacy Republicans, who generally come from rural states and resent what they consider the Ivy League elit-ism of the party's eastern wing, is former Kansas senator Robert Dole.

Senator Dole rose from poverty and became the first member of his family to graduate from college (Washburn Municipal University in Topeka, Kansas) despite war wounds that cost him use of his right arm. As Senate minority leader in December 1990, he urged Lamar Alexander, then secretary of the U.S. Department of Education, to reexamine admissions preferences for alumni children at private universities that receive federal funds. Two months earlier, an investigation by the U.S. Department of Education had concluded that Harvard was not violating the 1964 Civil Rights Act even though Asian American applicants were less likely to be admitted than whites with the same credentials. The department found that Harvard had the right to raise money through the use of legacy pref-erence, which accounted for much of the Asian-white gap.

"The last thing we need in American education is a caste system," Senator Dole wrote to Secretary Alexander. "These alumni perks have ab-solutely nothing to do with an individual's qualifications on merit."

In a 2004 phone interview, Dole said he still feels the same way. "It always seemed to me there ought to be a level playing field," he told me. "Affirmative action ought to be based on economic needs, not on gender or color. Legacy preference is almost the reverse. The richer you are, the better chance you have of getting in. I can see a reason for legacy preference in the early days. When a college or university was starting one hundred years ago, it needed a steady stream of supporters, and it offered certain advantages to bring in a family. They didn't have scholarships or Pell grants then, they were relying on these people. But now there's no reason for it."

SENATOR DOLE'S jawboning garnered little support from other legislators or government officials. Few politicians want to dismantle preferences for alumni children and other privileged applicants, because the system works to their advantage. Not only do their own children enjoy special consideration, but they can deliver admissions breaks for children of campaign contributors and key constituents.

Public universities give favored treatment to state legislators who control their appropriations; the University of Virginia, for instance, labels applicants sponsored by legislators as "special concern" cases. Elite private colleges need Washington's help for everything from campus expansion to scientific research. Yet, as nonprofit organizations, they can't endorse candidates or contribute to political campaigns without forfeiting their tax-exempt status (although individual administrators can and do donate). Instead, they buy influence through a different currency—admissions.

Graduates of the Ivy League and other premier universities pervade the federal bureaucracy and Congress. Universities look to these alumni, along with representatives from their districts and states, to spearhead their funding requests and safeguard their institutional interests. They cultivate alumni with cocktail parties, honorary degrees, awards, invitations to speak at commencement, and legacy preference.

Even politicians who are not alumni expect, and usually get, an admissions boost for their children and whomever else they recommend. Colleges view politically sponsored applicants from nonalumni families as akin to development cases, with the distinction that admission is expected to be followed by government funding rather than a private gift.

Trading admissions slots for political favors has become increasingly common as colleges seek ever more support for laboratories and other pork-barrel projects. Congressional funding for noncompetitive grants earmarked to specific colleges—an almost unknown practice twenty years ago—quadrupled from $495 million in 1998 to $2 billion in 2003, the *Chronicle of Higher Education* reported in 2004. During the same five years, higher education spending on lobbyists more than doubled to $61.7 million, surpassing expenditures for the same purpose by lawyers, labor unions, and the construction industry.

"Sometimes it's a quid pro quo," Daniel Saracino, Notre Dame assistant provost for admissions, acknowledged. "We've got a research grant worth $8 million and we need the support of senators to push it. We're going to keep them happy."

A longtime higher education administrator told me, "You have the problem of politicians who act like this is one of their donor or constituent services. The politician who may determine whether your building is going to be built calls you up and says it's very important that some kid is admitted." He then offered a hypothetical example. "If Charles Rangel [Congressman Charles B. Rangel, who represents Harlem] calls up Columbia and says, 'This kid's admission is important to me,' he's a very important person for Columbia with its expansion plans to build in Harlem. Making sure that everybody is as happy with you as possible is part of the thing. So much of this is by indirection. You hear from a trustee. Somebody says, 'I think it's very important to the congressman.'"

One higher education lobbyist explained to me how the game is played. "Schools pay very careful attention to those phone calls from politicians," he told me. "Every college has a bunch of cases like this. Let's say you need a 3.5 grade point average to get in. And the person a politician is advancing is a 3.3. Oftentimes that's enough to put them over. If they need a 3.5 but they have a 2.5, that's usually not enough.

"Colleges are willing to cut a little slack to everybody [in politics], along the lines of, 'Even the people who have opposed us might someday be our friend.' But there's a little bit of a hierarchy. The people at the very top of the list are the folks who have helped direct earmarked funding to a school.

"Once or twice a year, college presidents and very senior people come out and visit their members of Congress to talk about projects. During the course of this conversation, a member of Congress—I've been there when this has happened—will say, 'Little Johnny is getting up there. We'd like to bring him by.' This is a congressman who's been coming through for some time. The college president will go, 'That's just great. Have him give my assistant a call. Make sure to bring him in to see me.'

"That's the start of it. Let me carry that example a step further, based on actual experience. Little Johnny visits and loves the school. Four months later, the college gets a call from the congressman's chief of staff saying, 'Little Johnny loved that school. He's applied and hasn't heard yet. We're afraid he's on the bubble. Gosh, it would be great if Johnny would get in there.' That precipitates a series of calls. I got the sense from the school that he probably wouldn't have made it without the congressman's help. His test scores were toward the bottom of the bubble.

"Little Johnny got in."

HIS COLLEAGUES' warning failed to deter Michael Dannenberg, whose cordial, self-effacing demeanor concealed a dogged resolve. Dannenberg's conviction that legacy preference was an unfair perquisite for the privileged, and his sympathy for the high-achieving working-class applicants it displaced, were rooted in his own experience. Growing up without a father in Yonkers and Ossining, New York, home of Sing Sing prison, he was raised by his mother and grandparents, none of whom had college degrees. Disabled by childhood polio, his mother worked for the state Department of Motor Vehicles, while his grandfather was a clothing salesman. The family's principal recreation was going to Belmont or Aqueduct race tracks on weekends, where his grandparents would bet a few dollars on the horses. By the age of seven, Michael was reading the *Racing Form* and analyzing the odds. "I'm convinced I did well academically because of my time at the track," he told me.

Admitted to Cornell University and the State University of New York at Binghamton, Michael enrolled at Boston University instead because it offered the best financial aid package. BU was "total culture shock," he recalled. Many of his classmates had boosted their SAT scores by taking test-prep courses, which he hadn't heard of. "Everyone had a computer. I didn't have a computer. I was very unhappy. I didn't want to stay. There were all these rich kids, and I didn't fit in." But he persevered, writing for the student newspaper, where he found like-minded friends.

Supplementing his scholarship with federal aid and work-study jobs, he graduated magna cum laude in 1991 and headed to Washington with $1,000—his entire savings—to hunt for a job on Capitol Hill. That same spring, he read a cover story in the *Washington Monthly* headlined "Why Are Droves of Unqualified, Unprepared Kids Getting into Our Top Colleges?" The article, by John Larew, lambasted not affirmative action but legacy preference. "I remember thinking, 'This is terrible,'" Dannenberg said. "It stoked a flame for me with respect to fairness and educational opportunities. To me, legacy is a civil rights issue, a question of morality."

Answering an ad, Michael interviewed for a job with Rhode Island senator Claiborne Pell, sponsor of the need-based grants that bear his name. "I said at my interview, 'I know these programs, I've been a recipient,'" he recalled. As a legislative aide for Senator Pell, Michael pushed for financial rewards to states that generously funded elementary and secondary schools in low-income neighborhoods. After the proposal was narrowly defeated, he decided to go to law school. Now able to afford a test-prep course, he aced the LSATs and enrolled at Yale Law for his first encounter with the Ivy League.

Yale "was even worse than BU, it was old-money rich," he said. "I sat there thinking, 'Oh, God, I'm part of a club that I hate.'" One evening in his dorm, he began arguing about affirmative action with a conservative student in his constitutional law class. The student was a legacy at Yale Law, which gave preference to alumni children. Michael snapped at him, "You're the face of affirmative action." Infuriated, the classmate insisted that he had earned his admission, but Michael was unconvinced. "The truth is, in the elite schools, a lot of kids with better grades and test scores are turned down," he said.

He taught at Stanford after his law-school graduation in 1998, but then accepted Senator Kennedy's job offer, intending to resume his quest for equity in K–12 education. When the affirmative action issue heated up, he saw an opening to bring fairness to college admissions as well—and do something about the preference that had outraged him ever since he read the Larew article a decade earlier. In his view, an anti-legacy, pro-affirmative-action message would position the Democrats as the party that believed in rewarding merit as well as promoting diversity. He wouldn't be easily dissuaded.

To LIBERAL CRITICS, President George W. Bush is the face of legacy preference. They note that although he opposes affirmative action, he benefited from admissions breaks largely reserved for rich whites. Grandson of a Connecticut senator, son of a future president already prospering in the oil industry, the third-generation legacy was admitted to Yale despite coasting through prep school with mediocre grades, a 566 verbal SAT score, and few noteworthy athletic or extracurricular achievements.

His Yale record was equally undistinguished. "To those of you who received honors, awards, and distinctions, I say, 'Well done,'" he joked in his 2001 commencement address. "And to the C students, I say you too can be president of the United States."

But concentrating on one individual misses the larger picture. The president is part of Washington's legacy establishment—the bipartisan array of powerful insiders in the executive branch, Congress, and the judiciary who sent their children to their old schools or who are themselves legacies. There are also, to be sure, legacy establishments in other sectors of American society, from Wall Street to the media: one study found that 42 percent of corporate leaders graduated from twelve elite universities and 10 percent attended one of thirty-three exclusive prep schools, while "most of the media elite enjoyed socially privileged upbringings."

For Washington's power brokers, few tools have been more vital than legacy preference in catapulting forward political careers or consolidating a family's social status across generations. Political dynasties such as the Bushes (Yale) and Kennedys (Harvard) are built on legacy preference, ensuring their future generations continued access to elite higher education. Whatever their ideological bent, few members of the legacy establishment are eager to abolish the admissions edge that perpetuates their wealth and power—or even, I found, to be interviewed about it.

All three of the major-party candidates in the last two presidential elections are personally acquainted with legacy preference. Like President Bush, Massachusetts senator John Kerry was a Yale legacy with a C average in college, including four D's in his freshman year. "I always told my dad that D stood for distinction," Kerry told the *Boston Globe* in 2005.

Both Kerry and Bush belonged to Yale's Skull and Bones society, forging contacts that would help them in later life. Kerry is also, like the president, a Yale parent; his daughter, Vanessa, played varsity lacrosse there and graduated with highest honors in 1999. While his 2004 running mate, North Carolina senator John Edwards, a state university graduate who was the first member of his family to go to college, criticized alumni child preference, Kerry was noticeably silent on the subject.

Former vice president Albert Gore Jr., the Democratic presidential candidate in 2000, is a Harvard alumnus and ex-member of the university's board of overseers. He is not a legacy—his father attended a state teachers' college before becoming elected to the Senate—but appears bent on being patriarch of a Harvard clan. Although Harvard accepts only one in ten applicants, all four of Vice President Gore's children enrolled there. The first three, Karenna, Kristin, and Sarah, attended the National Cathedral School, an elite Washington private school for girls. All were outstanding students, although Sarah was cited by police as a sixteen-year-old high school junior for underage alcohol possession. She was "very up front" with Harvard about the incident, one person familiar with the situation told me. "She acknowledged she had been immature. There had been a number of huge issues that had to do with her father's public life and the pressure on the kids."

In addition to being legacies, Kristin and Sarah received athletic preference as lacrosse players. "They weren't top recruits, but they were certainly on a list that I submitted to the admissions office," recalled Carole Kleinfelder, former Harvard women's lacrosse coach. "On that second tier, you're not going to get anybody in who needs academic help. It's going to be somebody with legacy, somebody that's already got their foot in the door. It's another push." Sarah, whom Kleinfelder considered the stronger recruit, never played at Harvard, while Kristin was on the team for two years.

All three Gore daughters graduated with high honors from Harvard. Karenna subsequently attended Columbia Law School and gave a speech seconding her father's nomination for president at the 2000 Democratic convention. Kristin, who worked on the *Harvard Lampoon,* became a television comedy writer and also published a novel.

For their younger brother, Albert Gore III, the legacy edge apparently offset concerns about both his behavior and his academic record. As noted earlier, he was an average student. After St. Albans suspended him for smoking marijuana, he transferred to Sidwell Friends, and was later cited for driving nearly 100 miles per hour. While in college, he was ticketed for driving under the influence and charged with marijuana possession.

Gore's running mate in 2000 started a family tradition at Harvard's archrival. Connecticut senator Joseph Lieberman received undergraduate and law degrees from Yale, as did his son, Matthew. Counting Lieberman and Kerry, fifteen U.S. senators are legacies and/or alumni parents. The preferences start at the top, with majority leader William Frist's three sons.

Senator Frist, a Republican member of the education committee, joined the Bush administration in opposing affirmative action at the University of Michigan, but his sons have enjoyed preferences of a different kind. As noted in the introduction, Dr. Frist has close ties to Princeton as a graduate, ex-trustee, and donor. His eldest son, Harrison, enrolled at Princeton in 2002, although he had not been in the top fifth of his

St. Albans class. Princeton's admissions office, which evaluates candidates on a 1–5 academic scale, with 1 being the best, ranked him a 5, normally a near-certain rejection. But Princeton president Shirley Tilghman, who considered him one of her highest admissions priorities for the year, prevailed on the staff to accept him. As a Princeton sophomore, Harrison pleaded guilty to drunk-driving charges. A history major, he graduated without honors in 2006.

Princeton also admitted the senator's youngest son Bryan, who applied to its early decision program and was expected to enter in fall 2006. At St. Albans, Bryan was a "class leader and a very good student," said Sherrie McKenna, former director of college counseling. However, Bryan Frist did not make Cum Laude Society at St. Albans.

The senator's middle son Jonathan was arrested for drunk driving at the age of seventeen while still in high school. Because he was legally a minor, the disposition of his case is private. Like Harrison and Bryan, Jonathan did not rank in the top 20 percent of his class at St. Albans as signified by Cum Laude Society membership. Nonetheless, he enrolled in 2005 at highly ranked Vanderbilt University in Nashville, where nearly 80 percent of freshmen were in the top tenth of their high school class. A person familiar with his high school record said that he was "admissible" by Vanderbilt standards but "not in the top range by any means." Jonathan's father was not only Vanderbilt's home-state senator but also a former faculty member; Dr. Frist founded its organ transplant center in 1989.

One of Dr. Frist's likely rivals for the 2008 Republican nomination, Arizona senator John McCain, saw his legacy status as not a boon but a burden. "There were times in my life when I harbored a secret resentment that my life's course seemed so preordained," he wrote in his 1999 memoir, *Faith of My Fathers*. No doubt he was thinking partly of his college choice; he followed his father and grandfather, both admirals, to the U.S. Naval Academy. "When that baby was born, I assumed he was going to go to the Naval Academy," his mother told the *New Yorker*. Bowing to his parents' wishes, McCain reluctantly accepted what he later called his "unavoidable appointment." Displaying the independence that was itself a family tradition, the third-generation plebe rebelled against what he considered the academy's petty discipline and bullying upperclassmen and caroused through college, graduating fifth from the bottom of his class.

Even in the Senate, sometimes called a millionaires' club, several members with legacy connections stand out for their great wealth, which makes their children doubly attractive to college development and admissions offices. Three such senators belong to families on *Forbes* magazine's list of the four hundred wealthiest Americans: Senator Frist through his brother, health care magnate Thomas Frist Jr. (net worth $1.7 billion in 2005), and Senator Kerry through his wife, heiress Teresa Heinz (net worth $750 million in 2004; she dropped off the list in 2005). Minnesota Democrat and Yale graduate Mark Dayton is linked to two billionaire families: the Dayton retailing family (with an estimated net worth in 1998 of $1.3 billion) and, through ex-wife Alida, the Rockefellers. Their son, Andrew Rockefeller Dayton, attended Breck School in Golden Valley, Minnesota, before entering Yale as a third-generation legacy in 2002. Senator Dayton said that his son was admitted on merit and that Yale has never asked him for legislative help.

One senatorial son took a roundabout route to legacy status. John Bingaman, son of New Mexico senator Jeff Bingaman, believed his record at Sidwell Friends fell short of Ivy League standards and enrolled at New York University. "I felt I needed to spend a year elsewhere to prove myself," he told me. He then applied for transfers to Harvard, his father's alma mater, and Stanford, where his mother received her undergraduate degree and his father attended law school. Both universities give an edge to alumni children in the transfer process, and both accepted him. "Legacy could have played a role, but I'd like to think I was qualified to get into Harvard," John told me. "I did very well at NYU." He graduated from Harvard in 2002 with high honors in economics and now works in finance.

New York senator Charles Schumer also went to Harvard. His daughter Jessica matriculated there in 2002 and joined the *Harvard Crimson* as a photographer and writer. In a 2004 article, she recalled writing her college application essay about her "love affair" with the New York Yankees and lamented, "My job this summer in investment banking doesn't give me much time to follow the Yankees."

Since alumni children constitute nearly one-fourth of Notre Dame's student body, it's not surprising to find a legacy from that university ensconced on Capitol Hill. Daniel Lungren, a conservative Republican representative from California, comes from a classic Notre Dame family. His father, the late John C. Lungren, was president of Notre Dame's alumni association and President Nixon's personal physician. Daniel Lungren, two of his brothers, and his son graduated from Notre Dame, as did three of his nieces, while three of his sisters attended St. Mary's College across the street, and a fourth enrolled at Notre Dame for a year before transferring.

In a prior stint in Congress from 1979 to 1989, he said, he watched Fighting Irish football games and worked closely on legislation with other Notre Dame graduates on both sides of the aisle, such as former Kentucky congressman Romano Mazzoli, a Democrat and past president of the Notre Dame alumni club of Kentucky. "I've always felt that Notre Dame alums have a natural affinity and work together very well," said Lungren, who returned to Congress in 2004. "It used to be, you'd find members active and attending in the Notre Dame Club of Washington."

Congressman Lungren, who said he was "lucky enough" to be named alumnus of the year by the club, is a staunch defender of legacy preference. "I've recommended people, children of Domers, who had outstanding records and weren't accepted," he said. "But they do set aside a certain percentage [of slots for alumni children]. Look, it's a private institution. It can make the rules it wishes, so long as it's not discriminating on race, which it doesn't do.

"A university should stand for something. Notre Dame does stand for being a Catholic institution, and part of making sure that occurs is maintaining connections with graduates. One way of maintaining connections is considering legacy as part of their admissions policy."

MISSOURI SENATOR Christopher "Kit" Bond, who graduated from Princeton in 1960, was well positioned to help his alma mater. As chairman of a Senate appropriations subcommittee with jurisdiction over independent agencies, he wielded enormous influence over the National Science Foundation budget. In 1999, when NSF started a grant program for graduate students who taught in elementary and secondary schools, Princeton became concerned that the agency's existing graduate fellowship program, which had provided research funds for several of its Nobel laureates, would be neglected. The university lobbied Senator Bond, who successfully pushed to raise the stipends for the traditional fellowships to the same level as the new grants.

Princeton has been equally considerate of the senator. The same year Senator Bond bailed out the fellowship program, his son graduated from St. Albans, where he was not in the top fifth of his class, and enrolled at Princeton. According to a person familiar with his record, Sam was a "middle-of-the-pack" candidate. Due to legacy preference and perhaps his father's pivotal role in science funding, Sam was one of the priority cases recommended for admission that year by Princeton's then-president, Harold Shapiro. Sam, who graduated from Princeton without honors in 2003, became a second lieutenant in the Marines. (About 45 percent of Princeton seniors graduate with honors, high honors, or highest honors.)

Shana Stribling, the senator's deputy press secretary, acknowledged that Princeton is "near and dear to his heart" and lobbied him on the fellowships: "This was a pretty big program for them." But she said he has long supported funding for science and math research and that his advocacy for fellowships was unrelated to his son's admission. "Legacy always helps, but I don't think Sam would have had trouble getting in anywhere he was trying to go," she said.

"Senator Bond understood how important these fellowships were," recalled Nan Wells, then director of Princeton's office of government affairs in Washington. "What he saw especially was the need for native-born scientists. The chairman of our research board at Princeton talked to him."

If Princeton attracts more than its share of political offspring—some

more academically outstanding than others—that's not entirely an accident. Its aggressive lobbying operation in Washington, D.C., which Wells
headed from its founding in 1981 until 2002, keeps tabs on Washington
power brokers with children applying to Princeton, and passes word back
to the central administration. The president's office, in turn, includes these
students on the list of priority applicants that it sends to admissions.

"If you know someone, you'll make the university aware that their
application is coming in," Wells said. But, she emphasized, "there's never
any trade-off with admissions. Some universities do that sort of thing.
We didn't."

One applicant Wells was aware of was Louisine Frelinghuysen, daughter of Rodney Frelinghuysen, a Republican congressman from New Jersey.
Although Louisine was not a legacy—Princeton had rejected her father, who
graduated from Hobart College in Geneva, New York—she was descended
from one of the university's oldest families. There was a Frelinghuysen
in Princeton's very first graduating class, and dozens of family members
had gone there over the centuries, including two senators. Congressman
Frelinghuysen's father (also a congressman), two brothers, and two nephews
were all Princeton graduates.

Of equal significance to Princeton was that Rodney Frelinghuysen
bore no grudge for his admissions rebuff. Although he did not represent
Princeton's district, the congressman—New Jersey's senior representative
on the House appropriations committee—reaped millions of dollars in
government funding for the university's science research. In 1998, he
sponsored an amendment that increased the NSF budget by $70 million.
From his seat on the energy and water development subcommittee, he
took good care of Princeton's research into nuclear fusion.

In April 2001, when Louisine was a junior at Groton, Princeton presented her father with the university's Champion of Science award, calling him "instrumental in securing funding . . . for fusion research at the
Princeton Plasma Physics Laboratory. In this year's budget, he worked
with the White House and the secretary of energy to include $248.5 in the
energy budget for the fusion sciences program."

Louisine, who applied in 2002, was a stellar candidate: "exceptionally well qualified," Wells says. The congressman told me, "I married a woman who's very good at math and science. My daughter won one of the major science projects in high school with some other young man. She got in on her own steam, I assure you, I keep hands off." Still, Princeton accepts only about one in nine applicants and rejects many excellent students. In case Louisine needed a tip, the family ties and fusion funding supplied it.

Congressman Frelinghuysen favors legacy preference. "It's always good to have in the mix some of the sons and daughters of prior graduates," he said. "It often assists in their charitable giving."

Louisine Frelinghuysen isn't the only Groton-educated daughter of a member of Congress to go to Princeton. Christina Maloney had an SAT score of 1330 and ranked 46th out of 79 graduates of Groton in 1998—the same class that included Henry Park. She was rejected by Brown and Dartmouth and wait-listed by Bates and Davidson colleges. But she got into Princeton, where three-quarters of students have SAT scores of 1380 or above. Her father and grandfather attended Princeton, while her mother, Carolyn Maloney, is a Democratic member of Congress from New York City. Congresswoman Maloney told me that her daughter graduated from Princeton in 2002 with high honors in sociology. She added, "Every child at Groton could do the work at any college in America" because the school is so rigorous.

Politically connected Princeton legacies also include 2000 graduate Mary Bonner Baker, an actress and daughter of former Secretary of State James Baker III, a former Princeton trustee (and himself a legacy). Among the ranks of nonlegacy Princetonians are both daughters of Iowa senator Tom Harkin, an Iowa State University alumnus and a member of the Senate education committee. Amy Harkin graduated in 1998 and Jennifer Harkin in 2004, both without honors.

President Bush's niece Lauren was admitted in 2002 even though she applied after the deadline. The anthropology major graduated without honors in 2006. And despite the populist stance of her father, North Carolina State University alumnus and 2004 Democratic vice presidential candidate John Edwards, Catharine Edwards not only enrolled at Princeton but joined the blue-blooded Ivy club. She graduated with honors in politics in 2004.

Although West Virginia senator Jay Rockefeller is a Harvard man, the Rockefeller family has ties to Princeton as well. Princeton's Rockefeller College is named after the senator's father, John D. Rockefeller III, who graduated in 1929. The senator's youngest child, Justin, emulated his grandfather by enrolling at Princeton in 1998. Justin had attended St. Albans, where he was active in student government but did not rank in the top 20 percent of his class. He told me that Princeton also admitted his three older siblings, but they went to Yale and Stanford instead. A "little nervous" that Princeton would decide to reject him before he too could spurn it, he wrote to Fred Hargadon, then dean of admission, giving his word that he would matriculate if accepted.

At Princeton, Justin was concerned about the tendency of affluent white students to congregate among themselves. As vice president of Ivy, he sponsored a series of dialogues about race relations on campus and in the exclusive eating club itself. He and minority students participating in the discussions "really bonded," he told me. "There were tears, hugs, everything." He also sought, unsuccessfully, to replace portraits on the club walls of "1930s white guys," which he felt were intimidating to minorities, with more contemporary and diverse pictures. He graduated in 2002 with a degree in politics; although he did not earn honors, he was nominated for a prize for best senior thesis. He recently cofounded Generation Engage, a nonprofit aimed at boosting voting rates among eighteen-to-twenty-four-year-olds with no college experience.

Justin told me he has "absolutely no way of knowing" whether he and his siblings owed their Princeton admissions to their family name. "Ideally, college admissions would be based simply on merit, but we're not there yet as a society," he said, adding that he supports preference for minority and low-income applicants: "Someone who's come up through the ranks facing more adversity should absolutely be noticed, and his or her struggle taken into account."

Other senatorial offspring at Princeton also displayed a social conscience. Like their father, Maryland senator and Princeton trustee Paul

Sarbanes, Janet Sarbanes and her two brothers attended Princeton. And like their father, who fought against anti-Semitism during his student days, the three younger Sarbaneses were campus activists, with a passion for social justice stirred by childhood attendance at a predominantly African American elementary school in Baltimore.

Janet told me that she and her brothers were outstanding high school students; she finished second in her class at a private Baltimore school for girls. "My father loved Princeton," she said. "*Princeton* was a holy word in our house. We had all the benefits of being raised with the Princeton idea, of the well-rounded scholar-athlete with many extracurriculars. Culturally, we had all these advantages when it came time to apply. My parents were really strong that we should deserve to get into Princeton on the level of grades and sports and SAT scores. But we had the benefit of them knowing what it would take to get us into Princeton."

At Princeton, Janet said, she was surrounded by privilege. "I've never met people with as much wealth as I did at Princeton, and I never will again," she said. She spoke out for women's rights and was responsible for replacing references to "boys" and "sons" in the school song with gender-neutral lyrics. She passed out the alternative lyrics at football games, and buttons with the slogan "Expand the tradition." Janet graduated in 1989 with high honors in comparative literature and now teaches in the School of Critical Studies at California Institute of the Arts in Valencia, California.

Asked about legacy preference, she said, "There is an argument for keeping families involved in schools to maintain tradition and endowment, but it's certainly valuing that over diversity and equal opportunity." Later, she called me back to add, "In some ways, you could say my brothers and I make the argument for legacy admissions, because we were raised with this idea of Princeton as a kind of beloved community. When we got to the school and saw that it was failing to live up to that mission in various ways, we saw it as our responsibility to do something about it. So I told you about my involvement in women's rights, and my brother Michael was involved in getting Princeton to divest out of South Africa.

"There's this kind of alternative legacy tradition of making Princeton a more socially responsible place. That said, I certainly don't think it takes precedence over increasing the opportunities for socially and economically disadvantaged students to earn a Princeton degree."

DESPITE THE political risks, Senator Kennedy encouraged Michael Dannenberg to attack the admissions preference that had helped solidify the Kennedy family's political dynasty. In an April 2005 interview in his Washington office, relaxing in an easy chair with his Portuguese water dog, Sunny, dozing beside him, the senator described legacy preference as an "anachronism" violating his "core commitment" to access to higher education for low-income students. Because of admissions breaks for alumni children and early decision applicants, "a big chunk of the class is already spoken for," he said. Like legacy preference, the admissions advantage— estimated at 100 SAT points—for early applicants mainly helps affluent white students, in part because the requirement that candidates attend if accepted is a deterrent to low-income families who want to shop for the best financial aid deal.

Thick-skinned from a long and turbulent career, and with a Senate seat as safe as any in the country, Kennedy wasn't overly worried that critics would call him a hypocrite because he had enjoyed legacy preference, or dredge up his suspension from Harvard for cheating on a Spanish exam. ("Based on Teddy Kennedy's academic career, he's the one that ought to be giving us more guidance on this," Congressman Lungren said sarcastically when I brought up Kennedy's anti-legacy efforts.)

The senator—about whom a political opponent once remarked that if his name were Edward Moore instead of Edward Moore Kennedy, his candidacy "would be a joke"—said his Harvard admission wasn't due only to his famous surname. He ranked in the "bottom of the top quarter" at his prep school, Milton Academy, he said: "My last two years there, I did pretty well." None of his three children went to Harvard, he added, because they wanted to follow "different pathways" from their father. "It's a lot different now. There are so many good colleges."

Later, through an aide, the senator said he is "not convinced that legacy preferences are essential" to alumni giving. "Over the last fifty years, colleges have reduced their legacy preference, and financially they're in better shape than ever. . . . By and large, I think people give to their alma mater because of their personal experience and connection to the school."

Despite being a third-generation Notre Dame graduate, Danica Petroshius, then Kennedy's chief education adviser, backed Dannenberg as well. "The thing I can't get beyond, when I talk to higher education officials, is, Why is legacy important besides making donors happy?" Petroshius told me. "There are a lot of smart people out there who could find another way to make donors happy."

In early 2002, Dannenberg gained another key ally. Sharing a ride to New York City with an aide to North Carolina senator John Edwards, he railed against legacy preference. Impressed, the aide then pitched legacy to Senator Edwards as an issue for his upcoming presidential campaign. The senator "had an immediate visceral and ethical reaction that legacy preference was wrong," the aide told me.

That November, in a speech on education delivered at the University of Maryland, Senator Edwards derided legacy preference as "a birthright out of eighteenth-century British aristocracy, not twenty-first-century American democracy." The senator decided not to call for federal limits on alumni child preference, instead issuing a challenge to colleges and universities to end legacy and early decision voluntarily.

"It wasn't a hard call for John Edwards to say, 'Legacy preferences are wrong,' " a person familiar with his thinking told me. "It was more difficult to say, 'What's the federal role here? Bar them? A sunshine law? Just jawbone?' We spent a lot of time thinking about how to handle that. What ultimately became clear was that just the act of standing up and saying this was wrong is a big deal. There is a legitimate question about whether you want the federal government dictating policies like this. It wasn't necessary to cross that bridge."

Still, Edwards's speech was a breakthrough for the anti-legacy effort, and it combined with two events the next month to generate momentum and media attention for the cause. On December 2, 2002, the U.S. Supreme Court agreed to hear arguments in the Michigan case—or, more precisely, two cases, one involving law school admissions, the other undergraduate.

Three days later, Senate Republican leader Trent Lott appeared to endorse racial segregation by proclaiming at a one-hundredth-birthday party for South Carolina senator Strom Thurmond that the country "wouldn't have had all these problems" if it had elected Thurmond as president in 1948, when he was the candidate of the white-supremacist Dixiecrat party. Not only did Lott's remarks remind Americans why affirmative action was needed, but the senator himself, seeking to defend himself against charges of being a racist, went on Black Entertainment Television and criticized legacy preference for discriminating against minorities.

On December 20, Kennedy sought to capitalize on these developments. He and House education committee chairman George Miller wrote to President Bush, citing the Lott controversy and asking him to file a friend-of-the-court brief supporting affirmative action in the Michigan case. They also slipped in the first public signal of Kennedy's anti-legacy plans: "We will be working in the next Congress on a legislative initiative that will help universities to implement fair admissions programs that provide opportunities for minority and first-generation college students."

On January 15, 2003, I reported on the anti-legacy movement in a front-page *Wall Street Journal* article, which was followed by other articles, editorials, and opinion pieces in influential publications—including a *New York Times* column by conservative pundit William F. Buckley, who had run for a seat on the Yale Corporation thirty-five years earlier on a pro-legacy platform. "There are tribal instincts in life, colleges and universities are part of life, and nobody has proved that any harm whatever has been done by private colleges writing their own admissions policies," Buckley declared.

Despite this media flurry, not all of Senator Kennedy's Democratic colleagues were eager to wave the anti-legacy banner. Some of them were alarmed at the prospect of alienating the University of Michigan and other higher education allies that were spending time and money to defend affirmative action in court, and argued that an anti-legacy proposal could backfire by undermining the minority preferences it was intended to save. Congress, they noted, traditionally stayed out of college admissions. If Kennedy introduced a bill to ban legacy preference, the Republicans might retaliate by adding an amendment to prohibit considering race in admissions. The Democrats would then be hard put to justify eliminating one preference, legacy, that was allowed by the Constitution, and not the other, affirmative action, which was in legal jeopardy.

Bethany Little, an education staffer to Washington senator Patty Murray from 2001 to 2003, agreed with Dannenberg. "I felt like the best defense is a good offense," Bethany told me. "We should come out swinging. If you want to talk about what's really unjust in higher education, let's not talk about affirmative action, let's talk about legacy preference. The biggest single inequity still out there in college admissions is the legacy system. It seemed almost ridiculous to be having a debate about whether it was acceptable to consider race when for a lot of people it was perfectly socially acceptable to consider race and class anyway."

Although Dannenberg and his allies favored an outright ban on legacy preference, they needed a less drastic option to win over skeptical committee Democrats. They devised an alternative approach—penalizing colleges that practiced early decision and legacy preference and that also had significantly higher graduation rates for white students with college-educated parents than for minorities and first-generation college students. These schools would be required either to give up early decision or legacy policies or spend more money to reduce dropout rates of African American, Hispanic, and first-generation students. The proposal would affect more than eighty colleges, including five of the seven Ivies: Brown, Columbia, Cornell, Dartmouth, and Penn. Dannenberg hoped this idea would be more palatable to colleges than a ban, because it would not affect alumni donations.

Before committing to this idea, Democratic staffers wanted to gauge outside reaction. Since Democrats were still divided over the legacy issue, Dannenberg didn't want the proposal to be traced to Kennedy. Instead, he floated it through a friendly advocacy group, the Hispanic Education Coalition. One of its staffers, Marilyn McAdam, now deceased, "had pushed the coalition to realize that legacy policy was not going to benefit Hispanic students and this was an issue they should be vocal on," Bethany Little said.

The higher education community wasn't fooled. On April 29, a sympathetic lobbyist warned Kennedy's staff that any attack on legacy preference and early decision would "create a massive firestorm of protest from colleges and universities . . . Go there at your own peril."

The prediction was accurate; higher education groups, such as the National Association of Independent Colleges and Universities and the American Council on Education, organized a low-profile but intense campaign against the proposal. They didn't send out a "major blast" calling for colleges to denounce it publicly, one lobbyist told me, for fear that it would appeal to the media and public opinion. "We didn't want this crazy idea to take off," the lobbyist said. Instead, emissaries from private colleges in their home states visited the Democratic committee members, conveying the message that the proposal went too far and that any federal intervention in college admissions, even one designed to help minority students graduate from college, would in the end damage affirmative action.

Danica Petroshius told me that two lobbyists for private colleges buttonholed Kennedy in Massachusetts, urging him to abandon his anti-legacy stance. (One of the lobbyists, whom I subsequently contacted, said he did not approach Kennedy in person but wrote him a letter.) The response was "rough," she said. "As soon as they heard it was being floated, the lobbyists called us screaming. They said it was the biggest thing they would fight. We didn't even have a proposal yet, and they were already saying no. Behind the scenes, in the boardrooms, they talk about this more than they talk about Pell grants."

"We all heard from a lot of schools," Bethany Little said. "When I would talk to them, I explained what the policy would be, how unlikely they would be to be affected. We heard a lot of slippery-slope language— 'What you're saying isn't that bad, but it could open the door to federal control of admissions policy.' Certain members are more sensitive to the higher education lobby than others."

Asked about the reaction of the higher education lobby, Senator Kennedy smiled. "It was a firestorm up there," he said. "These were very good friends we worked with on education policy." He added that colleges have a tendency to cry wolf. When Congress adopted more stringent rules in 1998 for reporting data on campus crimes, he said, "you would have thought they'd have to close the universities down. Now it's routine to disclose that information."

Nevertheless, the blowback was effective. According to Bethany Little, some Democratic committee members began wavering, including a longtime friend of Kennedy's, Senator Christopher Dodd from Connecticut, who was besieged by complaints from private colleges in his state. Forced on the defensive, Dannenberg became demoralized. "Michael is a true believer. He believes strongly in our allies and that we're all after the same thing in the end," Bethany Little said. "He thought people would jump and say, 'This is an injustice we can do something about.' He was a little disillusioned."

"The prospect of losing this fight to ban legacy preference turns my stomach," Dannenberg emailed his girlfriend on June 2. "If I can't convince Democrats to get rid of something as wrong, as immoral, as legacy preferences, what's the point of being here?"

She answered, "The point is to raise it, raise it, raise it and keep fighting."

WHILE DANNENBERG fought on, the Supreme Court was poised to decide the Michigan cases. The Court had last weighed in on affirmative action in college admissions a quarter century earlier in *Bakke*, when by a 5–4 vote it had ruled against a white medical student who challenged his rejection by the University of California. Because of *Bakke*'s narrow margin, and because the majority was split over the rationale for affirmative action—was it necessary to remedy past discrimination, as four justices contended, or to promote diversity, as Justice Lewis F. Powell Jr. argued?—that decision failed to resolve the issue. Instead, the conflict became increasingly polarized, with courts or voters in a few states—including California, site of the *Bakke* case—banning affirmative action, but with some private and state universities, including Michigan, becoming more blatant in considering race in admissions.

Michigan's 150-point undergraduate admissions scale, which awarded an automatic 20 points to blacks, Hispanics, and Native Americans, smacked of a racial quota system—considered unconstitutional under *Bakke*. The law school's admissions process, also under challenge from a rejected white applicant, did not assign points but considered race in the context of each individual applicant's overall suitability, conforming more closely to *Bakke* guidelines.

Whatever the Court would decide in the Michigan cases was considered likely to shape private college admissions as well. Many observers of the relatively conservative Court believed that it would strike down race-based preferences. But they overlooked one element in affirmative action's favor—the Court's desire to preserve legacy preference. Dominated by Ivy Leaguers, the Supreme Court has long been a domain for the best and brightest of the legacy establishment. Among its most famous legacies are Harvard grad Oliver Wendell Holmes Jr., son of a well-known essayist who attended the school, and former president and chief justice William Howard Taft, one of a long line of his family members to attend Yale.

Five of the nine justices in 2003 or their children qualified for legacy preference. Two justices, Stephen Breyer and Anthony Kennedy, have family ties to Stanford University that span three generations. A third, Sandra Day O'Connor, is a Stanford graduate and mother of two Stanford alumni, and has served on the university's board of trustees. Justice Ruth Bader Ginsburg and her daughter Jane were the first mother and daughter ever to attend Harvard Law School. Justice John Paul Stevens followed in the footsteps of his father, Ernest Stevens, at both the University of Chicago and Northwestern University Law School. None of the justice's children went to Chicago, according to the university, but four of his nephews and nieces have attended.

These justices, like everyone else wrestling with the affirmative action debate, inevitably filtered it through the prism of their own personal history. Although legacy preference wasn't directly at issue in the Michigan case, it appeared to be on the justices' minds.

Both the Michigan law and undergraduate admissions processes gave preference to legacies as well as minorities. On the 150-point scale Michigan used to rank undergraduate candidates, alumni children received 4 points. During oral arguments on April 1, Justice Breyer drew the parallel. "What is the difference," the justice asked a lawyer representing the white students challenging affirmative action, between a university spurning a student because he isn't a minority, or because he isn't the child of an alumnus? The lawyer answered that the equal protection clause of the U.S. Constitution prohibits race discrimination but not discrimination on the basis of alumni affiliation—even if the effect is to favor whites.

Breyer was familiar with the legacy boost. His father, Irving, attended Stanford, as did his son, Michael, who graduated in 1997. That year, Justice Breyer gave the Stanford commencement address. After being introduced by his longtime friend Gerhard Casper, then president of the university, Justice Breyer confided to the crowd that "this morning I gave Michael a Stanford ring. . . . As I did so, I thought of my father, for it was his ring, given him on his graduation seventy years ago. Yesterday I walked through the Inner Quad and saw the three paving stones that mark my family's three graduations: my father's graduation, my own in 1959, and yours, Michael, now."

Before admitting Michael Breyer, Stanford placed him on its wait list—a frequent refuge for legacy applicants with borderline credentials. Former Stanford admissions dean Jean Fetter described the waiting list in a 1995 book as "an appropriate place to acknowledge any legacy preference." Susan Case, former director of college counseling at Milton Academy in Milton, Massachusetts, where Michael Breyer went to high school, confirmed that he was wait-listed by Stanford. "I don't know that legacy was the reason he was admitted," she told me. "He was a strong candidate in his own right." Another person familiar with his Milton credentials said the legacy connection "obviously contributed."

Justice Ginsburg and her husband, Martin, both attended Harvard Law School. (The justice completed her degree at Columbia.) Their daughter, Jane Ginsburg, told me she had excellent undergraduate grades and was accepted at three other top law schools besides Harvard. The younger Ginsburg—who became a professor at Columbia Law, where her mother used to teach—described her attitude toward being a legacy this way: "However you got in, you're in. Now you just have to prove you belong."

Justice Kennedy—son of Stanford alumna Gladys McLeod Kennedy—went to Stanford, as did his two sons and one daughter. Both sons, Justin and Gregory, graduated from Jesuit High School in Carmichael, California. Justice Kennedy's daughter, Kristin Marie, graduated in 1986 from St. Francis High School, a Catholic girls' school in Sacramento, where she was an honor-roll student and played on the tennis team, according to the school.

Sandra Day O'Connor wrote in *Lazy B,* her 2002 memoir about growing up on a cattle ranch by that name, that her father "always regretted that he did not attend Stanford." She fulfilled his dream, going there both as an undergraduate and a law student—as did her husband, John J. O'Connor III. Two of their three sons, Scott and Jay, enrolled at Stanford; the other, Brian, went to Colorado College. Jay, the youngest, was admitted to Stanford in 1980, while his mother was on the university's board of trustees.

Jay O'Connor, a technology executive in the San Francisco area, told me he applied to Stanford and four Ivy League schools and was accepted by all but Princeton, where he was wait-listed. In high school, he said, he was ranked near the top of his class and was editor in chief of the school newspaper and president of the debate team. He declined to divulge his SAT scores but said they "met or exceeded the standard ranges" published by the top-tier schools. "I was seen by all of the schools to which I applied as an outstanding academic candidate," he told me. "I don't know what happened inside any of those schools. I have no way of knowing that." He said that his brother Scott was an outstanding student and state champion swimmer in high school, and was also accepted at top universities with which their parents weren't affiliated.

Jay added: "I'm a big believer that you should make your own mark. Who your parents are shouldn't be relevant."

His mother evidently disagreed. Like Justice Breyer, Justice O'Connor had also delivered Stanford's commencement address—in 1982, when Jay was a sophomore, and Scott had already graduated. "There is no greater, more foresighted office in this land of ours than the admissions office of Stanford University," she told graduates, expressing the wish that "you will all be lucky enough to have your children attend this paradise on earth . . . that we call Stanford."

IF THE COURT had struck down affirmative action, Justice O'Connor's dream of a legacy paradise would have been imperiled. Civil rights advocates seeking payback would likely have mounted campus protests against legacy preference—and swung their full weight behind banning it. Indeed, in California and Georgia, where voters or federal courts had prohibited affirmative action, state universities had dropped legacy preference under pressure from civil rights groups. In a brief filed before the Supreme Court, minority students at Michigan and elsewhere cited legacy preference as one of several factors favoring whites that affirmative action was needed to offset. The implication was that the fates of minority and legacy preferences were intertwined; should the first be scuttled, the second would have to go as well, or admissions would tilt even more toward white privilege.

That prospect became moot on June 23, 2003, when, by a 5–4 vote, the Court upheld affirmative action in admissions to Michigan law school. Four of the five justices from legacy families voted to uphold affirmative action; the sole exception was Anthony Kennedy. Justice David Souter, a childless Harvard graduate, was the fifth affirmative action vote. In the less pivotal undergraduate case, the Court struck down Michigan's point system because it lacked "individualized consideration" and made race a "decisive" factor.

Justice O'Connor, who had been regarded as a swing vote, wrote the majority opinion in the law school case, *Grutter v. Bollinger,* reasserting Justice Powell's rationale that universities may consider race among other factors to promote their goal of student body diversity. In a tone reminiscent of her Stanford address twenty-one years earlier, the opinion brimmed with praise for the "educational judgment" and "expertise" of admissions decision makers. One of her key arguments was that Michigan law school took into account not only race but also a variety of "diversity factors"—such as whether applicants have traveled overseas, overcome hardships, or served their communities. Left unmentioned was another consideration that inhibited diversity, namely, legacy preference.

"The Law School actually gives substantial weight to diversity factors besides race," Justice O'Connor wrote. It "frequently accepts non-minority applicants with grades and test scores lower than under-represented minority applicants . . . who are rejected." Since many of these nonminority students admitted with low grades and test scores were likely to be alumni children, perhaps Justice O'Connor considered legacy preference a "diversity factor."

In a piercing dissent, a justice outside the legacy establishment suggested that elite colleges—and, by implication, their allies on the Court—cared more about saving preferences for alumni children than for minorities. Clarence Thomas, the only black justice on the Court, grew up in poverty and graduated from the College of the Holy Cross in Worcester, Massachusetts, and Yale Law School. His only child, Jamal, attended Virginia Military Institute. Justice Thomas complained that the "national debate" over legacy preference had indirectly contributed to Michigan's victory. He personally believed, he wrote, that the admissions process is "poisoned" by legacy preference: "This, and other, exceptions to a true meritocracy give the lie to protestations that merit admissions are in fact the order of the day at the Nation's universities." Nevertheless, alumni child preference is legal: "I will not twist the Constitution to invalidate legacy preference."

But colleges—and their allies on the Court—had no compunctions about twisting the Constitution to protect their favorite fund-raising tool. "Were this court to have the courage to forbid the use of racial discrimination in admissions, legacy preferences (and similar practices) might quickly become less popular—a possibility not lost, I am certain, on the elites (both individual and institutional) supporting the Law School in this case," he observed.

Whatever the motives for the Michigan decision, it deflated the anti-legacy push in Congress. The original reason for attacking legacy preference—to build public support for affirmative action—was now less compelling. "It took a little wind out of our sails," Bethany Little said. "The people we were getting the most traction with were people interested in the fairness argument. When we said, 'They might take away affirmative action in the face of this,' we had a real punch. When we had to give up the punch, we lost some political energy."

Dannenberg wasn't deterred. To counteract the colleges' lobbying blitz and sift reality from rhetoric, he organized a July 9 roundtable discussion for committee staffers. Panelists included journalist James Fallows, who had criticized early decision and legacy preference; two higher education lobbyists, Sarah Flanagan and Becky Timmons; and representatives of the Hispanic Education Coalition, which had circulated the proposal to require some colleges with legacy and early decision programs to fund efforts to reduce minority dropout rates.

Instead of producing harmony, the discussion highlighted the discord within the committee and between Kennedy's staff and their erstwhile higher education allies. "It was a very intense conversation, because the schools felt attacked," Bethany Little told me. "That was a shame, because I actually think there could have been a more productive policy discussion about solving the problem." She added that "the squabbling in the committee was exposed to outsiders."

In a July 21 follow-up memo to all Democratic committee staff, Flanagan blasted the proposal as an "extremely inappropriate" way to "insert Congress into individual college admissions decisions." She argued that while it was aimed at elite colleges, the proposal would actually hurt "small, struggling institutions" that take more chances on admitting minority students who are at risk of dropping out. "Because this proposal is so intrusive and potentially damaging," she warned, "college presidents in all sectors of higher education will vigorously and publicly challenge it."

Facing this threat, Kennedy decided to seek counsel—and political cover—from then Harvard president Lawrence Summers, a prominent advocate of increased access to elite education for low-income students. On August 5, Kennedy wrote to Summers, asking for his views on the Hispanic Education Coalition proposal, which the senator praised as a "modest and thoughtful recommendation." Harvard "does a good job in promoting diversity, so it would not be affected," Kennedy noted.

Summers's August 15 reply offered little comfort, toeing the lobbyists' Chicken Little line. "I must register a strong caution about any proposal that reaches into the college admissions process," he wrote. "Federal intervention in admissions has the potential to undermine fundamental values in higher education—institutional independence and the academic freedom of colleges and universities to compose incoming classes in accordance with their distinctive missions."

On September 5, the rift between Kennedy and private higher education became public when my colleagues in *The Wall Street Journal*'s Washington bureau reported that the American Council on Education had written to the senator, denouncing the proposal to penalize colleges that practiced early decision and legacy preference for disparities in graduation rates. Kennedy began having second thoughts, and Dannenberg realized that he just didn't have enough votes on the committee for the measure. Backing off the monetary incentive to pay more attention to minority and low-income students, Dannenberg and Senator Dodd's staff crafted a sunshine proposal. Colleges would have to report on the number, socioeconomic status, and race of students who were alumni relatives or admitted under early decision programs. But they would face no penalties, regardless of the data.

In October 2003, Kennedy proposed the reporting requirement as an amendment to the higher education act, prompting another round of media coverage. The senator and his staff insisted that the watered-down bill is a first step to restricting legacy preference. "It's a continuum," Kennedy told me. Dannenberg believed that the bill would "name and shame" colleges that favor the privileged in the same way that test-score reporting mandated by the No Child Left Behind law has exposed deficient secondary schools.

Nevertheless, Dannenberg's crusade was losing momentum. The scaling back of the bill signaled to colleges that, with affirmative action safe, Senator Kennedy no longer considered the battle against legacy preference as a priority. In the summer of 2005, with the sunshine bill awaiting a hearing or vote in committee, Dannenberg left Kennedy's staff to join the New America Foundation, a Washington think tank, as director of education policy. Soon afterward, the senator agreed to omit the reporting provision from the education committee's reauthorization of higher education. According to a spokeswoman, the senator felt there wasn't enough bipartisan support for it and didn't want to jeopardize a deal with Republican colleagues on federal financial aid for college students. "It's clearly a long-term project," the spokeswoman said.

Today, the anti-legacy movement in Congress appears moribund. In March 2006, the House defeated, by a vote of 337 to 83, a proposal by a Republican member to require colleges to report "raw admissions data" on race, legacy status, and other factors. Dannenberg himself is no longer looking to Congress for leadership, but he hasn't given up the cause. He's organizing a campaign to persuade students and alumni to link their giving to colleges to fair admissions policies. Dannenberg envisions current and prospective donors pledging to withhold their gifts unless colleges either abolish legacy preference or boost financial aid for low-income and minority students.

"Maybe we can't get the government to push colleges, but we might be able to get students—the donors of the future—and current alumni to do it," he said. "A lot of folks think legacy preferences are morally wrong, even if they are in line to benefit from them. It's no different from other civil rights issues."

9

THE **CHALLENGE** OF

WEALTH-BLIND

ADMISSIONS

How Caltech Raises
Standards—and Donations

It was the most controversial first-place pick in the history of *U.S. News & World Report*'s influential rankings of American colleges. In 1999, when the magazine anointed the California Institute of Technology as the nation's best university, the cognoscenti scoffed as vigorously as if Stephen King had been awarded the Nobel Prize in Literature. How could a tiny engineering school in California surpass Harvard, Yale, Princeton, Stanford, and Caltech's larger, better-known East Coast counterpart, the Massachusetts Institute of Technology? The magazine yielded to the criticism and changed its criteria—reducing the importance of one measure, expenditures per student, in which Caltech led the field by a wide margin. Caltech, which otherwise might have stayed on top for years, slid back to the bottom half of the top ten, saving the Ivies and other traditional powerhouses from perennial embarrassment.

Yet there is a good reason, left unmentioned in that ruckus, for putting Caltech a notch above the rest: the Pasadena school comes closer than any other major American university to admitting its student body purely on academic merit. Caltech doesn't compromise admissions standards to attract donations or foster a wealthy alumni base. Nobody gets into Caltech because their families are rich, famous, or well connected; they get in because of their talent and passion for science, period.

The preferences of privilege so familiar on other campuses are alien to Caltech's culture. It's the only one of the country's top twenty universities that does not take into account an applicant's alumni affiliation, according to a *U.S. News* survey. Of 549 students admitted to Caltech in 2005, only eight—1.5 percent—were alumni children, far below the proportions at other elite schools.

The Caltech application asks candidates where their parents went to college, and some students and faculty on the admissions committee say they actually hold alumni children to a higher standard. Being a legacy "could have a negative effect," said physicist Michael Cross, a member of the freshman admissions committee. "If they've done a summer research project at Caltech through their parents' connections, that's less impressive than if they found a position on their own."

Unlike their counterparts at other universities, Caltech's president and development staff don't prod the admissions office to lower standards for children of prospective donors. Of Caltech's fifty-four trustees, including many of its biggest benefactors, only two have children who went to Caltech. Despite being a short drive away, Caltech isn't on the Hollywood map; most children of movie stars and moguls don't want to work that hard. They'd rather spend four years in Providence, Rhode Island, coasting through Brown's anything-goes curriculum, than stay in sunny California and endure Caltech's five required semesters of math and physics.

Athletic prowess doesn't count for much in Caltech admissions either. Its squads adhere to the amateur ideal: any student who wants to can play. Caltech doesn't even field intercollegiate teams in upper-crust sports such as crew, squash, sailing, and horseback riding.

Caltech does have a tuition benefit package for employee dependents—free tuition at the institute, 50 percent paid elsewhere. Yet, despite the significant financial incentive, Caltech faculty rarely lobby for their children, nor does the admissions office favor them. For instance, Cross's son, an outstanding student, applied early to Caltech but was deferred to the regular pool and enrolled instead at MIT, Caltech's archrival.

"Obviously, there isn't any strong preference for faculty children, since he didn't get in," said the physicist. "I wasn't disappointed. I wasn't sure Caltech was the right place for him."

Another physicist on the freshman admissions committee, Robert McKeown, told me that he wasn't encouraging his daughter to apply to Caltech, despite the potential tuition savings. "She's a very good math and science student, but she doesn't have the passion or drive in science or math that we look for," McKeown said of his daughter, with an objectivity that was almost scary. "She's just below the cut for admissions at Caltech."

Without underperforming rich kids dragging down the overall quality, Caltech each year enrolls an outstanding freshman class; the average SAT score of entering students in 2003 was 1505, including a remarkable 775 in math, just 25 points below the maximum. Moreover, instead of perpetuating aristocracy, Caltech exposes promising youngsters from working-class and immigrant families to the best scientific education, preparing them for research careers. About 85 percent of Caltech students graduated from public high schools, 60 percent receive financial aid—as against the 40–45 percent typical of the Ivy League—and fully one-quarter speak a language other than English at home.

Ben Golub's parents, both computer programmers, emigrated to the United States from Russia when he was seven. As a scholarship student at a private high school in New Jersey, he quickly exhausted its math offerings. In his senior year, he studied math at Princeton, where he disliked what he perceived as students' preoccupation with money and political connections. He noticed that wealthy undergraduates flocked to easy majors "where you don't need a lot of raw intellectual power to get by with a decent GPA. I don't know many obscenely rich people who want to be scientists or engineers or physicists. They want to be businessmen or bankers. The academic world is so tough."

Nobody ever accused Ben of lacking intellectual power. The high school valedictorian with the 1590 SAT score chose Caltech over Princeton, Harvard, and Stanford. As a sophomore in 2004, with an almost perfect 3.9 grade point average, he was named by the student government to the Caltech freshman admissions committee, where he joined admissions staff and eminent faculty in evaluating candidates. "Anyone who tried to use wealth and pull strings at Caltech would be laughed out of the room," he said. "It's how smart you are that counts."

JUST AS Copernicus disproved the medieval notion that the sun revolves around the earth, Caltech disproves the modern dogma that the survival of private higher education revolves around admissions breaks for the rich. Administrators at other great private universities often concede privately that lowering standards for alumni and donor children seems inappropriate and even undemocratic. But they contend that a private institution can't risk alienating a wealthy alumnus by rejecting his son or daughter any more than a public university can afford to antagonize the chairman of the legislative committee that supplies its state funding. If these preferences were ever curtailed, the argument goes, gifts to private education would dwindle, class sizes would grow and laboratories crumble, and scholarships for needy students would dry up.

In fact, Caltech is one of three prestigious private colleges—the other two are the Cooper Union for the Advancement of Science and Art in New York City and Berea College in Berea, Kentucky—that flourish without preferences for upper-class students, be they alumni children or polo players. They don't have development lists, country club sports, or vigorous fund-raising operations targeting well-off parents of newly admitted students. Nor do they have socially exclusive clubs or fraternities that encourage wealthy students to segregate themselves from the hoi polloi.

Instead, this trio judges applicants based on merit while taking into account socioeconomic disadvantages—such as coming from a single-parent family or attending an inner-city high school offering few advanced courses—that might have limited the candidates' accomplishments but not their potential. As a result, all three enroll lots of low-income students, unlikely fodder for future fund-raising appeals. More than 80 percent of Berea's student body qualifies for Pell grants—the federal financial aid program with the strictest income limits.

Despite such seemingly self-destructive policies, Caltech, Berea, and Cooper Union attract enough gifts to maintain academic excellence and meet students' financial need. Tuition for all students at Berea and Cooper Union is free, while Caltech keeps its tuition, $25,335 in 2004–5, about 15 percent below other top universities. To boost resources, all three schools are pursuing ambitious fund-raising campaigns. Their experience shows that while it's easier to attract rich givers and build an endowment by compromising admissions, there are other means toward the same ends. It is possible to be both need-blind and wealth-blind.

Caltech, Berea, and Cooper Union differ widely in their locales, histories, and curricula. But an examination of them reveals certain common traits that help them safeguard the integrity of their admissions process and the quality of their student bodies while still persuading donors to pony up. These characteristics suggest an alternative model for colleges that want a cleaner admissions system but fear the fiscal consequences. Similarities include:

1. *Small size.* Caltech has only about 900 undergraduates; Cooper Union, 950; Berea, 1,550. Just as it's harder for a fugitive to disappear in a village than a metropolis, so it's harder for an underqualified student to hide on a small campus than a large one. Scarcity makes each slot in the freshman class more precious; the students all know each other, and the professors all know them too. Moreover, small enrollments mean a limited curriculum and fewer "gut" majors and courses.

Small institutions are also less likely to have graduate schools in business and law, which often yield rich alumni with few qualms about pressuring the undergraduate admissions office. Business and law schools "create people who are good at using influence," said Caltech admissions director Richard Bischoff.

2. *Branding.* Caltech, Cooper Union, and Berea not only eschew legacy preference but also, due to their small size, have relatively few alumni. Fortunately, these three schools aren't just special places to their own graduates. They have developed distinctive identities and reputations that appeal to other potential funders—philanthropists, charities, and the federal government.

Caltech is synonymous with excellence in scientific research; its alumni and faculty, including such seminal thinkers as Linus Pauling and Richard Feynman, have won thirty Nobel Prizes. The Richter scale, used to measure earthquakes, was developed at Caltech.

One dean at an elite university described the difference between fund-raising for Caltech and for the Ivy League. If an Ivy League university is seeking money from a corporation, this person said, "The first thing they say is, 'Who is an alum in that company?' Then they go see the alum and say, 'You had a great time as an undergraduate, wouldn't you want to make that possible for somebody else?' " Whereas the Caltech pitch, he said, is "We have the best program. If you support us, you'll help science and national prosperity."

Businessman and Caltech trustee Wally Weisman, who is heading the institute's current fund-raising campaign, graduated from Stanford, as did his three children. John Diekman, a successful venture capitalist, is neither a Caltech graduate nor a prospective parent; he has degrees from Princeton and Stanford and is childless. Yet in 2004, he joined the institute's board, which normally entails a significant donation. "I always admired Caltech," he told me. "It's the absolute cream of the crop when it comes to science and engineering. The horsepower of its kids is just extraordinary. I couldn't have gotten in."

Renowned nationally for its programs in art, architecture, and engineering, Cooper Union is also a uniquely New York City institution—a niche likely to impress philanthropists there. New York's skyline and image owe much to Cooper Union alumni such as Milton Glaser, who created the "I ♥ NY" logo for the famous advertising campaign, and architect Daniel Libeskind, who won the competition to redesign the World Trade Center site after the September 11, 2001, attacks. "There was a time when virtually every city agency that had anything to do with technology was headed by a Cooper engineering graduate," said Cooper Union president George Campbell. Berea College has accumulated a startlingly large endowment by promoting its progressive history—founded by an abolitionist minister, it was the South's first interracial, coeducational college—and its mission of educating and uplifting impoverished Appalachian families.

3. Faculty involvement in admissions decisions. At most universities, faculty broadly oversee undergraduate admissions, but they leave reading applications and sifting the wheat from the chaff to professional admissions staff. At Caltech, though, admissions staff, students, and faculty—including 2004 Nobel Prize winner H. David Politzer—hash out admissions decisions together; no freshman is admitted without at least one professor reading and commenting on his or her file. At Cooper Union, nine professors look over each portfolio submitted by an applicant to the art program, and two faculty members review each would-be architect.

Faculty participation hinders wealth from intruding on the admissions process. Having risen to their lofty status on their own merit (or so most of them believe), faculty vigorously uphold academic standards in admissions, as long as they aren't pushing their own children. Protected by lifetime job tenure, they're in a stronger position than admissions staff to withstand pressure from the development office or president. Also, while admissions staff are conversant with class ranks and test scores, faculty members are better qualified to judge subjective criteria such as student essays, research projects, and recommendations.

"I don't think faculty would take well to having any pressure put on them by wealthy parents," said Hugh Taylor, emeritus professor of geology, who chaired Caltech's freshman admissions committee in 2004–5.

4. Creative fund-raising. Colleges that don't accommodate donors via admissions preferences have to compensate with other rewards. Gordon Moore, cofounder of computer chipmaker Intel, earned his doctorate at Caltech amid what he called a "fantastic intellectual climate." Although their two sons did not attend Caltech—one went to San Jose State, the other to the University of Santa Clara—Moore and his wife in 2001 pledged $600 million to the institute, the largest gift in the history of higher education. Instead of an admissions quid pro quo, Caltech thanked him with a rare honor: it named an asteroid after him: 8013 gordonmoore.

Moore was touched. Caltech "presented me with a neat framed picture showing the discovery photo," he emailed me. "It is not a very bright object—none of the new asteroids are—but it is an unusual recognition. ... At least it will not hit the earth in the next several million years."

Caltech also arranges for donors who endow scholarships to have lunch on campus with the recipients, so they can take pleasure in learning firsthand how much their generosity helps students. Because Caltech's science whizzes are often shy and socially awkward, they're carefully coached before these lunches to use the correct cutlery and to express their appreciation.

Berea takes this approach even further—it sends students on the road with fund-raisers. For the final week of a course on philanthropy and volunteerism, students travel nationwide to meet donors—including many nonalumni who have never set foot on the Berea campus—and assure them that the college is still committed to helping the underprivileged.

One such student, Melvin Cowan, was raised in Lexington, Kentucky, by his mother, an off-and-on restaurant cook who earned less than $10,000 a year. Growing up, Melvin said, he was a "problem child" who "should have been a statistic. I should have been in the penitentiary. If you'd have told me when I was twelve or thirteen that I'd go to college, I'd laugh in your face." A Lexington community center changed his outlook by introducing him to art and dance. Then, after his freshman year of high school, the African American teen from the city found himself on a bus to rural Berea to attend a summer program for disadvantaged youth.

"I remember my first time coming to Berea for Upward Bound," he said. "I wondered, 'Where are they taking me?' All I saw was grass. I didn't see any malls, any restaurants." He came to enjoy the campus so much that he returned the next three summers and then enrolled at Berea College. A communications major, Melvin participates in a wide variety of community service programs. He coaches a dance team composed of nine middle school students with special needs, is establishing a Berea student association to teach at-risk youth about higher education, and has written a forty-page manifesto titled "A Young Social Revolutionist's Guide to Self-Awareness and Social Action."

In January 2005, Melvin traveled to Florida with a member of Berea's development staff and told his story to a dozen donors. "I satisfied any questions donors might have about what's going on at the college, what are students like, what their money is being used for," he said. "We talked to people who have never seen the campus in their life and are major givers to the college. They love the college's mission. They love what it stands for. That's why they donate heavily." Melvin, who intends to go into business for himself, said he won't neglect the college, even if he becomes too rich for his children to enroll: "I will donate to Berea. I want to have at least several scholarships in my name."

COOPER UNION has few alumni more devoted than Marilyn Hoffner and Albert Greenberg. The couple, both graphic designers, have both served as president of Cooper's alumni association. Hoffner worked at Cooper for twenty-four years, heading its fund-raising and alumni offices. Her husband was on the board of trustees and listed himself in the Manhattan phone book as Albert "CU" Greenberg. Their license plate is CU1948, memorializing the year they graduated. They named their only son Peter Cooper Greenberg, after the industrialist and inventor who established Cooper Union in 1858 in the belief that education should be as free as air and water. The younger Greenberg was "interested in architecture from the minute he was born," his mother said. An excellent student at a New York City prep school, he applied in 1980 to an array of colleges with premier architecture programs and enrolled at Yale, where he would graduate with distinction in that field before studying at Harvard.

Cooper Union turned him down. His mother said a dean told her that his drawings weren't quite good enough. The rejection disappointed his parents, but it didn't shake their loyalty to their alma mater. If anything, they were proud that Cooper held Peter to the same rigorous standards as every other applicant. "When other alums call and say, 'Help me get our kid into Cooper,' we have a good answer," Hoffner said. "We didn't interfere with the process, and there's nothing you can do anyway. I don't think you can get anybody in."

Based in an eight-story brownstone overlooking the Bowery in Lower Manhattan, Cooper spurns a lot of top-notch students. One of the most selective schools in the country, it accepts only 12 percent of candidates, about the same proportion as Stanford and Yale. Being New York City's preeminent art school, it sees a lot of well-connected applicants, but it pays little deference to wealth and celebrity. Preference for the privileged "could play, if we let it, a major role, especially with politicians and donors and people like that who would expect something in return for their generosity," longtime admissions dean Richard Bory told me a few months before he retired in July 2005. "That's one of the reasons we're so negative about any kind of legacy."

If an applicant cited a relationship to an alumnus or prospective donor, Bory said, Cooper's admissions staff would ask for a letter directly to the dean disclosing the tie. In a typical year, about 10 percent of applicants have letters sent on their behalf from people with presumed clout— Bory recalled a recommendation from movie stars Ted Danson and Mary Steenburgen. Bory then tracked those students—not to give them an edge, but to make sure he could defend an adverse decision.

"I like to be informed," Bory said. "In case somebody asks me, 'Why didn't my kid get in? I was going to give $20 million,' I can say, 'If you take a look, his SAT II is a little low.'" In eighteen years as admissions dean, he added, he's received only three or four phone calls asking why a student was rejected. "Some of the most prominent New Yorkers' children and grandchildren have not been admitted to Cooper," he said. "They all accept the fact. We don't get the pressure. If you had to use the word *pure,* this is probably a very pure admissions process and an extremely egalitarian one."

While rebuffing many a well-connected applicant, Cooper Union beckons to talented newcomers. According to Bory, 35 to 40 percent of Cooper students weren't born in the United States and 27 percent are Asian American. Then there's Erik Pye, born and raised in Austin, Texas. Family upheaval left him a high school dropout and homeless at the age of sixteen, sleeping in half-constructed strip malls and on the roofs of parking garages. But he always knew he'd be an artist, ever since as a three-year-old he spilled baby powder to illustrate snowfall and painted walls with his mother's nail polish. "When I was homeless in Austin, I used to sit in

Denny's with a cup of coffee and draw all night," he said. Occasionally, he silkscreened T-shirts and sold them to pay for food.

He eventually earned a high school equivalency degree and spent three years in the army at Fort Drum in upstate New York. As he was being discharged, another soldier told him about an art school in New York City that was both prestigious and free. "I said, 'That's the place for me,'" Erik recalled. "I walked out of the meeting and looked it up on the Internet."

He enrolled at Onondaga Community College in Syracuse, New York, and began applying to Cooper Union. Rejected once, he redoubled his efforts and improved his portfolio. In 2001, he was admitted, and borrowed $1,500 for living expenses from "a guy I met in a coffee shop." At Cooper, he told me shortly before his 2005 graduation, "I explored lots of avenues of art I could never afford otherwise," including printmaking, video, and sculpture. Cooper has "incredible access to the market, the art world, the avant-garde," he said. "There's people of every social and economic description here, from the very rich to the very poor. They're all very talented and all superworkaholics. I've been working my butt off." Among his projects: a full-length documentary, which he hoped to sell to Home Box Office, on the New York City drag nightclub scene.

For decades, Cooper Union coasted financially on income from its endowment, which consists largely of valuable real estate holdings, including the landmark Art Deco Chrysler Building as well as the ground under it. Cooper receives $16.7 million a year in tax-equivalency payments from the lessee of the Chrysler property—amounting to 47 percent of Cooper's operating expenses. Perhaps because their educations had been free, and because Cooper had not aggressively sought donations, many alumni were unaccustomed to the concept of giving back. In 2000, when George Campbell took over as president, he began asking alumni groups for money and was startled by the negative reaction. "I was pulled aside," he said. "They said, 'We're not used to hearing this conversation from the president. We want to hear about academic programs. We don't want to be solicited.'"

That same year, annual budget deficits and pressing needs for state-of-the-art facilities prompted Cooper to launch a capital campaign, with a goal of raising $250 million by 2012. "There really has not been a culture of giving here," Campbell said. "The school was fairly comfortable for many years. We're dependent on endowment, and we haven't really asked alumni over the years to give back and sustain this great legacy. We had to change that culture. The school clearly cannot sustain itself without a significant amount of continuing resources."

Contributions to Cooper Union in Campbell's first half decade were 70 percent higher than in any prior five-year period. As of 2005, Cooper Union had amassed $75 million toward its campaign goal. The biggest gifts, according to a person familiar with the campaign, have come from nonalumni: local philanthropists and foundations who regard Cooper as part of the Big Apple's core. "The argument they make is that they're integrally woven into New York City, part of what makes it a civic place," this person said. "Unlike the Ivies, they don't get most of their philanthropic support from alumni."

Ronni Denes, Cooper's vice president of external affairs, acknowledged that alumni would be more generous if their children received an admissions edge. "Legacy preference would make a difference because people work hard at building paths for their children's future," she said, recalling a dinner party conversation with a businessman who explained to her why he contributed heavily to his Ivy League alma mater. "He said, 'I hadn't heard from my university for years, until I began to make money,'" she remembered. "'Then two fund-raisers showed up at my door. I said, 'I've been out of school for twenty-five years. Nobody cared what I was doing before. Why should I care about my university now?' They said, 'Because you have two children.'"

Nevertheless, Denes said, legacy preference isn't compatible with Cooper Union. "It would change the character of the institution," she said. "There is an egalitarian, merit-based idealism that exists here because every single student knows that no matter how rich or how poor they are, they were tapped because they bring something remarkable. They're being given something remarkable as a result of it. We work these kids very hard. They earn their scholarships. If we had legacy preference, we could buy a parcel and build a gym. But right now, our kids don't really need a gym. They need the kind of nurturing we give them."

President Campbell said he hears from "a few alums who are very upset their child didn't get in, and say explicitly they aren't going to contribute. We look them up, and by and large those are people who haven't contributed significantly anyway. That doesn't significantly hurt Cooper." He urged all American colleges to abolish preferences for children of alumni and donors: "If legacy were eliminated, Cooper wouldn't be unique anymore. But from an idealist's point of view, I'd like to eliminate it. If in fact we didn't have all of these other preferences, some of these folks would get squeezed out. You'd have more seats. You'd probably have a higher minority population."

K. C. DENDOOVEN, a Las Vegas publisher of illustrated books on national parks and other tourist destinations, isn't a Berea College alumnus or parent; he graduated from a technical school in Michigan. He didn't visit Berea until 2004, doing field research for a book about the college for its 150th anniversary in 2005. Yet DenDooven has been donating to Berea for years, ever since reading a magazine article about the obscure Kentucky college where tuition is free but every student has to work at a job at least ten hours a week, from making brooms for sale to clerking in the admissions office. "It intrigued me," said the publisher, who sends Berea $2,050 a year. "Some rich spoiled kid can't go there and park his Ferrari out front because the old man has a ton of dough."

Like DenDooven, Marie Gebbie has no Berea ties. In fact, the college discouraged her from applying because she grew up in Dayton, Ohio, outside its Appalachian service area. Instead, the carpenter's daughter worked her way through night school. Yet late in life, when she started a profitable bag-distribution business in the Chicago area, she began giving to Berea. In addition to her $3,000–5,000 annual donation, she's set aside at least $200,000 for the college in her will. "I like to give an opportunity to other people that I didn't have when I was their age," she said. "It gives me pleasure to know a deserving person is going to get a college education, and have an opportunity to better his or her life."

People such as DenDooven and Gebbie have made Berea higher education's unlikeliest fund-raising magnet. A nondenominational Christian campus located on a mountain ridge thirty-five miles south of Lexington, Berea encourages "plain living, pride in labor well done, zest for learning, high personal standards, and concern for the welfare of others," according to its mission statement, known as "The Great Commitments." Students have few distractions; situated in a "dry" county that prohibits the sale of alcohol, Berea has no fraternities nor sororities, and few students are allowed to have cars on campus before their senior year.

While Caltech and Cooper Union give no break to wealthy students, Berea actually bans them. It maintains an income limit that, among other things, amounts to a legacy deterrent. No one from a family of four earning more than $51,000 is eligible to attend Berea (with a few exceptions, such as faculty and staff children), ruling out most children of alumni. Even Kentucky coal miners earn too much to send their children to the college. As if the income ceiling weren't enough protection against privilege, Berea also restricts its geographic reach, taking 80 percent of its students from Kentucky and southern Appalachia, a largely impoverished nine-state region. In the mid-1990s, the Cincinnati, Ohio, area was added to this target area to encourage recruiting of black students. Berea's student body is now 19 percent African American, and blacks—who at most colleges drop out more often than whites—graduate at the same rate as other students. One explanation: minorities on other campuses often grow discouraged or resentful because they can't afford the same amenities (cars, restaurants, extracurricular activities) as richer white students. Berea's minorities have less cause to feel like second-class citizens because their white classmates are poor too.

The demographics of Berea's student body would make any Ivy League fund-raiser shudder. The average family income is $27,000, and most students come from families in which neither parent graduated from college. While foreign students are a cash cow for other colleges, the thirty whom Berea admits each year meet the income guidelines and, like everyone else, pay no tuition. "There are many more poor internationals out there than there are rich," observed Joseph Bagnoli, associate provost for enrollment management. Bagnoli, also a Berea alumnus, issued a challenge to the Ivy League and other premier private universities to stop catering to the wealthy: "Attempt to disprove the implicit assumption that the elite actually deserve their privilege. . . . Make a bona fide attempt to not only admit but graduate students who are at a socioeconomic disadvantage. This would mean not only providing scholarship funding but also the support necessary to help them achieve high academic standards."

Berea already fulfills that challenge. Considering the deprived social and educational backgrounds of many of its students, Berea's academic standards are formidable. It accepts only one-fourth of applicants, and the average freshman SAT score is a respectable 1090. Although poverty is often a barrier to completing college, 60 percent of Berea students earn their bachelor's degrees in five years or less, and nearly half go on to graduate school; among southern colleges, Berea is second only to Davidson College in North Carolina in the number of alumni who obtain doctoral degrees. Among comprehensive colleges, defined as undergraduate institutions that award less than half their degrees in liberal arts, *U.S. News & World Report* ranks Berea as the best in the South.

One of its most notable graduates is John Fenn, a Virginia Commonwealth University professor who shared the 2002 Nobel Prize in chemistry. When he was eleven years old, his father, an electrical engineer, was laid off from a job as a factory manager in New Jersey and the family moved to Berea, where his parents joined the faculty. Berea "was a remarkable place," Fenn told me. "The people at Berea were there because they wanted to learn. What turned me on to chemistry was a freshman chemistry teacher I had at Berea. He told us about the real world, what was going on in industry. He made the subject live."

While shunning the rich, Berea has become flush itself. Its $862 million endowment in 2005 ranked 22nd per student among U.S. private colleges and universities, just behind Wellesley and four spots ahead of Dartmouth. As of September 30, 2005, it had raised $125 million toward a campaign goal of $150 million for the college's 150th anniversary.

Part of this success can be attributed to hidden savings in its business model: the student work requirement ensures cheap labor, while Pell grants and other need-based federal aid offset a portion of scholarship costs. Still, in an apparent paradox, Berea's greatest source of financial strength is its hostility to wealth and privilege—epitomized in the income limit, the work requirement, the free tuition, and a turbulent history of bucking the powers that be.

Berea's founder, the abolitionist minister John Gregg Fee, was disowned by his slaveholding parents. Pro-slavery mobs drove Reverend Fee and other Berea pioneers out of Kentucky shortly before the Civil War; they returned in 1864, as the North was slogging toward victory. Forty years later, when the Kentucky legislature banned interracial education, the integrated college fought the state law all the way to the U.S. Supreme Court—and lost. It then helped support a nearby school for black students until Kentucky repealed the law in 1950. Recent initiatives, such as a campus "eco-village"—housing with passive solar heating and lower water use for single-parent and married students and their children—continue this progressive tradition.

Berea skillfully markets its populist identity through direct mail to likely donors across the country, drawing widespread grassroots support that more than compensates for its relatively low rate of alumni giving and paucity of major gifts of a million dollars or more. Berea gains between 1,000 and 2,500 new donors a year, and people with no personal connection to the college often remember it in their wills. In 2003–4, Berea raised nearly $27 million—a staggering 62 percent of it in bequests.

Berea "built a huge endowment," said one fund-raising consultant. "It hired guys who worked out of their houses all over the place, mostly in the Midwest, developing relationships with people in church congregations who died and left money to the college."

It also attracts gifts from affluent alumni children and grandchildren who attended other colleges themselves but are grateful to Berea as the springboard of their family's upward mobility. Bill Robbins's grandparents were tenant farmers living in a shack in southern Indiana; indoor plumbing and electricity were luxuries beyond their means. His father, Earl Robbins, left school in eighth grade to become a farm laborer too. But when Earl was eighteen, a cousin at Berea encouraged him to go to a secondary school it ran for penniless dropouts. Earl borrowed $10 from an uncle and set out for Kentucky. At Berea, Earl "found a world he didn't know existed," his son said. Earl finished high school in two years, then earned a bachelor's degree at Berea and a master's degree at the University of Kentucky. He taught agriculture, opened an insurance business, and ultimately became a Berea trustee and donor. Bill recalled that Earl, who died in 2004, "liked to take the checks over to Berea and present them to the development office in person."

By the time his three children were ready for college, Earl was making too much money for them to attend Berea. But Bill and his siblings never forgot that without Berea they might still be hitching up mules. They give regularly to Berea, underwrite a lecture series there, and are exploring the possibility of endowing a $1.5 million faculty chair.

Bill now runs the insurance business and breeds Thoroughbred horses. He sent both of his children to private colleges; his son went to Harvard, married a Harvard legacy, and became a mutual fund analyst, culminating the family's plows-to-privilege saga. Berea "meant everything to my family," Bill said. Although the income limit prevented subsequent Robbins generations from enrolling at his father's alma mater, Bill wouldn't have it any other way. "Berea ought to reserve its places for children who couldn't be educated otherwise," he said. "If it made room" for rich students, "maybe my dad wouldn't have been able to go there."

AFTER A WINTER of drenching rains, the Caltech campus looked especially lush when I visited in March 2005. Olive, sycamore, and eucalyptus trees were all in leaf and purple, sweet-smelling wisteria overhung the Spanish-style archways.

But the students scattered here and there in the "superquiet study area" on the second and third floors of Sherman Fairchild Library were oblivious to the burgeoning spring. With backpacks, water bottles, and calculators on the tables beside them, they worked on their end-of-term exams, neatly sketching graphs and solving problems. No proctors were in sight as the students timed themselves by their watches or the library clock to finish in the allotted three or four hours. The self-policing of exams illustrates Caltech's honor code: "No member of the Caltech community shall take unfair advantage of any other member."

In a different way, so does the indifference of its undergraduate admissions screeners to wealth and power. It would be unfair to other Caltech students and faculty to let in legacies, development cases, faculty children, or athletes who couldn't pull their weight in class or on the collaborative research for which the institute is renowned.

It would also be unfair to the privileged students themselves. Caltech's grueling curriculum leaves no refuge for less than brilliant minds— white or black, rich or poor. Caltech students take six courses a semester, two more than at most colleges. The institute doesn't offer summer courses and rarely grants course credit for advanced placement tests or classes taken at other universities. Nor is a failing grade erased from a student's transcript, as it is at some universities, if he or she retakes and passes the course. "Everyone understands the enormous challenge represented by admission to Caltech," president David Baltimore, a Nobel laureate, told me in his office. "Only the rare, special student can handle Caltech. If we were a different type of school that could handle a wider range of students, somebody could say, 'My child can handle the school, they just have to get in.'"

Caltech professor H. David Politzer, who shared the 2004 Nobel Prize in physics, said he would not have survived as an undergraduate: "I'm too slow. The pace here is outrageous." Politzer, who graduated from the University of Michigan and received his doctorate from Harvard, said Caltech demands more gray matter than the Ivy League. "At Harvard and Yale, grades don't mean squat. The goal is to become CEO of some Fortune 500 company or president of the U.S. At Caltech, there isn't much else" besides academics.

If anything, Caltech holds affluent applicants to a higher standard, because they've had more opportunities for education and research. Thus, a 720 score on the physics SAT II subject test by a lonely wonk from a mediocre high school in rural Kansas or Louisiana might in Caltech's eyes signal greater potential than an 800 by a suburban student from a top high school in suburban New York. Still, it only budges so far for disadvantaged students.

"There have been heartbreaking cases in our applicant pool—fabulous kids everyone loved," Erica O'Neal, assistant vice president for student affairs, told me. "You could see passion jumping out of the file. Yet there are holes in the transcript" because they attended inferior high schools without high-level math and science courses. "The ultimate decision has to be no."

Just as Caltech makes no concessions to wealth, it won't sacrifice merit for diversity's sake. Caltech struggles to attract minority students, in part because the relatively few blacks or Hispanics who have the preparation in advanced math needed for Caltech likely have their pick of the Ivy League and other elite universities. Only one of 207 Caltech freshmen in 2004 was African American; overall, blacks make up 1 percent of the student body and Hispanics 7 percent. Women, an underrepresented group in the sciences, comprise about 30 percent of Caltech undergraduates, a lower proportion than at MIT (43 percent)—which is precisely why Vicki Loewer, with a 1560 SAT score including perfect scores on the math part and the math SAT II, chose Caltech over MIT.

"I don't want to wonder why I got in," Vicki, a chemical engineering major with a 3.88 average and a member of the freshman admissions committee, told me one morning as we sat at an outdoor café on campus. Although she was wearing casual clothes, she told me she had dressed up especially for the interview; during exam week, she usually wore blue pajamas everywhere, including to admissions committee meetings. Vicki, whose father is a Baptist minister and whose mother is chief of staff to a federal education official, graduated from a public magnet high school in suburban Washington, D.C.

"I have excelled here. I found my stride," she told me. "We have more freedoms than students at other schools. Caltech lets you embrace all your weird, freakish tendencies. . . . I intend to give lots of money to Caltech when I have it."

A Caltech senior in 2005, Vicki wanted to stay there for graduate school, but her department urged her to go elsewhere to broaden her experience. Wooed by Princeton, MIT, the University of Texas, and other premier schools, Vicki chose MIT, which she described to me as a "good runner-up" to Caltech. She was awarded a $30,000-a-year graduate fellowship from the National Science Foundation.

At her first Caltech admissions committee meeting, Vicki told me, she asked if she was supposed to factor race and gender into her evaluations and was told no. "I would have had trouble taking them into account," she told me. "It would be horrible if the school was full of stupid women. That's my nightmare. It doesn't make sense for science to be run that way. It wouldn't be logical to let someone in who wasn't that good." Asked how the admissions committee would respond if asked to admit an applicant because the family might donate to Caltech, she said, "We would throw things."

The freshman admissions committee consists of admissions office staff, sixteen students, and sixteen faculty; only about half of the students and faculty show up at any given meeting. Of 2,300 applications from U.S. students in 2005, the admissions staff turned down the bottom one thousand applicants outright and forwarded each of the others to a faculty member and a student for review. If staff, professor, and student agreed that a candidate should be rejected, admitted, or placed on the waiting list, that was final. If they disagreed—as they did on 210 applicants in 2005—decisions were hashed out over three mornings and two afternoons in March by committee subgroups of half a dozen people, including at least one admissions staff member, professor, and student. The admissions office evaluated international applicants by itself, because it was most familiar with grading and testing policies overseas.

Faculty participation in undergraduate admissions used to be more extensive. For decades, each professor on the committee would travel for two or three weeks each winter to a specified territory, such as the upper Midwest or (a more coveted assignment) Hawaii, and interview candidates there. Back at Caltech, they would advocate for their favorites before the full committee, and usually prevail. "It was a fantastic experience for the professors, and for the teachers at these various schools," recalled Caltech archivist Judith Goodstein, a committee member in the 1980s. "The teachers understood if they had a shining star in their student body, somebody gifted in math or science, that kid, regardless of background, stood a chance of being accepted." A number of such applicants interviewed by Caltech professors, Goodstein recalled, later joined the faculty themselves.

Goodstein does remember one instance of pressure from Caltech fund-raisers—a call from the vice president of development complaining that she had not interviewed a donor's son. "I went back and looked at the kid's folder and it was just average," she told me. "We did do a courtesy interview, but I don't think I did it. I bristled at the notion that somebody in development would tell me I had to go see a kid. I don't think the kid came to Caltech."

According to Professor Michael Hoffmann, who chaired the admissions committee at the time, these faculty tours stopped in the late 1980s because fewer professors were willing to spare time from research. "It was just harder to get somebody to commit as the pressure in the academic world became higher," he told me.

Several prominent faculty remain extraordinarily dedicated to undergraduate admissions, none more so than Politzer. When his Nobel Prize was announced in October 2004, Politzer skipped Caltech's press conference heralding the award. Yet the next morning, he was the first member to show up at the freshman admissions committee meeting. Politzer says faculty participation safeguards the quality of Caltech's student body. "Again and again, I find I have a very different perspective than a staff member as to the attractiveness of a particular student," he told me. "I make a scientific judgment of the merit or aptitude or intensity shown by their work. The staff people, who don't have backgrounds in science, don't have a way to distinguish between endeavors of young people that to my mind might have enormously different levels of intensity, aptitude, and commitment."

In one case, he said, the admissions staff wanted to turn down an applicant with a math SAT score below 700. But the youngster's research, which to the admissions reader "looked like a science fair project," would actually have made "a fine senior thesis at Caltech, except he did it on his own, not with a faculty member," Politzer said. "I liked him, and I recommended him."

IN 1926 Pasadena was one of the richest municipalities in the United States, a mecca for wealthy midwestern retirees. On March 9, in the home of railroad tycoon Henry Huntington, one hundred local businessmen each pledged $1,000 a year for ten years to the fledgling California Institute of Technology, which had changed its name just six years earlier from Throop College of Technology. The Associates, as the group was known, helped sustain Caltech through the Great Depression; over the years, members of the group have contributed to more than fifty Caltech buildings, including several dormitories named after them.

Today, the Associates continue to be a valuable and primarily local Caltech resource. Of its 1,448 members—who now pay either $35,000 all at once or $3,000 a year for twenty years—only 380 are alumni. Like the group's founders, most current Associates didn't attend Caltech, nor did their children. They're southern California businessmen, motivated by the civic pride that Caltech cultivates. In return for their gifts, they can travel overseas with Caltech faculty, are invited to public and private lectures, and enjoy meals, meetings, and celebrations at the Athenaeum, the elegant inn on campus where Albert Einstein and other visiting scientists have stayed.

"Caltech is so small that it doesn't overrun Pasadena," said Caltech trustee and Associates member Stephen Onderdonk, explaining the affinity between the institute and local business circles. His wife's grandfather, Fred Alberston, was a founding Associate. "A lot of the local community are members of the Associates," the Pasadena businessman said. "People use the Athenaeum for wedding and other social engagements. Caltech welcomes community participation."

Caltech archivist Judith Goodstein said, "It was so important for the institute to have the names of prominent members of the community be listed as founding Associates. It became quite a successful organization with a glittering array of names well known in LA. There are a serious number of significantly wealthy individuals, leaders of the business or legal world, who seem to really get a charge out of rubbing shoulders with Nobel Prize winners."

The Associates and other nonalumni boosters are one key to Caltech's prosperity. As at Cooper Union and Berea, Caltech fund-raisers have to overcome several handicaps—a tiny pool of twenty thousand graduates, one-fifth the alumni base of other elite universities; no admissions break for donors; and a student body heavily drawn from public high schools and immigrant and lower-income families. One-third of alumni donate to Caltech, far below Princeton (61 percent), Harvard (48 percent), Dartmouth (47 percent), and Yale (45 percent).

"From a fund-raising point of view, all those kids are still paying off loans," said Gary Dicovitsky, the vice president for development. "They don't have a buffer for their own children. They have to save, save, save and can't give until later in life. That's not a dream for a fund-raiser, but I wouldn't have it any other way."

Still, its $1.4 billion in assets in 2005 ranked Caltech 18th among private institutions in per-pupil endowment, ahead of MIT, and it has raised more than $1 billion toward a $1.4 billion campaign goal. Besides its nonalumni support, Caltech has also benefited enormously from its ability to groom successful entrepreneurs. These self-made multimillionaires who amply repaid the institute for its role in their fortunes include the late Arnold Beckman, who earned a doctorate in chemistry in 1928 and invented the electronic pH meter and other scientific instruments; 1954 alumnus Benjamin Rosen, chairman emeritus of Compaq Computer Corp.; and billionaire Intel cofounder Gordon Moore, who earned his Ph.D. at Caltech in 1954, one of America's wealthiest men.

Moore, whose father (a deputy sheriff in California) never finished grammar school, told me that Caltech's $1.4 billion campaign is "pretty tough sledding," even with his $600 million gift. "We don't have the alumni base to draw on that bigger schools do. We have to appeal broadly to people who don't have a connection to Caltech."

Caltech also appeals to the federal government. Its faculty generated $227 million in fiscal 2004 in federal research grants, of which about one-third covers overhead for facilities and administration. In addition, NASA paid Caltech $1.6 billion that year to manage the Jet Propulsion Laboratory in Pasadena, including an "award fee" of $21 million pegged to performance. Compared with research-based funding in its operating budget, Caltech's tuition revenue is so small that the institute has on occasion considered eliminating tuition altogether.

According to Politzer, Caltech trustees once debated whether to use a major gift to replace tuition. "I think we could have done it, "he told me, "but I've heard there was a trustee who said, 'This is America: people believe you get what you pay for. Do it, and you will denigrate your value in the marketplace.' "

Toward the end of my Caltech visit, I saw disturbing signals of what might be called "legacy creep"—impending deference toward alumni and donors in admissions. Dicovitsky, the vice president for development, told me he planned to ratchet up Caltech's fund-raising from parents of current students; such programs, as we have seen at Duke, can lead to favoring applicants whose parents are expected to donate. Bischoff, who was hired as admissions dean in 2004 after holding the same job at the University of Chicago, confessed he is considering changing Caltech's practice of sending the same letter to all rejected applicants, substituting a gentler one for spurned legacies.

I asked Baltimore whether it would be easier to achieve Caltech's $1.4 billion campaign goal if it offered admissions preferences to the wealthy. The campaign "has stretched us enormously to find new donors," acknowledged Baltimore, who later in 2005 would announce his retirement. "We have to sell the vision of Caltech, the overriding excellence of everything we do, the participation in great intellectual adventures, the importance of Caltech to the economy. We're doing a much, much harder thing [than other universities], hewing to our idealism while still raising money."

Yet he assured me that Caltech would never compromise its standards. "People should be judged not by their parentage and wealth but by their skills and ability to contribute to society," he said. "Any school I'm associated with, I want it to be a meritocracy."

10

ENDING THE

PREFERENCES

OF PRIVILEGE

Suggestions
for Reform

On May 23, 2004, giving his first commencement address as president of Amherst College, Anthony Marx called for America's elite colleges to reclaim their mission as engines of upward mobility.

"America today—and our great colleges and universities—have hit a wall of blocked opportunity," President Marx told more than one thousand graduates, family members, and faculty gathered in Amherst's verdant quadrangle. "At our top colleges, only one-tenth of our students are drawn from the poorer half of the population, only 3 percent from the bottom quarter. . . . If we believe in diversity of class, ethnicity, origin, and interest among our students, then we must also embrace economic diversity."

Nearly six months later, a little-noticed session on the same campus demonstrated why Amherst and other premier colleges have so few low-income students—and how the impulse for change crumbles before the imperative to mollify alumni and donors.

On the Saturday morning of homecoming weekend, before the football game with archrival Williams College, Amherst hosted what it billed as an "admissions workshop" for alumni and their children—a perk denied other applicants. Braving the season's first snowstorm, about forty-five parents and students gathered in Converse Hall to hear a presentation by Katharine Fretwell, Amherst's director of admissions. Fretwell walked the audience through Amherst's admissions process and statistics—the college accepts one-fifth of its 5,500 applicants, expecting 400 to enroll—and asked for questions. A gray-haired graduate in a white sweater raised his hand. "I think this is a question everyone in the room wants to ask," he said. "I feel a little bad about asking it, but is there an advantage to a family relationship?"

The director paused to choose her words, recognizing that her answer would be of critical importance to the alumni whose gifts filled Amherst's coffers—and who likely wondered whether the president's ambition for economic diversity would leave their children in the cold.

"There can be," she assured the audience, noting that the application form asks candidates about relatives who attended Amherst. "We do communicate with the alumni office as we go through the admissions cycle."

Then the admissions director recited a litany of statistics that starkly documented the edge Amherst College gives to legacies. Over the last fifteen years, she said, Amherst had admitted 50 percent of alumni children, as against 20 percent of all applicants. Amherst, she continued, rates applicants on an academic scale from 1 (outstanding) to 7 (unqualified). The college accepts 85 percent of applicants given a 1 rating, with most of the exceptions being impoverished foreign students to whom it can't afford to give financial aid. Legacy status comes into play with candidates given a 2 rating—strong students who have taken challenging courses and scored in the 1400s on their SATs. Amherst admits 40 percent of such candidates overall—but 100 percent of alumni children with a 2 rating.

As the workshop ended, Fretwell revealed an exclusive entrée for the privileged few. She had already told the audience that in the interest of fairness Amherst does not interview applicants; the college lacks the staff to visit all 5,500 candidates in their hometowns, and holding optional meetings on campus would discriminate against low-income students who can't afford to travel. Now Fretwell confided to the departing crowd that, despite the ban on official interviews, she and admissions dean Thomas Parker were always available for informal "conversations" with graduates and their children. All they had to do, she told them, was call the admissions office and identify themselves as alums.

It has become fashionable for college presidents to grab headlines by promising to admit more low-income applicants. In recent years, Harvard, Yale, Princeton, and the University of Virginia have all expanded financial aid for such students in hopes of boosting their enrollment. But such initiatives should be eyed with skepticism until Marx and his brethren answer the vital question "Who will lose out?"

Admissions is a zero-sum game. Elite colleges are reluctant to increase their enrollment because their inaccessibility enhances their prestige. Hence, pledges to make room for poor students run up against the reality that a large proportion of slots at these institutions are reserved for the rich. At Amherst College, for instance, alumni children make up 10 percent of the student body. Another 15 percent are recruited athletes who tend to be "wealthier and less ethnically diverse than other students," according to a 2005 report; the college fields men's and women's varsity teams in upper-class sports such as squash and golf. Thus it's no wonder that President Marx's policies have not matched his inspiring rhetoric. He told me in January 2006 that Amherst planned to enroll an extra twenty-five low-income students a year at most. When I asked if he would consider abolishing legacy preference to make space for more, he responded, "This college is what it is because of close to two hundred years of alumni investing in the place. We value that historical connection."

Like Amherst, few colleges are eager to alienate alumni and donors by curtailing favoritism toward their children. Colleges have boxed themselves into a corner by degrading admissions into a fund-raising tool; even if they want to be more democratic in admissions, they're afraid to jeopardize the flow of checks. Nor are colleges eager to reduce affirmative action for minority applicants. Hence, their flexibility is limited; any extra slots for low-income candidates have to come largely at the expense of students who don't qualify for any preferences and already face the highest odds against admission. That prospect would leave the colleges favoring the poor *and* the rich—and locking out middle-class candidates with outstanding credentials.

This dilemma appears to be playing out at Harvard. In February 2004, former president Lawrence Summers announced that he was eliminating tuition for students from families earning under $40,000 and reducing it for students from families with incomes between $40,000 and $60,000. (In 2006, Harvard said parents earning under $60,000 would no longer have to make any payment.) Nevertheless, even Summers—whose resignation in 2006 deprived Harvard of its most powerful advocate for socioeconomic diversity—clung to the preferences of privilege, insisting that the legacy boost is "integral to the kind of community that any private educational institution is."

Lacking available slots, the 2004 financial aid initiative boosted enrollment from families earning under $60,000 by 51 students out of a freshman class of 1,620—a significant but not overwhelming increase. It's a good bet that most of them nudged out outstanding unconnected candidates, rather than legacies, athletes, or development cases.

One unhooked middle-class applicant whom Harvard passed over was Samantha Baras, who was in the top 10 percent of her class at Brookline High School in Brookline, Massachusetts. (Among her high school classmates who enrolled at Harvard: President Summers's stepdaughter.)

Samantha scored 1480 on the SATs—without test preparation or retaking the test—as well as an 800 on the SAT II writing test and the maximum 5 on three advanced placement tests. A vegetarian who plans to be a doctor, she wrote her college essay on her mixed emotions about dissecting animals in biology class: "Nothing feels as bad as that first cut. Nothing feels as good as finding what I'm looking for—whether it's the sixth stomach chamber of an obese earthworm or a specific vein of a frog. . . . How is it possible for me to live as an enthusiastic vegetarian and dissector?"

Rejected by four Ivy League universities—Harvard, Brown, Penn, and her first choice, Columbia—she enrolled at New York University, which gave her a merit scholarship. As a freshman there, she compiled an impressive 3.8 average. "NYU is a great school and it has worked out very well for me," she told me. "There is no question that there are many exceptionally high-performing students at NYU, sharing a similar story to mine, who deserve the same opportunity as Ivy League graduates to rise to the top of our society."

Samantha's credentials were "way up there," said Brookline High principal Robert Weintraub, who added that he called Columbia and other Ivies on her behalf, to no avail. "Samantha does not have legacy. That's sort of a strike against her in terms of getting into highly selective schools. We have tons of parents who've gone to Harvard who live in Brookline."

To expand access for low-income students without abandoning the middle class, colleges have little choice but to dismantle the preferences of privilege. If they don't do so voluntarily, public pressure may eventually prod Congress to penalize schools engaging in these preferences by withholding federal aid or revoking their nonprofit status.

As we have seen, Senator Kennedy proposed requiring colleges to report data on admissions of alumni children. That would be a valiant first step, but more sweeping change is needed—and would likely draw wide public support. I recommend the following reforms:

1. End legacy preference. Most Americans want to abolish legacy preference, as Oxford and Cambridge in England have already done. Requiring alumni children to compete on even terms would help restore fairness to admissions and improve access to elite universities for unconnected middle-class and working-class applicants.

Colleges' fears that their traditions and endowments would decline without legacy preference are exaggerated. Since alumni often can afford private schools, test-prep services, tutors, and independent counselors, their children would still enjoy many advantages over other candidates. Moreover, without an admissions entitlement, legacies would likely strive harder in high school. As a result, some alumni children would be accepted on merit, enabling them to share college customs and family lore with classmates. Those who get in would have the self-confidence of knowing they did it on their own, rather than by relying on their parental pedigree.

Nor would alumni contributions to colleges necessarily plummet, as the examples of Caltech, Berea, and Cooper Union show. For most alumni, giving to their alma mater doesn't hinge on whether it accepts their children; it stems from other motives, such as gratitude for their own education or desire to promote research or teaching in an overlooked field. The few alumni who do respond to an admissions rebuff by reducing or withholding donations are dismayed largely because they were counting on legacy preference to save the day. If they didn't expect preference, they wouldn't be so disappointed. They might also offset their reduced charity to their alma mater by giving to the colleges where their children do enroll.

Elite colleges could compensate for losing legacy preference by creating other rewards and naming opportunities for donors—much as Caltech named an asteroid after Gordon Moore. And with their endowments in the billions of dollars, they could easily withstand a small decline in giving.

Even a prominent higher education lobbyist says colleges could prosper without legacy preference. The credo that legacy is essential to fundraising is "the kind of traditional thinking it's very hard to break out of," said Gerald Cassidy. "If you keep track of your alumni, and you initiate them early into giving small amounts so they get used to giving, you can raise a lot of money without legacy preference. Particularly if you've conditioned them to the fact that there aren't preferences that could work for their children."

Ending legacy preference would require a seismic shift in attitudes among college administrators—a cultural upheaval that apparently hasn't taken hold at Texas A&M. In January 2004, the state engineering school announced that it was dropping legacy preference, which had amounted to a maximum of 4 points on a 100-point admissions scale. It acted under pressure from legislators and civil rights groups; upset that the university had decided not to practice affirmative action for minority applicants, they demanded that A&M also toss out legacy preference for alumni children, an overwhelmingly white group.

According to A&M administrators, the change has not decreased legacy enrollment at all, apparently because alumni children still have an unofficial edge. Robert Walker, vice president of development, explained that he and his staff advise children of alumni and donors to answer essay questions on the application by writing "everything they can about grand-parents, parents, aunts, and uncles that were Aggies. We don't give them any credit for that, but the people who read it can't help" but notice the family ties. "It helps them psychologically."

2. Establish a firewall between fund-raising and admissions. As we've seen, most elite universities profess to separate these two functions but actually pursue children of prospective donors, celebrities who create buzz, and politicians who bring government funds to the campus.

A true firewall would mean that college fund-raisers and the president's staff would respect the integrity of the selection process and stop imposing "development cases" on admissions. No longer would movers and shakers such as Dave Zucconi and Joel Fleishman have a say in both fund-raising and admissions. Colleges would rein in the parent fund-raising committees that have morphed into admissions networks for affluent suburbs such as Lake Forest, Illinois. To avoid the appearance of a quid pro quo, every college should adopt a policy that it will neither accept nor negotiate donations from any parent whose child has applied to the institution or is on the waiting list. If the child has been admitted and decided to enroll, there should be a minimum waiting period of, say, two years until the parents can donate.

Once colleges could no longer dangle admissions slots, they would be forced to compete on quality for nonalumni donations and government funding. Like Caltech, Berea, and Cooper Union, they would attract gifts based on the excellence of their academic (and athletic) programs and the appeal of their missions. To meet its fund-raising target, each college would then have a financial incentive to improve its educational quality and define what makes it valuable and unique—ultimately benefiting students, employers, and American society as a whole.

3. Develop conflict-of-interest policies for college admissions staff. Any college admissions staff member who is related to or has socialized with an applicant or an applicant's family should not evaluate, advocate for, or vote on that candidate. Obviously, admissions staffers are likely to be biased in favor of applicants they know. But even if personal relationships furnish valuable insights into an applicant, as Harvard and other elite colleges contend, the trouble is that admissions deans and staffers are more likely to be acquainted with children of alumni and donors than with first-generation students from immigrant or low-income families. Conflict-of-interest rules would give underprivileged applicants a fairer shake.

4. Abolish athletic preference and scholarships for upper-crust sports.
I would not entirely eliminate preference for athletes in admissions. Unlike the legacy and development boosts, which credit an applicant for parental achievement, athletic preference rewards a candidate's own hard work and excellence. But the growing number of slots set aside for athletes at elite institutions supposedly devoted to academics has gotten out of hand.

Recognizing the problem, several colleges—including Amherst and other members of the New England Small College Athletic Conference— have considered capping athletic admissions in some sports. But, as in the fallout from Title IX, such caps are likely to hurt working-class sports such as wrestling, while wealthy alumni and donors shield upper-class sports from cuts.

In my view, athletic preference and scholarships should be reserved for recruits in major sports that most American children have an opportunity to try. Currently, for boys, the most popular sports are football, basketball, track and field, baseball, soccer, wrestling, cross country, golf, tennis, and swimming and diving; for girls, basketball, track and field, volleyball, softball, soccer, tennis, cross country, swimming and diving, competitive spirit squads, and golf. Colleges discriminate against minorities and low- and middle-income students by reserving slots—and, outside the Ivy League, scholarships—for athletes in sports only rich white people tend to play. Also, strictly by the numbers, it takes more skill to be recruited in a mass sport such as basketball or baseball than in sailing or squash.

Colleges could still field teams in less popular sports, but recruits would be evaluated on their academic credentials and would not be eligible for athletic scholarships. Without admissions preference for prep-school sports such as women's crew and horseback riding, colleges would comply with gender-diversity requirements by taking more female athletes from low- and middle-income families and public school backgrounds.

5. Eliminate admissions preference for faculty children and tuition assistance plans that put pressure on admissions offices to do so. It has become standard practice for universities to compensate faculty members and other employees by reimbursing part or all of their children's college tuition. It would be fairer to professors without college-age children for universities to drop this benefit and pay higher salaries across the board instead. If a college does offer such a reimbursement program, the tuition break should be fully "portable"—that is, the children should receive the same subsidy no matter where they enroll. As we've seen, if the college limits the benefit to faculty children in its own student body, then the admissions staff feels obliged to accept them—and avoid the wrath of professors forced to pony up full tuition elsewhere. Coming from highly educated families that value learning, faculty children start with an academic edge and don't deserve an admissions advantage.

In addition, to avoid an appearance of conflict of interest, university presidents, provosts, and other highly paid administrators should be discouraged from sending their children and relatives to their own institutions—particularly if they stand to benefit from a tuition break.

6. Provide equal access for Asian American students and for international students who need financial aid. If elite colleges were truly committed to socioeconomic diversity, they would regard the proliferation of outstanding Asian American applicants as an opportunity, not a problem. They would rush to propel into the higher ranks of American society a group of students who not only boast outstanding test scores and grades but also are immigrants or immigrants' children from low- or middle-income families that sacrificed in hopes of a better life for the next generation. Asian American students also bring a variety of cultures, languages, and religions to stir the campus melting pot. Colleges should counter anti-Asian bias through sensitivity training sessions and hiring more Asian American admissions deans, directors, and staff.

In 1990, the federal Office for Civil Rights found that Asian American students needed higher test scores than whites to be admitted to Harvard. But it bought Harvard's argument that preferences for legacies and athletes, who were mostly white, accounted for the gap, rather than race discrimination. Scaling back those preferences would deprive elite universities of excuses for setting a higher bar for Asian Americans and compel them to confront the question of racism.

By the same token, elite universities that proclaim themselves to be "need-blind" in domestic admissions should dig into their billion-dollar endowments to extend that same policy to foreign students. Limiting international recruits to the jet-setting children of royalty and business tycoons discriminates against talented lower-income applicants, induces cynicism abroad about American higher education, and gives domestic students a narrower understanding of the rest of the world.

BY ELIMINATING preferences for legacies, development cases, faculty children, and athletes in patrician sports, elite colleges would open up a substantial number of seats—an estimated one-quarter of the freshman class. These slots should be filled on merit in the broadest meaning of the term. Candidates should be evaluated not on their parents' wealth but on their own achievement and potential. That doesn't mean that colleges should automatically accept applicants with the best test scores or grades, although those are important credentials. Admissions decisions inevitably are, and should be, subjective. Relying on the best judgment of their staff and faculty, colleges should consider anything germane to a candidate's cause, including essays, recommendations, and economic or social disadvantage. Thus Anthony Marx could fulfill his goal of socioeconomic diversity and revamp Amherst's economic profile by allocating more spaces to outstanding students from low-income families. Other colleges might supplant the beneficiaries of privilege with students who are especially gifted in music and art, or tenacious in overcoming illness, abuse, family disruptions, racial discrimination, or inferior high schools. Any of these approaches would be more attuned to American values of hard work, equal opportunity, and upward mobility and more likely to yield a capable leadership class than kowtowing to wealth.

There remains the thorny question of affirmative action. Eliminating admissions breaks for legacies and other predominantly white groups would weaken the case for minority preference. Ideally, a fair, accessible college admissions system based on individual merit would make no exception for any entitled group, but would inspire students of all races—and their teachers—to redouble their educational efforts. Perhaps in twenty-five years, as Justice O'Connor foresaw in her Michigan opinion, affirmative action will no longer be needed.

For now, though, only an admissions preference can compensate for the persistent achievement gap between white and Asian students, on one hand, and black and Hispanic students, on the other. By ensuring diversity, affirmative action both enhances intellectual and social interaction on campus and fosters minority representation in the upper realms of government, business, and the military, to which selective colleges provide a gateway.

Affirmative action aside, substituting outstanding students for those who coasted in on their parents' wallets would improve the colleges' academic rigor and social cohesion. The Ivy Leagues could toss out "gut" courses patronized by legacies and development cases and make their humanities and social sciences curricula as demanding as Caltech's engineering program, yielding more-knowledgeable and better-prepared graduates. The meritocratic ethic would spill over into daily campus life; with everyone arriving through the same admissions process and fewer students from fancy neighborhoods and prep schools, social segregation would abate. To survive, eating clubs and other insular groups would become more open to students of all backgrounds.

All American schoolchildren are taught that if they work hard enough, they can fulfill their ambitions, even become president. The elite colleges that unlock the door to success in our society contradict that promise, and sow anger and disillusion, by compromising standards to admit children of the rich, famous, and powerful. Ending the preferences of privilege would revitalize the social compact, replenish the ranks of leadership with deserving newcomers, and bear out de Tocqueville's description of America as a democracy with "an almost universal equality of social conditions."

NOTES

I am indebted to many confidential sources for providing or confirming information in this book. Where sources interviewed on the record are named in the text, they are not noted here to avoid repetition.

While none of my *Wall Street Journal* articles on admissions are reprinted here in their entirety, quotations and other material taken from them are scattered through the text. In particular, much of the Duke University material in Chapter 2 is taken from "At Many Colleges, the Rich Kids Get Affirmative Action," *Wall Street Journal*, February 20, 2003. Some information in Chapter 4 on legacy preference is drawn from "Preference for Alumni Children in College Draws Fire," *Wall Street Journal*, January 15, 2003. Information and academic data for Groton School's class of 1998, used in several chapters, are from "For Groton Grads, Academics Aren't Only Keys to Ivies," *Wall Street Journal*, April 25, 2003. Much of the discussion in Chapter 7 of "life challenges" criteria at the University of California originally appeared in "Extra Credit: To Get into UCLA, It Helps to Face 'Life Challenges,'" *Wall Street Journal*, July 12, 2002. The section on the Supreme Court and legacies in Chapter 8 relies on "For Supreme Court, Affirmative Action Isn't Just Academic," *Wall Street Journal*, May 14, 2003.

Except where otherwise noted, admissions data on individual universities—such as average SAT scores, acceptance rates, percentage of fresh-

men who ranked in the top 10 percent of their high school class, and proportion of students on financial aid—come from *U.S. News & World Report*'s website, www.usnews.com. University endowment data are from the
NACUBO Endowment Study, courtesy of Damon Manetta, manager, public affairs, National Association of College and University Business Officers. Data on individuals' wealth come from the Forbes 400 list of richest
Americans, available at www.forbes.com.

INTRODUCTION: THE TENNESSEE WALTZ

3   IN A 1997 ARTICLE: David L. Evans, "The Pitfalls of a Pure Meritocracy," *Con-
tempora Magazine*, July 31, 1997, p. 32.

4   PRINCETON'S RAREFIED IVY EATING CLUB: J.W. Victor, former president of
Princeton Inter-Club Council, confirmed that Lauren Bush and Caitlin Edwards were
Ivy members. Justin Rockefeller said in an interview that he was in Ivy.

6   POSTED TO LATIN AMERICA: See Daniel Golden and Charles Forelle, "Just How
Far Does Diversity Go?" *Wall Street Journal*, June 26, 2003, p. A6, which describes how
a Jewish student born in Panama qualified as Hispanic for purposes of law school
admissions.

8   IT SUSPENDED EIGHTH-GRADER: Bill Turque, *Inventing Al Gore* (Boston: Hough-
ton Mifflin, 2000), pp. 304–5. Turque confirmed in an interview that the marijuana incident took place in the Bishop's Garden.

9   HIS NAME WASN'T EVEN LISTED: Josh Cherwin, spokesman for former vice
president Gore, told me that Albert III did graduate. Harvard occasionally omits
names of graduates from the commencement program at the family's request.

10   INCOME AND WAGE GAPS: For a summary of research on economic stratifica-
tion, see Stephen J. McNamee and Robert K. Miller Jr., *The Meritocracy Myth* (Lan-
ham, Md.: Rowman & Littlefield Publishers, 2004), pp. 52–65.

10   "A GROWING BODY OF EVIDENCE": *The Economist*, January 1, 2005, pp. 22–23.

11   ONLY 3 TO 11 PERCENT OF STUDENTS: For 3 percent, see Anthony P. Carnevale
and Stephen J. Rose, "Socioeconomic Status, Race/Ethnicity, and Selective College Admissions," in Richard D. Kahlenberg, ed., *America's Untapped Resource: Low-Income
Students in Higher Education* (New York: Century Foundation Press, 2004), Table 3.1,
p. 106. For 11 percent, see William G. Bowen, Martin A. Kurzweil, and Eugene M.
Tobin, *Equity and Excellence in American Higher Education* (Charlottesville: University
of Virginia Press, 2005), pp. 98–99. Bowen and colleagues also conclude that only
3 percent of students at elite colleges are "both first-generation college-goers and from
low-income families."

11   BOTH WERE MEDIOCRE STUDENTS: For Bush's academic record, see Jerome

Karabel, "The Legacy of Legacies," *New York Times,* September 13, 2004, p. 23. For Kerry's, see Michael Kranish, "Kerry, Bush Grades Nearly Identical," *Boston Globe,* June 8. 2005, p. 1.

11   MAINTAINS A CHAPTER: All information on Cum Laude status of St. Albans graduates in this book was provided by David Baker, then the school's director of communications.

12   COMMITTED $25 MILLION: "Celebration Marks Official Dedication of Frist Center," *Princeton Weekly Bulletin,* November 6, 2000.

12   OPPOSES AFFIRMATIVE ACTION: "Frist Shares Bush Position on University of Michigan," Associated Press, January 17, 2003.

16   SIX DAYS AFTER: Furstenberg did not reply either to that email or to a follow-up email that I sent him asking if my intervention had been responsible for Jamie's admission to Dartmouth.

16   A SUBSEQUENT NEWSPAPER REPORT: Anne Marie Chaker, "Bad News for Wait-listed Students," *Wall Street Journal,* June 16, 2005, p. D1.

16   REFUSED TO HEAR: Lee Williams, "She Took It to the 'Street,'" www.dailyprince tonian.com, February 28, 2000.

17   SUSPENDED FOR SEVEN MONTHS: Certification of Disposition, *State of New Jersey v. William Harrison Frist Jr.,* Princeton Borough Municipal Court, July 12, 2004.

19   SUGGESTED IN HIS DISSENT: *Barbara Grutter v. Lee Bollinger,* Supreme Court of the United States, No. 02–241. See Justice Thomas's discussion of legacy preference beginning, "Much has been made of the fact that elite institutions utilize a so-called 'legacy' preference," and accompanying footnote.

19   GIVEN $25 MILLION: "$25-Million Bass Gift Applauds Stanford Contributions to Mankind," Stanford News Service, June 13, 1991.

20   HEADMASTER RICHARD COMMONS: In September 2004, Commons warned Groton alumni that "the book may present information in a manner that is unfavorable to Groton." In a second letter, on March 22, 2005, addressed to the "Groton Family," he complained that I had been "contacting members of the Groton community" asking for "copies of specific issues of the *Groton School Quarterly.*" The *Quarterly* lists academic honors and college destinations of Groton graduates.

1: HOW THE "Z-LIST" MAKES THE A-LIST

23   NO PRESS COVERAGE ALLOWED: I attended the dinner as a member's guest.

24   THE FIRST ISSUE OF ITS NEWSLETTER: The committee's newsletter is called *Re:sources.*

25   BY EXAMINING: Many COUR members are listed in *Who's Who in America* (New Providence, N.J.: Marquis, 2005). It provides names of children, which I then checked against Harvard alumni and student directories. I also found names and college affiliations of alumni children in Harvard class reunion reports, kept in the Har-

vard Archives in Pusey Library. To identify children of COUR members who are neither alumni nor in *Who's Who,* I relied on confidential sources.

25   AT LEAST 336: The number of COUR children accepted to Harvard was likely
higher, as some of those admitted would enroll elsewhere.

26   "LAST YEAR WE COMPLETED": Harvard College Class of 1962 Fortieth Anniversary Report, p. 162.

26   CHAIRS A $400 MILLION: *Re:sources,* May 2004, p. 9.

29   ZOFNASS . . . DONATED: Harvard College Fund Annual Report, 2003–4.

30   GIVEN GENEROUSLY TO HARVARD: Harvard College Fund Annual Report,
1998–99, and Development News, 2005, "Alumni and Friends of Radcliffe Fund Four
Radcliffe Institute Fellowships."

31   REAPED $648 MILLION: Steven Syre, "A 648M Smile," *Boston Globe,* May 3,
2005, p. E1.

32   ENDOW TWO PROFESSORSHIPS: *Harvard University Gazette,* October 24, 2002.

32   A HARVARD FUND-RAISING AWARD: "John Harvard's Journal," *Harvard Magazine,* March–April 2003, p. 82.

34   DONATED BETWEEN $500,000 AND $1 MILLION: Campaign Leadership Gifts,
Harvard College Fund Annual Report, 1998–99; Harvard College Fund Annual Report, 2000–1.

36   HAS GIVEN $30 MILLION: Interview with Albert F. Gordon.

37   HER PARENTS GAVE HARVARD: Harvard College Fund Annual Report, 2003–4.

37   NOTED: Harvard College Class of 1974 Thirtieth Anniversary Report.

38   THE *HARVARD CRIMSON* REPORTED: Dan Rosenheck, "The Back Door to the
Yard," *Harvard Crimson,* June 6, 2002, p. B1.

38   AMONG OTHER DONATIONS: Harvard College Fund Annual Report, 2003–4.

39   TOUTS DEFERRAL: William Fitzsimmons, Marlyn McGrath Lewis, and Charles
Ducey, "Time Out or Burn Out for the Next Generation," www.admissions.college.
harvard.edu, 2000.

39   CARIBBEAN VOYAGE: *The Tell-Tale,* fall edition 2001, volume 1.

40   NOT IN THE TOP 10 PERCENT: Celene was not in the Cum Laude Society, which
at Nightingale-Bamford includes only the top 10 percent. Interview with Joyce Mitch-
ell, director of college advising, Nightingale-Bamford.

41   BY EXAMINING HONORS DATA: Honors for graduating seniors are listed in
Harvard commencement programs, available at the archives in Pusey Library. I was
unable to locate graduation information for a number of COUR children who enrolled at Harvard, probably because they either took longer than four years to graduate, dropped out, or transferred.

43   BETWEEN $250,000 AND $500,000: Harvard College Fund Annual Report,
2000–1.

44   "ONE OF THE LARGEST OWNERS": Peter Grant, "Multifamily Affair: Kushner Aims to Be a Player," *Wall Street Journal*, September 6, 2000, p. B10.

44   25,000 APARTMENTS: Company overview, www.kushnercompanies.com.

44   KUSHNER, HIS FAMILY, AND HIS BUSINESS ASSOCIATES: Jeff Pillets and Clint Riley, "Paying for Power: The Kushner Network," *Bergen Record*, June 16, 2002, p. 1.

45   ANNUAL INSTALLMENTS: A $250,000 payment to Harvard by the Charles and Seryl Kushner Charitable Foundation was recorded in a public filing for fiscal 2001 with the New Jersey Division of Consumer Affairs.

46   NEARLY $100,000: The Center for Responsive Politics, www.opensecrets.org.

47   MAJOR GIFTS TO NEW YORK UNIVERSITY: Interview with NYU spokesman John Beckman.

47   NEVER CONSUMMATED: Interviews with Beckman and Alan Hammer, acting chairman of Kushner Cos.

2: RECRUITING THE RICH

52   MAUDE WAS NOT INDUCTED: Lawrenceville School provided a list of inductees.

53   JOKED WITH PROTESTANT FRIENDS: Maude refers to the "WASP Club" in her entry in the 2001 Lawrenceville yearbook.

53   BUNN VENTURES: Tim Landis, "What's in a Name? Plenty of History and Success If It's Bunn," *State Journal-Register*, Springfield, Ill., April 29, 1999, p. 7A.

53   MORE THAN A DOZEN: George W. Bunn Jr., University of Illinois at Springfield Oral History Collection. Mr. Bunn told interviewer Sally Schanbacher in 1972 that "this last fall, our family sent the fifteenth boy to Lawrenceville."

56   "AUTOMATICALLY ADMITTED": "Q and A: Rick Levin," *Yale Alumni Magazine*, November/December 2004, p. 28.

57   NONGOVERNMENTAL REVENUE: Voluntary Support of Education Survey, RAND Council for Aid to Education. Ann E. Kaplan, survey director, provided tables on sources of giving to universities.

58   BARON MAURICE: "Phony Baron Given Three-Year Sentence," Associated Press, January 31, 1991.

62   FUND-RAISING PROWESS: Susan Kauffman, "Duke's Money Machine," *Raleigh News & Observer*, December 15, 1996, p. 1.

62   GAVE ANOTHER $10 MILLION: Duke News Service, "Anne and Robert Bass Make Second $10 Million Gift to Support Undergraduate Education," January 25, 2001.

64   ALL-LEAGUE HONORS: Martin London, letter to Stuart Karle, August 17, 2004.

64   SENT INFORMATION: London letter.

64   HIS ONLY CAREER TACKLE: Tim was redshirted in the 1995 season, did not play in a game in 1996, and recorded one tackle as a backup free safety in 1997, according to Stanford football records.

65   FORD FOUNDATION: Interview with Howard E. Covington Jr.

66   "ELEVATE DUKE": Howard E. Covington Jr. and Marion A. Ellis, *Politics, Progress and Outrageous Ambitions* (Durham: Duke University Press, 1999), p. 379.

67   RAIDED YALE FAMILIES: For instance, although plumbing fixtures billionaire Herbert Kohler Jr. graduated from Yale, his daughter Laura Elizabeth Kohler went to Duke.

69   FAMILY MEMBERS PLEDGED: Duke Policy News, "Sulzbergers Support Child Policy Program," 1998.

70   IMPRESSIVE CURRICULUM VITAE: www.pubpol.duke.edu/people/faculty/fleishman/fleishmancv.pdf.

71   ONCE OFFERED THE PRESIDENCY: Anthony Flint, "Brandeis Chooses Thier as President," *Boston Globe,* May 6, 1991.

71   CONDUCTED A WINE TASTING: Interview with James Gorter.

71   THE GORTERS LATER ENDOWED: "Filling Bass Chairs," *Duke Magazine,* May–June 2001.

72   HE ALSO OWNED OR HELD OPTIONS: I am grateful to Charles Forelle, *The Wall Street Journal* Boston bureau's resident math whiz, for poring over U.S. Securities and Exchange Commission records to determine Fleishman's corporate compensation and stock holdings.

74   A FRIEND AND POLITICAL SUPPORTER: Interview with Stephen Swid.

75   BRODIE REBUFFED: Interview with Brodie.

75   MITCH HART LEFT: Interviews with Hart and Brodie.

77   "DUKE'S UNDER-CAPITALIZATION": Robert Bliwise, "Duke's Master Builder—A Leader and Her Legacy," *Duke Magazine,* July–August 2004.

77   ONE-THIRD REDUCTION: Steven Wright, "Data Raises Admissions Questions," *Duke Chronicle,* January 11, 2001.

78   "NEVER WANTED TO ADMIT": Rachel Toor, *Admissions Confidential* (New York: St. Martin's Press, 2001), pp. 209–11.

82   NOT THE CUM LAUDE SOCIETY: Interview with David Miller, Lake Forest High School.

3: THE FAME FACTOR

85   DEPICTED: Jennet Conant, "School for Glamour," *Vanity Fair,* February 1998.

86   "PSYCHOPATH": Jill Goldsmith, "Mouse Memo Blasts Ovitz," *Daily Variety,* October 21, 2004.

87   ON ITS WEBSITE: Parents Weekend 2004 Schedule of Events, brownparents weekend.rawdata.net/event_schedule.php.

87   NINE HUNDRED STUDENTS PACKED: Maichael Janusonis, "Brown Honors Scorsese," *Providence Journal,* January 28, 2003, p. 1.

87 AMONG THE GUESTS: President Simmons joked that Hoffman and DeVito had disrupted her speech at Ovitz's house.

92 ACCEPTED BY A SECOND IVY LEAGUE UNIVERSITY: Princeton allegedly accessed Yale's admissions decision on Lauren Bush without authorization. Alexander Clark, Preliminary Security Report, Yale University Office of Undergraduate Admissions, June 20, 2002.

93 "HUNTER-WARRIOR TYPES": Peter Carlson, "The Relatively Charmed Life of Neil Bush," *Washington Post,* December 28, 2003, p. D1.

95 VIED WITH HIS DAUGHTER'S CLASSMATES: Interview with Adam Vitarello.

95 MORE THAN ONE-QUARTER: Brown accepted 196 of 763 transfer applicants in fall 2003, or 26 percent, according to www.usnews.com/usnews/edu/ranking.

100 "SHERMAN PRIZE": Clyde Haberman and Albin Krebs, "Just an Ordinary Student," *New York Times,* September 11, 1979, p. B8.

100 ARRESTED DURING DEMONSTRATIONS: UPI, "Brown U. Says Amy Didn't Make Grade," *Newsday,* July 19, 1987.

100 LOITERING, AND DISORDERLY CONDUCT: Associated Press, "Fonda Daughter's Sentence: Public Service," *New York Times,* November 5, 1989.

101 CHARACTER WITNESS: UPI, "Anne Brown, Socialite and Noted Author," *Newsday,* November 22, 1985.

103 ON ITS BOARD FROM 1988 TO 2000: Gregorian curriculum vitae, provided by him.

103 GIVEN THE LIBRARY $1 MILLION: Vartan Gregorian, *The Road to Home: My Life and Times* (New York: Simon & Schuster, 2003), pp. 290–91.

103 SOPHIA LOREN WAS LOOKING: Interview with Eric Widmer.

105 EXPELLED FROM BROWN: Ben Grin, "Putting Past Behind Him, Ted Turner '60 Builds Strong Relationship with University," *Brown Daily Herald,* April 29, 2004.

105 LARGE WHITE CADILLAC: Juliette Wallack, "Zucconi '55 Remembered for His Character, and Car," *Brown Daily Herald,* February 24, 2003, p. 1.

106 TALE OF THAT VISIT: Interview with Eric Widmer.

108 CAUGHT OFFERING: Katherine Boas, "Football Team Barred from Winning Ivy Title," *Brown Daily Herald,* September 6, 2000, p. 1.

108 COULD HAVE NO FURTHER CONTACT: Shannon Tan, "Zucconi '55 Moves to Development Office amid Ivy League Sanctions," *Brown Daily Herald,* September 12, 2000, p. 1.

108 "I AM AMUSED": James H. Rogers, "Mail Room," *Brown Alumni Magazine,* January–February 2001.

108 "INSENSITIVITY TO QUALIFIED SONS": Roger Williams, "Mail Room," *Brown Alumni Magazine,* March–April 2001.

108 ORGANIST SOFTLY PLAYED: Interview with William Nicholson.

109 $20–25 MILLION: "Witness: Ovitz Pay Play at Disney 'Unreasonable,'" Dow Jones News Service, October 25, 2004.

109   A $25 MILLION PLEDGE: Kenneth Weiss, "Ovitz Gives UCLA Hospital $25 Million," *Los Angeles Times,* February 20, 1997, p. B1.

109   FALLEN BEHIND: The only major gifts—six figures or above—from the Ovitz Family Foundation to UCLA from 1997 to 2004 were $1 million in 1997, $1 million in 1998, and $500,000 in 2000, according to records the foundation submitted to the Internal Revenue Service. The *New York Post* reported on January 25, 2002, that UCLA was "frustrated by Ovitz's delays and now despaired of ever being fully paid."

109   TYPICALLY GIVING EACH OF THEM: Form 990s, Ovitz Family Foundation.

109   OFFERED TO HELP PLACE: Bernard Weinraub, "Hollywood Ending," *New York Times,* January 30, 2005.

4: ENDURING LEGACIES

118   THE BIGGEST GROUP: Interview with Daniel Saracino.

119   ENDOWING A SCHOLARSHIP: Interview with Terry Desmond.

121   "SERVE TO REPRODUCE": William G. Bowen, Martin A. Kurzweil, and Eugene M. Tobin, *Equity and Excellence in American Higher Education* (Charlottesville: University of Virginia Press, 2005), p. 167.

122   THAN EITHER AFRICAN AMERICAN OR HISPANIC: At the University of Pennsylvania, for example, 15 percent of freshmen in 2004 were alumni children, while 7 percent were African American and 7 percent were Hispanic.

122   "A DECIDEDLY BETTER CHANCE": Bowen et al., *Equity and Excellence,* p. 103.

122   DAVIDSON COLLEGE: Interview with Nancy Cable, former dean of admissions at Davidson.

123   FREE COLLEGE COUNSELING: Interview with Jill Caskey, director of Brown Alumni College Advising Program.

123   ITS COUNTERPART: Interview with Robert Alig, University of Pennsylvania assistant vice president of alumni relations.

124   54 PERCENT OF CORPORATE LEADERS: Thomas R. Dye, *Who's Running America? The Bush Restoration* (Upper Saddle River, N.J.: Prentice Hall, 2002), p. 148.

124   "THE GREATER GOOD": T. S. L. Perlman and Deborah Perlman, "Let In by Lottery," *Princeton Alumni Weekly,* October 23, 2002.

125   "TIGHT LIMITS": Bowen et al., *Equity and Excellence,* p. 171.

125   "NO SPECIAL EXCEPTION": "Bush Opposes 'Legacy' College Admissions," CNN.com, August 6, 2004.

125   A MAY 2004 POLL: "Public Views on Higher Education: a Sampling," *Chronicle of Higher Education,* May 7, 2004.

125 DUE TO A C: Sarah Harris and Gordon Rayner, "His Oxford Dream Dashed, Euan Blair Is Bristol-Bound," *Daily Mail*, August 24, 2002.

126 "CANCER CREEPS INSIDIOUSLY": R. J. Innerfield, "Losing Legacies," *Princeton Alumni Weekly*, May 15, 2002.

127 BEFORE WORLD WAR I: Interview with Jerome Karabel.

127 THE COLLEGES' SOCIAL SCENE: See discussion of Harvard finals clubs and Gold Coast residence halls in Marcia Graham Synnott, *The Half-Opened Door: Discrimination and Admissions at Harvard, Yale and Princeton, 1900–1970* (Westport, Conn.: Greenwood Press, 1979), pp. 23–32.

127 JEWISH UNDERGRADUATES AT HARVARD TRIPLED: Dan A. Oren, *Joining the Club: A History of Jews and Yale* (New Haven: Yale University Press, 1985), pp. 49–50.

127 AT COLUMBIA: Oren, *Joining the Club*, p. 43.

128 "ASIDE FROM THEIR DISDAIN": David O. Levine, *The American College and the Culture of Aspiration, 1915–1940* (Ithaca: Cornell University Press, 1986), p. 154.

128 WHICH IN 1922 DEVELOPED: Levine, *The American College*, p. 142.

128 YALE'S BOARD OF ADMISSIONS VOTED: Oren, *Joining the Club*, p. 59.

128 AND 29.6 PERCENT: Synnott, *Half-Opened Door*, p. 155.

128 NEEDED A 60 AVERAGE: Synnott, *Half-Opened Door*, p. 154.

128 HELPED ROLL BACK: Synnott, *Half-Opened Door*, p. 155.

129 SIMILARLY, AT HARVARD: Synnott, *Half-Opened Door*, p. 112.

129 CLARK SLASHED: Nicholas Lemann, *The Big Test: The Secret History of the American Meritocracy* (New York: Farrar, Straus and Giroux, 1999), p. 149.

129 LED BY CONSERVATIVE COLUMNIST: Lemann, *Big Test*, p. 150.

129 "THE ONLY PREFERENCE": Quoted in Lemann, *Big Test*, p. 151.

129 A 1990 REVIEW: Compliance Review No. 01-88-6009, Office for Civil Rights, United States Department of Education, October 4, 1990, p. 1. Admissions staff comments, pp. 27–28.

130 UNIVERSITY-COMMISSIONED STUDY: McKinsey Report for the Notre Dame Alumni Association.

130 214 NOTRE DAME CLUBS: Interview with Charles Lennon, executive director, Alumni Association.

131 A SUBSTANTIALLY HIGHER YIELD: Interview with Daniel Saracino.

131 AVERAGE 80 POINTS LESS: Interview with Daniel Saracino.

131 TOLD THE *CHICAGO TRIBUNE*: Meg McSherry, "A Case for Special Cases," *Chicago Tribune*, May 25, 2003, p. 1.

132 AN ASTONISHING 74 PERCENT: Interview with Louis Nanni, Notre Dame vice president for university relations.

133 IN HIS AUTOBIOGRAPHY: Ed R. Haggar, *Big Ed and the Haggar Family* (Austin, Tex.: Eakin Press, 2001), p. 55.

136   GAVE $33 MILLION: Julie Flory, *University of Notre Dame News*, "Groundbreaking Ceremonies Planned for New Performing Arts Center," September 5, 2001.

5: TITLE IX AND THE RISE OF THE UPPER-CLASS ATHLETE

150   ARRAY OF SEGREGATED SPORTS: All data are from "NCAA Student-Athlete Ethnicity Report, 1999–2000—2002–2003" and pertain to Divisions I, II, and III for 2002–2003. Percentages for each sport don't add up to 100 percent because I have omitted categories such as "other" and "American Indian."

151   MIDDLEBURY COLLEGE: Middlebury Ad Hoc Committee, 2002, pp. 7–8, cited in William G. Bowen and Sarah A. Levin, *Reclaiming the Game: College Sports and Educational Values* (Princeton: Princeton University Press), p. 352, n. 33.

151   ONLY 6 PERCENT OF RECRUITED: Bowen et al., *Equity and Excellence*, p. 172.

151   68 PERCENT OF THE STUDENT BODY: Email from Carol Wood, May 15, 2005.

152   GIVEN TWELVE ADMISSIONS SLOTS: "Admissions Slots by Sport," University of Virginia, document provided to author in response to public records request.

152   INCREASED FROM 332: NCAA, "Sports Sponsorship and Participation Report, 1982–2003," p. 153.

153   DOUBLE THE COLLEGIATE AVERAGE: According to the NCAA "Participation Report," the average college in 2002–3 fielded 16.5 teams.

153   TYPICAL URBAN PUBLIC SCHOOL: East Boston High School profile, Massachusetts Department of Education website, www.profiles.doe.mass.edu.

153   EASTIE OFFERS: "Boston Public Schools High School Sports 2004–2005," Boston Public Schools Department of Athletics.

153   IT HAS TEAMS: www.andover.edu/athletics/teams.

154   ATHLETES LAGGING BEHIND: Bowen and Levin, *Reclaiming the Game*, p. 92.

155   "THE MORE SELECTIVE": Bowen and Levin, *Reclaiming the Game*, p. 77.

155   SINK TO THE BOTTOM: Bowen and Levin, *Reclaiming the Game*, pp. 130–43.

155   "TROUBLING ISSUES": Bowen and Levin, *Reclaiming the Game*, p. 139.

155   AVERAGE FOR WOMEN ROWERS: "University of Virginia Selected Athletic Data," UVA Institutional Assessment and Studies, April 5, 2005.

158   A LATE VIRGINIA POLO PLAYER: Email from Carol Wood, April 13, 2005.

159   "DEAN BLACKBURN'S ATTENTION": Email from Carol Wood, June 24, 2005.

160   ACQUIRED TEETH: Title IX Legislative Chronology, Women's Sports Foundation.

160   KEY FIGHT: Mike Szostak, "End in Sight at Last for Title IX Case," *Providence Journal-Bulletin*, June 24, 1998. Also, Jessica Gavora, *Tilting the Playing Field* (San Francisco: Encounter Books, 2002), pp. 70–90.

161   ENDORSED NINE "EMERGING SPORTS": Interview with NCAA administrators Judy Sweet and Wendy Walters.

161   TALL, STRONG WOMEN: Barbara Carton, "You Don't Need Oars in the Water to Go Out for Crew," *Wall Street Journal*, May 14, 1999, p. 1.

161   MORE THAN QUADRUPLED: NCAA, "Sports Sponsorship and Participation Report," pp. 35, 63.

161   GREW FROM 31: NCAA, "Participation Report," p. 173 (women's rowing), p. 177 (men's rowing).

162   VARSITY RIDERS NEARLY DOUBLED: NCAA, "Participation Report," pp. 48, 64. Squad size, p. 173.

163   130 COLLEGES DROPPED: NCAA, "Participation Report," pp. 191, 204. Wrestling organizations say the figure is much higher.

163   CUT ITS FIFTY-SEVEN-YEAR-OLD VARSITY: Tim Leone, "Fans See Curtain Close on Bucknell Wrestling Team," *Harrisburg Patriot,* February 11, 2002.

163   BUCKNELL RESTORED WRESTLING: Susan Crawford, "Philanthropy Assists a Sport That Struggles with Title IX," www.bucknell.edu.

164   SUBSTANTIAL MINORITY REPRESENTATION: Undergraduate Enrollment Data, NCAA Division 1 Athletics Certification Interim Report, University of Virginia, Appendix 6A, July 2001.

164   "MAKES FINANCIAL SENSE": Final Report, Virginia 2020 Strategic Planning Task Force for the Department of Athletics, March 1, 2002, p. 47.

164   ALUMNI PAID $250 APIECE: Email from Carol Wood, June 1, 2005.

165   BATTED ONLY TEN TIMES: He had no hits in two official at-bats in 2003, and also walked and was hit by a pitch. He had two hits in six at-bats in 2004.

168   "READILY ADMITS": Bob Ryan, "Walking on Wild Side: Being Here Dream to These Players," *Boston Globe,* April 4, 2004, p. E13.

171   ELIMINATING BASEBALL SCHOLARSHIPS: Dan Heuchert, "Bottom of the Ninth," *Alumni News Magazine,* winter 2002.

6: A BREAK FOR FACULTY BRATS

182   DATA GATHERED: Email from Professor Malcolm Getz, January 31, 2005. Getz calculated these percentages at my request from data that he and Professor Siegfried had compiled for their article "Where Do the Children of Professors Attend College?" Working Paper No. 03-W02, Department of Economics, Vanderbilt University, February 2003.

182   HIRED AFTER 1996: Interview with Manuel Monteiro, associate vice president for human resources, Boston University.

183   BU TOOK 79 PERCENT: Email from Kelly Walter, February 1, 2005.

183   157, OR 2.9 PERCENT: Email from Alissa Kaplan Michaels, March 4, 2005.

184   NO-INTEREST LOANS: Steve Stecklow, "Teacher's Perk," *Wall Street Journal,* April 15, 1997, p. 1.

184   "COMMITMENT AND DEDICATION": Compliance Review No. 01-88-6009, Office for Civil Rights, United States Department of Education, October 4, 1990, p. 9.

184   FIFTY-TWO GRADUATES: Princeton High School, 2004–5 School Profile.

184   NOT AMONG THAT TOP 12 PERCENT: "Town Topics," June 24, 1998, p. 33. Seniors graduating with honors were identified by asterisks.

184   95 PERCENT OF PRINCETON STUDENTS: Email from Cass Cliatt, August 1, 2005.

185   ONE OF THE STRONGEST PREDICTORS: Interview with Professor Ronald Ferguson.

185   AVERAGE SALARY: "Annual Report on the Economic Status of the Profession, 2004–5," American Association of University Professors, Table 4, p. 33.

186   58 PERCENT ADMIT RATE: Communication from Doris Davis, Cornell associate provost for admissions.

186   ONLY 14 OF 87: Ithaca High School College Profile 2004.

187   "THE OTHER LEGACIES": Laura Randall, "The Other Legacies: Fac Brats," New York Times, January 16, 2005, Section 4A, p. 12.

187   $9 MILLION A YEAR: Interview with Manuel Monteiro.

188   58.1 PERCENT PAY: "2004 Comprehensive Survey of College and University Benefits Programs," College and University Professional Association for Human Resources, August 2004.

189   "FAIRNESS CONCERNS": Staff of the Joint Committee on Taxation, "Options to Improve Tax Compliance and Reform Tax Expenditures," January 27, 2005, p. 45.

190   RAISED ITS BAR: Interview with Lee Coffin.

190   SCALED BACK PROPOSED CUTS: Stecklow, "Teacher's Perk."

190   A STANFORD SPOKESWOMAN: Email from Kate Chesley, March 1, 2005.

191   SIGNED A PETITION: Patrick Healy, "Faculty Demands Administration Response to Petition on Remission," Tufts Daily, December 3, 1991, p. 1.

191   BACKED DOWN: Letter to university community from President Jean Mayer, June 1, 1992.

191   CRAFTED THE CAP: Maureen Lenihan, "Faculty Threatens Tufts with Lawsuit over Tuition Remission," Tufts Daily, February 26, 1992, p. 1.

191   $294, 210: IRS Form 990, 2002–3, Trustees of Tufts College.

193   THE NEXT FACULTY MEETING: It took place on March 2, 2005, in the Coolidge Room of Ballou Hall.

7: THE NEW JEWS

200   HIRED A RABBI: Daniel Golden, "Religious Preference: Colleges Court Jewish Students in Effort to Raise Rankings," Wall Street Journal, April 29, 2002, p. 1.

200   PROPORTION OF JEWS: Email from Greg Perfetto, Vanderbilt associate provost for institutional research, January 26, 2005.

201   "GREASY GRIND": Yale Dean Frederick S. Jones, quoted in Synnott, Half-Opened Door, p. 15.

202   POPULARIZED THE TERM: Lemann, Big Test, pp. 174–84.

202   "ASIAN OR PACIFIC ISLANDER": Statistical Policy Directive No. 15, "Race and Ethnic Standards for Federal Statistics and Administrative Reporting," Office of Management and Budget.

202   NO LONGER QUALIFY: Lemann, *Big Test,* p. 244.

202   "LOWER RATE THAN WHITE": Compliance Review No. 01-88-6009, Office for Civil Rights Department of Education, October 4, 1990, pp. 1, 2, 35, 40.

202   STEREOTYPING: Compliance Review, pp. 24–26.

203   "ADVERSELY AFFECTED": Compliance Review, p. 1.

203   THREE PRINCETON RESEARCHERS: Thomas J. Espenshade, Chang Y. Chung, and Joan L. Walling, "Admission Preferences for Minority Students, Athletes and Legacies at Elite Universities," *Social Science Quarterly* 85, 5 (2004): pp. 1422–46.

203   ENTERING ASIAN AMERICAN FRESHMEN: Institutional Self-Study Instrument Report, Yale University, p. 44.

204   GAINED A VICTORY: "Revisions to the Standards for the Classification of Federal Data on Race and Ethnicity," Office of Management and Budget, Federal Register Notice, October 30, 1997.

204   OBTAIN COLLEGE DEGREES: "Recommendations from the Interagency Committee for the Review of the Racial and Ethnic Standards to the Office of Management and Budget Concerning Changes to the Standards for the Classification of Federal Data on Race and Ethnicity," Office of Management and Budget, Federal Register, July 9, 1997, Part II.

206   "BECAUSE OF THEIR RACE": Kai Chan, "Admissions Policies Unfair to Asians," www.dailyprincetonian.com/archives/2004/11/29/opinion/11584.shtml, November 29, 2004.

206   "CONSIDER EACH APPLICANT": Email from Eric Quinones, May 27, 2005.

207   "SELF-SEGREGATION": Sam J. Cooper, "Gank Post Upsets Asian Associations," www.dailyprincetonian.com/archives/2003/02/27/news/7445/shtml, February 27, 2003.

208   ADOPTED A FORMULA: Daniel Golden, "Schools Find Ways to Achieve Diversity Without Key Tool," *Wall Street Journal,* June 20, 2003, p. 1.

209   "EXTRAORDINARY ACADEMIC PERFORMANCE": "Comprehensive Freshman Admissions Policy," www.admissions.ucla.edu/prospect/Adm_fr/FrSel.htm.

210   TO 65 IN 2004: Interview with Diana Schmelzer.

211   ACCUSED HIS FLAGSHIP: John Moores, "College Capers," www.forbes.com/forbes/2004/0329/040_print.html, March 29, 2004.

211   "SOMEWHAT FEWER ASIAN": Eligibility and Admissions Study Group, Final Report to the President, University of California, April 2004, p. D-5-4.

216   81.8 PERCENT OF FOREIGN: "Primary Source of Funding by Academic Level," Open Doors 2004, Report on International Education Exchange, Institute of International Education.

217   63 PERCENT OF ALL: "Undergraduate Financial Aid Estimates for 2003–04 by Type of Institution," 2003–4 National Postsecondary Student Aid Study, National Center for Education Statistics, June 2005, pp. 5–6.

217   OFTEN, IT'S INTERNATIONAL: Presentation to alumni by Amherst College admissions director Katharine Fretwell, November 13, 2004.

221   CLOSELY FOLLOWED THE NEWS: Groton's student newspaper, the *Circle Voice,* polled students on their attentiveness to the princess's death.

8: THE LEGACY ESTABLISHMENT

228   MICHIGAN VOTERS: "The EPIC-MRA Report," January–February 2003, Volume 11, Number 1, p. 7.

229   "SOMEWHAT IRONIC": Justice Harry Blackmun, concurring opinion, U.S. Supreme Court, *University of California Regents v. Bakke,* 438 U.S. 265 (1978).

229   "CASTE SYSTEM": "Education Fairness," News from Senator Bob Dole, December 19, 1990.

231   FUNDING FOR NONCOMPETITIVE GRANTS: Jeffrey Brainerd, "Lobbying to Bring Home the Bacon," *Chronicle of Higher Education,* October 22, 2004, p. A26.

233   READ A COVER STORY: John Larew, "Why Are Droves of Unqualified, Unprepared Kids Getting into Our Top Colleges?" *Washington Monthly,* June 1, 1991.

234   566 VERBAL SAT SCORE: Jerome Karabel, "The Legacy of Legacies," *New York Times,* September 13, 2004, p. 23.

235   10 PERCENT ATTENDED: Dye, *Who's Running America,* p. 148.

235   "MEDIA ELITE": Dye, *Who's Running America,* p. 109.

235   "D STOOD FOR DISTINCTION": Michael Kranish, "Kerry, Bush Grades Nearly Identical," *Boston Globe,* June 8, 2005, p. 1.

235   UNDERAGE ALCOHOL POSSESSION: Peter Pae and Amy Argetsinger, "Md. Teenagers Say Drinking Is Commonplace," *Washington Post,* October 2, 1995, p. B01.

236   PUBLISHED A NOVEL: Kristin Gore, *Sammy's Hill* (New York: Hyperion, 2004).

236   FIFTEEN U.S. SENATORS: Aside from those mentioned in the text, Senate legacies include John Warner (Washington and Lee University), John Sununu (Massachusetts Institute of Technology), and Russell Feingold (University of Wisconsin). Other alumni parents include Feingold, Gordon Smith (Brigham Young University), and Orrin Hatch (also BYU).

237   "A SECRET RESENTMENT": John McCain, *Faith of My Fathers* (New York: HarperCollins, 2000), p. 53.

237   "WHEN THAT BABY": Connie Bruck, "McCain's Party," *New Yorker,* May 30, 2005.

237   "UNAVOIDABLE APPOINTMENT": McCain, *Faith of My Fathers,* p. 108.

240   NSF STARTED A GRANT PROGRAM: Interview with former NSF director Rita Colwell.

240 **WITHOUT HONORS IN 2003:** Princeton officials Eric Quinones and Cass Cliatt furnished honors information for Princeton graduates.

241 **"INSTRUMENTAL IN SECURING":** "U.S. Reps. Frelinghuysen and Holt Receive Science Coalition Awards," News from Princeton University, April 16, 2001.

247 **"TRIBAL INSTINCTS":** William F. Buckley Jr., "Civil Rights for Old Boys," *New York Times,* January 24, 2003, p. 23.

257 **DENOUNCING THE PROPOSAL:** Jackie Calmes, "A Special Weekly Report from *The Wall Street Journal*'s Capital Bureau," *Wall Street Journal,* September 5, 2003, p. A4.

257 **KENNEDY PROPOSED:** Daniel Golden, "Bill Would Make Colleges Report Legacies, Early Admissions," *Wall Street Journal,* October 29, 2003, p. B1.

9: THE CHALLENGE OF WEALTH-BLIND ADMISSIONS

261 **CHANGED ITS CRITERIA:** Interview with Robert Morse, director of data research, *U.S. News & World Report.*

262 **ONLY EIGHT:** Interview with Richard Bischoff.

262 **OF CALTECH'S FIFTY-FOUR TRUSTEES:** Communication from Gary Dicovitsky, March 17, 2005.

263 **LANGUAGE OTHER THAN ENGLISH:** Cooperative Institutional Research Program freshman survey, Higher Education Research Institute, University of California at Los Angeles, fall 2004.

266 **THIRTY NOBEL PRIZES:** "Annual Report 2003–2004," California Institute of Technology, p. 4.

268 **CAREFULLY COACHED:** Interview with Caltech assistant vice president Erica O'Neal.

268 **STUDENTS TRAVEL NATIONWIDE:** Interview with Joanne Singh, Berea associate vice president for development.

271 **COOPER RECEIVES $16.7 MILLION:** Email from Jolene Resnick, April 5, 2005.

272 **70 PERCENT HIGHER:** Email from Resnick, April 5, 2005.

274 **"THE GREAT COMMITMENTS":** There are eight commitments: the first is "to provide an educational opportunity primarily for students from Appalachia, black and white, who have great promise and limited economic resources."

274 **TO ENCOURAGE RECRUITING:** Email from Joseph Bagnoli, March 23, 2005.

274 **GRADUATE AT THE SAME RATE:** Presentation to the Berea College Board of Trustees by the Office of Institutional Research and Assessment, May 2004.

275 **SECOND ONLY TO DAVIDSON:** Email from Joseph Bagnoli, March 23, 2005.

276 **WAS DISOWNED:** *Berea College History,* video, Berea College public relations.

276 **2,500 NEW DONORS:** Interview with Joanne Singh.

278 **SIX COURSES A SEMESTER:** Interview with Erica O'Neal.

279 **WAS AFRICAN AMERICAN:** Interview with Richard Bischoff.

279   AT MIT (43 PERCENT): Student body profile (2004–5), Office of the Provost, Institutional Research, web.mit.edu.

282   ONE HUNDRED LOCAL BUSINESSMEN: Alice Stone, *The Associates of the California Institute of Technology: Patrons of the Century's Science* (Pasadena: California Institute of Technology, 1991), p. 5.

282   JUST SIX YEARS EARLIER: Judith R. Goodstein, *Millikan's School* (New York: W. W. Norton, 1995), p. 75.

282   1,448 MEMBERS: Communication from Gary Dicovitsky, March 17, 2005.

283   TWENTY THOUSAND GRADUATES: Interview with Gary Dicovitsky.

283   GENERATED $227 MILLION: Interview with Richard Seligman, senior director, Caltech Office of Sponsored Research.

10: ENDING THE PREFERENCES OF PRIVILEGE

287   HEAR A PRESENTATION: "Admission Workshop for High School Students and Their Parents," Converse Hall, November 13, 2004.

289   HAVE ALL EXPANDED: Marcella Bombardieri, "Elite Colleges Go After Low-Income Recruits," *Boston Globe*, July 16, 2005, p. 1.

289   "LESS ETHNICALLY DIVERSE": "Faculty/Administration Conference on NESCAC Athletic Admissions," January 15, 2005, p. 6.

290   ELIMINATING TUITION: "Harvard Announces New Initiative Aimed at Economic Barriers to College," *Harvard University Gazette*, February 28, 2004.

290   "INTEGRAL TO THE KIND": Daniel Golden. "Boss Talk: Shaking Up Harvard," *Wall Street Journal*, June 8, 2004, p. B1.

290   51 STUDENTS: Email from Joseph Wrinn, July 6, 2005.

290   STEPDAUGHTER: Her name is Yael Levine. Although her mother, Harvard English professor Elisa New, and Summers were widely known to be a couple at the time of Yael's admission, they were not married until December 2005.

292   ACTED UNDER PRESSURE: Todd Ackerman, "Legislators Slam A&M over Legacy Admissions," *Houston Chronicle*, January 4, 2004, p. 1.

294   CONSIDERED CAPPING: "Faculty/Administration Conference," p. 6.

294   MOST POPULAR SPORTS: "NFHS 2003–04 High School Athletics Participation Survey," National Federation of State High School Associations, 2004.

ACKNOWLEDGMENTS

One of my greatest pleasures in reporting on college admissions, both for *The Wall Street Journal* and for this book, has been making the acquaintance of so many bright, dedicated people who share my concern about preferences for the rich.

Unfortunately, those who risked their jobs to help me must remain anonymous. Others I am delighted to thank by name: Keith Brodie, Juliet Chung, Michael Dannenberg, Al Gordon, Jennifer Hahn, Peter Hawkins, Alec Klein, David Leebron, Bruce Poch, Jonathan Reider, Mary Anne Schwalbe, Philip Tinari, Rachel Toor, and Juliette Wallack.

My colleagues in the Boston bureau of *The Wall Street Journal* have provided invaluable support. I would like to thank bureau chief Gary Putka for recognizing the importance of this topic and prodding me to investigate it and John Hechinger, Charles Forelle, David Armstrong, and Barbara Glickler for scrutinizing—and greatly improving—all or part of the manuscript. I am indebted as well to colleagues elsewhere in the *WSJ* empire, including John Lippman, Bryan Gruley, James Bandler, Elizabeth Bernstein, David Wessel, and Jessica Vascellaro.

I also thank *Wall Street Journal* managing editor Paul Steiger, senior deputy managing editor Dan Hertzberg, page one editor Mike Miller, and assistant news editor Carrie Dolan for their thoughtful handling of my articles, and Stuart Karle, Jonathan Albano, Alison Gooding, and Mia Israeli for their sage legal counsel. Ken Wells and Rose Ellen D'Angelo of the *Journal*'s book department were helpful and encouraging far beyond the call of duty, as were former *Journal* editors Steve Adler, Joanne Lipman, and Amy Stevens, and national news editor Laurie Hays.

My longtime friend and former *Boston Globe* colleague Charles Stein read the manuscript and offered typically sagacious suggestions. Other *Globe* friends—Brian Mooney, Gerard O'Neill, and Alex Beam—shared the wisdom of their publishing experience. I am indebted to left-coast journalists Steve Proctor, Steve Fainaru, and Mark Fainaru-Wada for their assistance, to David Groff for his thoughtful guidance on my book proposal, and to Garen Hartunian for Internet advice.

Some college and prep-school officials were more accommodating than others to my inquiries. Daniel Saracino and Matthew Storin of Notre Dame, Coach Kevin Sauer of Virginia women's crew, spokesmen Eric Quinones of Princeton and Mark Nickel of Brown, and David Baker, formerly of St. Albans, were particularly patient and helpful.

I'm grateful to my indefatigable agent, Lynn Johnston, who came up with the title and shepherded this project from start to finish, my insightful editor, Rachel Klayman, her able assistant, Lucinda Bartley, and the rest of the impressive Crown team, including Steve Ross, Kristin Kiser, Matthew Martin, John Mahaney, Donna Passannante, Tammy Blake, and Melanie DeNardo.

Special thanks go to my wife, Kathy, my son, Steven, and my stepchildren, Sean and Caroline, for their love, friendship, and understanding. I would also like to express my love and gratitude to my mother, Hilda Golden, my sister, Olivia, and my late father, Morris Golden. A Russian Jewish immigrant who went to City College on the GI Bill and became a professor of English literature, he taught me the importance of the written word and the meaning of the American dream.

INDEX

About the Author

DANIEL GOLDEN is deputy bureau chief at the Boston bureau of *The Wall Street Journal*, where he has covered education since 1999. Previously, he was a reporter at the *Boston Globe*. His journalistic career has taken him to remote locations around the world: a leper colony in Nigeria; an apartment complex for the poor in Medellín, Colombia, built by a billionaire drug lord; a funeral on Pine Ridge Indian Reservation in South Dakota for a teenager born with fetal alcohol syndrome and killed in a drunk-driving accident. The recipient of numerous journalistic honors and awards, including the Pulitzer Prize and the George Polk Award, he holds a B.A. from Harvard College. He lives with his wife and children in Belmont, Massachusetts.